CONTENTS

A DOG'S HEART

Based on Mikhail Bulgakov's classic satire

A major new staging in collaboration with radical theatre makers Complicite, as Simon McBurney makes his much-anticipated operatic directorial debut.

20 Nov – 4 Dec 2010

English National Opera
Live at the London Coliseum
eno.org · 0871 911 0200

EN O

THE RETURN OF ULYSSES

Young Vic   EN O

The epic legend re-imagined

ENO and the Young Vic's South Bank Show Award-winning partnership continues with a stunning new staging of Monteverdi's classic opera based on the second half of Homer's *Odyssey*.

24 Mar – 9 Apr 2011

An English National Opera and Young Vic co-production
Live at the Young Vic
youngvic.org · 020 7922 2922

Supported by
ARTS COUNCIL ENGLAND

GRANTA

12 Addison Avenue, London W11 4QR

email editorial@granta.com

To subscribe go to www.granta.com

Or call 845-267-3031 (toll-free 866-438-6150) in the United States, 020 8955 7011 in the United Kingdom

ISSUE 113

EDITOR	John Freeman
DEPUTY EDITOR	Ellah Allfrey
ARTISTIC DIRECTOR	Michael Salu
ONLINE EDITOR	Ollie Brock
EDITORIAL ASSISTANTS	Emily Greenhouse, Patrick Ryan
PUBLICITY	Saskia Vogel
DESIGN INTERNS	Daniela Silva, Francesca Ulivari
FINANCE	Geoffrey Gordon, Morgan Graver, Craig Nicholso
MARKETING AND SUBSCRIPTIONS	Anne Gowan, David Robinson
SALES DIRECTOR	Brigid Macleod
SALES MANAGER	Sharon Murphy
TO ADVERTISE IN THE UK CONTACT	Kate Rochester, katerochester@granta.com
TO ADVERTISE IN THE USA CONTACT	Emily Cook, ecook@granta.com
IT MANAGER	Mark Williams
PRODUCTION ASSOCIATE	Sarah Wasley
PROOFS	Kelly Falconer, Katherine Fry, Lesley Levene, Jessica Rawlinson, Vimbai Shire
ASSOCIATE PUBLISHER	Eric Abraham
PUBLISHER	Sigrid Rausing

In the United States, *Granta* is published in association with Grove/Atlantic Inc., 841 Broadway, 4th Floor, New York, NY 10003, and distributed by PGW. All editorial queries should be addressed to the London office.

Granta USPS 000-508 is published four times per year (March, June, September and December) by *Granta*, 12 Addison Avenue, London W11 4QR, United Kingdom, at the annual subscription rate of £34.95 and $45.99.

Airfreight and mailing in the USA by Agent named Air Business, c/o Worldnet Shipping USA Inc., 149–35 177th Street, Jamaica, New York, NY 11434. Periodicals postage paid at Jamaica, NY 11431.

US POSTMASTER: Send address changes to *Granta*, PO Box 359, Congers, NY 10920-0359.

Granta is printed and bound in Italy by Legoprint. This magazine is printed on paper that fulfils the criteria for 'Paper for permanent document' according to ISO 9706 and the American Library Standard ANSI/NIZO Z39.48-1992 and has been certified by the Forest Stewardship Council (FSC). *Granta* is indexed in the American Humanities Index.

ISBN 978-1-905881-23-9

CONTENTS

PEN AMERICA #13

Featuring fiction by Don DeLillo, poetry by John Ashbery, Patti Smith and Jonathan Lethem in conversation, & much more. Visit **pen.org/journal**

cover art: *Couple* by Daisy Rockwell (2010)

Foreword

Nineteen seventy-five marked the end of the dictatorship in Spain. The repressive regimes in South American countries would hold out until the following decade, but other cultural changes were afoot. In Europe, the tradition of exiled South American writers living and working in Paris gradually came to an end. Instead of looking north for their intellectual meridian, a young generation of émigrés began seeking publication in post-Franco Spain.

The writers in this collection were all born in or after 1975.

Many of these writers have not suffered in their own skin the social and moral circumstances that haunted their predecessors. When asked, the majority expressed scepticism, with varying degrees of reticence, nervousness or irony about the idea of an author having an active role in public life. Mario Vargas Llosa, whose bid for the presidency of Peru in 1990 was the theme of *Granta* 36, is perhaps the most obvious example of a public and influential figure following the intellectual model of Camus or Sartre. While writers such as Julio Cortázar, Ariel Dorfman and Isabel Allende adopted a moral and political stand against unacceptable political conditions and wrote sweeping social epics, the writers in this issue, by contrast, tell stories which are quotidian. For them, censorship, blacklists, exile and persecution are historical facts rather than actual memories, although it is obvious that they have had to fight other difficulties and fears.

This generation – and those before it – has been able to forge new paths, unfettered by the shadows of yesterday's literary masters. Not surprisingly, a variety of manifestos has been launched over the past few decades: Chile's 'McOndo' (an Anglo version of García Marquez's Macondo); 'Crack' in Mexico, playing with the idea of the 'Boom' generation; and, most recently, the 'Nocilla' – chocolate spread – generation in Spain. Despite these stabs at collective self-identification, talent is individual and unpredictable, and the work of a single writer can suddenly upset all readings of the past and future. Who could have imagined fifteen years ago that the writings of the outcast Chilean, Roberto Bolaño, who washed ashore in

Barcelona via Mexico, would exercise so wide an influence on writers in Spain, Latin America and across the world?

If a good part of contemporary Spanish literature seems eccentric to Europe, Latin America has always been the literary Far West. No other language shares the same territorial expanse (or population) in contiguous nations. The controversy over whether there are national literatures in Latin America long ago became the realm of historians. The literary homeland, as this collection shows, is the language itself. *Granta* has never before put together a selection of the best young writers in a language other than English. The publication of this edition almost simultaneously in English and Spanish represents the culmination of a dialogue which began seven years ago with the first issue of *Granta en español.*

We invited four writers to serve as jurors: the Argentinian writer and film-maker Edgardo Cozarinsky, who has lived between Paris and Buenos Aires for many decades; the British journalist Isabel Hilton, previously a correspondent in South America, who currently divides her time between England and China; the novelist Francisco Goldman, an American of Guatemalan descent who lives between New York and Mexico City; and the Catalan writer and literary critic, Mercedes Monmany, who lives in Madrid. The two of us, co-editors of the Spanish edition of *Granta*, were also members of the jury.

It has been an ambitious endeavour. We limited eligibility to writers under thirty-five, with at least one novel or story collection to their name. We searched exhaustively for recommendations and discoveries, receiving over three hundred submissions, from over twenty countries. We read everything, and agreed to a shortlist. Early on, we renounced the possibility of a unanimous vote, establishing instead a system of four rounds in which each successful author had to receive at least one majority vote. In the end, we chose twenty-two authors, only a handful of whom had been previously published in English.

The fiction in this issue is profoundly diverse, ranging from an ironic and demanding story by Pola Oloixarac, which dissects the political and moral shortcomings of the preceding generation, to the symbolism of Sònia Hernández and the clarity and outspokenness of Lucía Puenzo. Elvira Navarro deconstructs the final hours of a doomed relationship, while Samanta Schweblin's original voice turns the kaleidoscope of narrative suggestion slightly askew.

Many of the male writers represent women in a less passive and traditional role than have previous generations, or write in the first person as female narrators. Thus, Rodrigo Hasbún explores a couple's sentimental unravelling from the points of view of both characters and Alberto Olmos describes the desolation and emptiness of his main character, a female consumer in the frozen limbo of modern-day life. Federico Falco's story explores the hidden motivations of a young girl infatuated with Mormon missionaries in the Argentinian provinces, and Andrés Barba writes about female isolation and the extremes of a warped relationship to the body.

Spanish readers will recognize the trademark style of Patricio Pron and the intense technical innovation of Carlos Labbé. Pablo Gutiérrez, Alejandro Zambra and Javier Montes all have in common an almost Poundian purification of the dialect of the tribe. Andrés Neuman explores the language as an outsider – an Argentinian who has come of age in Granada – in a story about hatred between university professors. Matías Néspolo, Andrés Felipe Solano and Santiago Roncagliolo delight in particular locations. There is a strong sense of revision of various sentimental customs and literary traditions in the pieces by Antonio Ortuño, Andrés Ressia Colino, Oliverio Coelho and Carlos Yushimito. Many of them have chosen to live in foreign countries or are naturally more open, thanks to their backgrounds, to influences beyond the Spanish-speaking world.

With this selection, *Granta* and *Granta en español* aim to seal a pact – a secret handshake of sorts – with the reader, which we hope will prove the value of our shared references. In ten years' time we will see if our choices were correct, how many of the writers in this collection will have lived up to their promise, how many of them will endure.

We wish to thank Luigi Spagnol and Stefano Mauri for their sponsorship of this project through Duomo Ediciones, the members of the jury for their willingness and endurance, and Angels Balaguer, Laia Salvat, Doris Castellanos and Ella Sher for their indispensable help.

Aurelio Major and Valerie Miles
September 2010

COHIBA

Lucía Puenzo

TRANSLATED BY VALERIE MILES

LUCÍA PUENZO
ARGENTINA
1976

Puenzo is a writer, screenwriter and director. Her first film, *XXY*, won the Critics' Week Grand Prize (2007), a Goya for the Best Foreign Film and more than twenty international prizes. Her second, *El niño pez*, opened the Panorama section at the Berlin Film Festival in 2009, won prizes in Spain, Romania and Tokyo, and was part of the official selection in Tribeca and Havana, as well as at many other festivals. Her novels are *El niño pez* (2004), *9 minutos* (2005), *La maldición de Jacinta Pichimahuida* (2007), *La furia de la langosta* (2010) and *Wakolda* (2011). Her books have been published in France, Spain, Germany, Italy, the United States and Brazil. 'Cohiba' is a new story.

His hand brushes against mine in the darkness. His skin is hot and rough. Short hair, curls combed flat with some amateur pomade that shines even in the penumbra of the movie theatre. His smell insinuates itself over the rest. He looks at me out of the corner of his eye. I look back. Everything he has is new: the white shirt, the watch, the open backpack with a few books on Afro-Cuban art. He is a young professor or a student about to graduate. Thirty years old, no more. I move my hand from the armrest and hide it between my legs. On-screen, the actor speaks directly to the camera, challenging the Empire: junk food is to blame for the world's obesity. He introduces us to his vegan girlfriend and the doctors who are going to accompany his body as it falls over the precipice, stuffed with trash for an entire month. The man lets his hand fall on to my leg in a smooth move that nobody else sees. It takes but a second – a caress – for everything else to disappear . . . the people, the movie. He is all that exists now, his slow, deliberate breathing. I lie in wait, hunching closer to the woman on my right. I could ask him to let me go by, tell him that I have to go to the bathroom and wait in the lobby. But I don't do anything. The woman scoots over a bit so that my arm stops touching hers. All three of us stare ahead in silence. On-screen the American body begins to decompose. Swollen, flaccid, lacking all desire, it vomits in the car park of a McDonald's and the cinema bursts into laughter. The man on my left laughs along and leans his leg into mine. This time I stay put. He realizes it's become a battle of wills (he likes that). He settles his backpack down on his left leg so the stranger sitting on his other side can't watch him. His hand moves over to his pants, he unbuttons them and pulls down the zipper. Without turning my head, I can see him take it out. He strokes it with his right hand, holding on to the backpack with his left. Up and down, faster and faster. He laughs when everyone else laughs (up, down) without taking his eyes off the screen (up, down). A German man lounges in the row just in front of us, oblivious to the fact that he is aiming at his neck (up, down) his breathing gets deeper, falters, nobody notices (up, down) his hand goes crazy, his breathing envelops both of us (I will not . . .) he finishes himself off with the applause, eyes fixed on the screen, spattering the back of the German's seat, the tips of his blond hair, painting the wood in spasms, signing it with a last drop of semen.

He keeps still, composing himself while the credits announce that the American has won all the independent cinema awards. When the lights come on, he gets up and asks to be allowed by. He's the first person up, even though we are seated in the middle of the row. People move their knees to let him go by; someone complains about his haste. He abandons the theatre fleeing like a rat, cowardly, his eyes nailed to the floor. He walks hunched over, uncomfortable with his height. Little by little, the theatre begins to empty, but I can't tear my eyes from his work of art, the most ephemeral expression of modern art. The German's girlfriend in the row ahead caresses his hair and pulls her sticky hand away.

The lobby is swarming with people. All the countries of the world simmering in a single broth. He is nowhere to be seen. The shouts of a British group stand out from among the sweaty babel, arguing with a mulatto guard. They demand to be allowed to stay in the cinema to see the next Japanese film, refusing to stand in yet another line. One of them is a member of the jury of the Havana Film Festival. The guard talks to them about equal rights and even about revolution. As I am about to cross the doorway, I feel his breath on the back of my neck. He's right there, holding his body against mine. In the chaos of people pushing to get out nobody notices anything strange about the way his hands grab my waist. *Look at me, at least once.* His voice is low, serene, dark as his skin. He doesn't have a closed, inland accent. *Please. Look at me.* He slides his left hand downwards. The right hand continues past it and stops in the middle of my stomach. For a moment I am surprised by how natural his hands feel holding my body (as if he knew it by heart). The crowd pushes us forward. I escape his grip and cross the doorway.

Forty degrees wait for us outside. Cubans and foreigners mingle in a line that is three blocks long, credentials hanging from their necks. I look for the Brasileira, the Basque's red shirt, the Hungarian's gigantic body. People shove their way down the tiny stairs. Some arrive to the showing late; others get dragged there by the current. I fight the desire to look at him until someone stumbles and pushes me up against the naked back of a mulatto woman with grey eyes. She turns her head around and laughs like a snake charmer. Our skin slides off one another's; there's nothing to grab. Black people of all shades are scattered among the Europeans. A hand slips up from beneath the jumble of bodies and grabs mine before the mulatto woman is able to say anything. The Brasileira flashes her string of white teeth. She has a mole just above her lip and a birthmark on her neck, the trace of an eternal kiss. Lightly smudged make-up from the night before gives her a halo of glamour, like a classic film star. Her breath is sweet with alcohol; she has carried a flask of rum in her purse since the first day and takes short pulls from it as if it were filled with Bach Flower Remedies.

She goes down the remaining stairs two by two, cutting across diagonally, barking for them to let us through, it's an emergency. The Basque waits at the corner, tying the laces of his orthopaedic shoe. One leg is twenty centimetres shorter than the other and he weighs only fifty kilos. He's warned me five times since we first met (seventy hours ago to be exact) that he's of no use as anyone's protection. The Hungarian woman is exactly the opposite, both in size and in spirit. Her stories are as exuberant as her body. She crosses the street in between cars, devouring a melting ice-cream cone. *We have one hour before the next movie shows,* she says in perfect Spanish. *Let's go to the cemetery.* She walks on, not bothering to wait for an answer. She's a director's assistant in Budapest, she's used to giving orders. She was married to a Cuban for a decade, she knows the island by heart, her youngest daughter was born in Varadero and grew up eating fish and oranges. She has been insisting on taking us to the place where her husband proposed matrimony since the day we arrived.

The street is a psychotic migratory wave: people walking in groups, nobody going in the same direction. They walk with the same sluggish gait, crushed by the heat and lack of air. Along the banks a string of large, run-down houses and mansions from the colonial period now converted into human dovecotes, one family per room, are all in the same state: peeling paint, broken glass, tall weeds, holes in the ceilings and walls. The residents sit out in the doorways in plastic chairs, watching the parade of foreigners pass by. A blonde woman with sun-creased skin doesn't bother to hide an expression of scorn at the swooning state of some of the representatives of the First World. The Brasileira is the only one who stares back, unblinking, until the blonde woman smiles at her and moves on to the next foreigner.

The cemetery is located in the centre of Havana; an entire city block full of dead people. The closer the tombstones are to the centre, the older. Some no longer bear any trace of a name or a date; they're just blocks of stone sticking out from among the vegetation. We cross the threshold at that magic hour: when everything looks a little nicer than it really is. The setting sun does not alleviate the heat. Instead, the humidity grows denser. When the Basque considers the photos he could have shot in this light, his eyes cloud up. His limp marks the rhythm of the walk and he ponders over how dangerous his Cuban adventure could have been: he arrived a day before the workshop began and decided to spend the day walking around on his own at the Malecón fair. He was about to buy *Trilogía sucia de La Habana* for fifteen dollars when a black man whispered in his ear that he could get it for him for only ten. In one fell swoop the Basque managed to pick up a book, a guide and the hope of a lover. By noon he had already treated the man to three mojitos, lunch, the book, his sunglasses . . . He was ecstatic: Havana exceeded his fantasies. He took photos left and right (he wanted to bring it all back with him) until the guide offered to take a photo of him. Further and further away he walked, pursuing a panoramic shot of the Malecón. When he was about fifty metres away, he called out for the Basque to smile, then took off at a run.

The Hungarian comes to a halt at a grave marked by a huge domino tile instead of a regular headstone. A double six is engraved in the stone, weather-worn from decades in the open air. *Right here,* she says, *this is where I said yes.* The woman buried before us had been her friend, her love, a compulsive domino player who had followed her from Budapest to Havana. She died in a macumba session (unable to withstand the passage of the Immaculate Conception over her body). The artisan who contrived the domino marker was the Hungarian's ex-husband. They had met right here: she points to the García Lorca Theatre in front of the cemetery and asks us to accompany her. I continue to watch them over my shoulder. Everything seems unreal, the logic of dreams: faceless men, friend-strangers, the dramas of other people's lives . . . Ever since we left the movie theatre, I have felt him still lingering, watching me, swallowed into the Cuban night every time I turn round.

A white marble lobby, chandeliers, Persian rugs . . . The García Lorca Theatre is one of the few refurbished buildings in Havana. It boasts the grandeur of epochs past that can't be found anywhere else on the island. *La Bohème* will begin in ten minutes. The Brasileira sets to seducing one of the guards in a way that is as natural to her as breathing is for the rest of us mortals. She bats her eyelashes until he falls into a trance. The guard lets us stand in the line reserved for Cuban residents. The people coming in are wearing long dresses and summer suits. They are foreigners, although there are also some Cubans who are not a part of the dying socialism found outside, in the streets. The Hungarian shows her old residency card and buys four tickets, while the Brasileira puts on lipstick in front of a mirror. The duo enter the lobby, dragging along their Basque-Argentine millstone. They hold their heads so high that nobody notices the Hungarian's girl-explorer Bermudas, nor the Paulista's skin, so damp with perspiration it looks almost bathed in oil. The soprano shrieks as if they were about to tear her to pieces. With a sigh of agony, the Brasileira sneaks off to the bathroom before the intermission.

The hallway is empty and dark (in Cuba they conserve light even in the opera). Old-fashioned armchairs with corduroy upholstery and gold ribbing decorate the vestibule but in the bathroom there is nothing: no paper, no soap. A thread of water trickles from the tap, a tiny light bulb moves in circles, like a pendulum, above the hypnotized stare of the Brasileira, who follows it from below, spread out in one of the easy chairs, arms hanging over the edge, neck stretched backwards. For a second it looks broken – snapped – but she picks her head up when she hears someone come in. She lifts her dress with one hand and pulls her thong down with the other as she walks into one of the stalls. She doesn't sit down but, barely bending her knees, opens her legs. She does a little wiggle-dance before pulling her thong back up. *Tenho um presentinho pra você*. She pulls a roach from her bra and holds it in her fingertips as if it were a diamond.

That's how it was from the first day on: she would finish waking up as the sun went down. I arrived at the school at five in the morning on Sunday. The airport taxi stopped at the entrance gate so the security guard could confirm my name on the list. He assigned me a room in the last apartment module, gave me a set of keys and a warning: my Brazilian room-mate had arrived the day before. The headlights illuminated five Rationalist buildings strewn amid a field as barren as an African savannah. The taxi left me in front of the last apartment module, a cement rectangle with acrylic windows. Something tickling my left foot made me look down: it was a tiny frog; there were two more on my bag. All around me, the ground was littered with frogs.

The Brasileira was singing in the shower when I got in. The bedside lamp in her room was on, a scarf hung over the shade. Her clothes were scattered across the floor: papers, books, speakers, records, incense, oils, creams, make-up, sweets, powdered milk . . . The bed was unmade, photos stuck to the wall. An empty milk carton was left on the kitchen table. A pair of panties and a lace bra hung from a rocking chair made of ribbons of blue plastic that sat on the living-room balcony. For someone who had landed less than twenty-four hours earlier, it was a prodigy of chaos. I set her underclothes down on the table. They were still wet, recently washed. Outside there was no sign of dawn. A herd of rickety goats passed in front of the apartment building, harangued by a mulatto every bit as skinny as them. She came out of the bathroom in the nude. After a few steps she stopped, when she saw first my bag and then me, sitting in front of the balcony. She leaned against the wall, hands behind her back. We talked until daybreak. Not once did she ever try to dress or to cover herself up, but let a small puddle of water form at her feet, which the breeze that came in from the balcony slowly but surely dried up. At seven, she said we needed to sleep for a few hours before meeting the maestro.

At five minutes to ten in the morning, a black car with smoked windows appears like a mirage at the end of the palm-lined road. The ten of us attending the workshop wait in front of the rest of the students, the cameras, the journalists at the bottom of the stairs. There is a rumour going around that this will be the last workshop the maestro teaches. Birri – the school's director – helps him out of the car. García Márquez emerges sheathed in a blue jumpsuit, cleaning a pair of spectacles that get lost for a moment in Birri's white beard when they separate from their embrace. *Smile for the hyenas*, he whispers, giving us hugs in front of the journalists' cameras. We follow him up a floor, to the classroom. He doesn't let anyone else in except us. Inside, the microphones are already turned on. Every word is recorded and belongs to the Film School of San Antonio de los Baños. *So . . . who has the big idea?* García Márquez asks. He's having fun with us. Or, rather: he's making fun of us. *Your mission is to deliver one good idea, only one,* he says, fishing around in his jumpsuit pockets until he finds what he's looking for: an inhaler. He takes a hit from it and his eyes come back to life. *If you don't have one, go out and find it.* Intimidated to the point of going mute; when he leaves ten minutes later not one of us has been able to decide yet whether his voraciousness is of the vampire variety or is merely contempt. One thing has become clear: screenwriters, for the maestro, are no more than a breed of lackeys.

So, from the very first day, García Márquez has turned his students into a pack of hunters. The big one is our prey and it can be found anywhere (past, future, fiction, reality). On the second night, standing in the doorway of the theatre, roach hanging from her lips, the Brasileira looks into the darkness and sighs . . . *I won't leave until I find it*. She walks away, down a narrow, cobbled street that runs between the back of the theatre and the cemetery wall which is covered in captions dedicated to the people at rest on the other side. Car headlights cut out silhouettes of Havana's nocturnal citizens. At sunset, clandestine taxis come out: clients pile in, sitting on top of each other until there is no room left to breathe. If one prefers to walk, the eyes grow accustomed to the dark and the silhouettes slowly recover their features. The Brasileira's whistle reaches me from the corner. I see her for a second, waving her arm, illuminated by the headlights of a passing car, then the darkness swallows her up again. The glow coming from one of the theatre signs is the only light along the whole block. I hear a sound – *tsss* – to my right and turn my head to see a flare of embers suspended in mid-air. As my vision adjusts I can just make out the Brasileira: she's holding the roach with the tips of her fingers, the back of her head resting against the cemetery wall as she fills her lungs with smoke. *Você viu isso?* She points to a small door that is barely lit. Two foreigners dressed in pastel colours wait in front of a black man with the body of a boxer and an unctuous, adolescent hooker at his side. Above the door someone has written by hand: WELCOME TO GARCÍA LORCA'S HELL.

When the door opens, beams of light tint the European brand-name clothing. The Europeans descend and the black man is about to shut the door when the Brasileira takes the offensive, sweetened by the sounds of Afro-Cuban music and hip hop. A fresh round of eyelash batting ensues and he lets us through. Downstairs, people are dancing, packed into a fifty-square-metre basement decorated with leftover stage props, the waiters dressed in period costumes. To be more precise, the people who are dancing are black; the white people watch them with respect as they move in ways they themselves will never be able to. A few drunken men (white) pluck up the courage to shake their spastic bodies amid such elegance, while a few chosen women (white) are escorted to the floor and led around like rubber dolls. It takes a minute before I register a stab of pain on my forearm. My sudden movement – clumsy – spills the drink of the man standing next to me. He is about to curse at me when he realizes what his cigar has done to my skin: a round burn, as perfect as a birthmark in raw flesh (the same spot where that other man first touched me).

The theatre lobby above is limbo to the hell that's below. People strike affected poses as they wait for the intermission to end, never realizing that below their feet others are shaking their bodies to the point of trance, or that the waiters doling out drinks below are dressed in outfits very similar to those serving glasses of sherry with plastic smiles above. The Hungarian and the Basque are lounging near the bathroom, nearly prostrate with boredom and having nothing to say to each other. Their eyes light up when they see me (not because of me, but because of their hope that the Brasileira is behind me). It takes all of five strides for her to be nearly on top of me, followed by the Basque (double the number of strides, half the speed). *The last guagua from Heladería Copelia to the school leaves in an hour*, the Hungarian says. They agree to go down to hell as long as they can catch the bus back.

To go down is always harder than it is to come up: there are more people than just a few minutes earlier, dancing in place wherever they stop, wedging their bodies in alongside foreign bodies. The Hungarian waves a few bills at the bar until she's able to exchange them for mojitos. My cigar burn is getting worse – a damp red circle stains one napkin after another – and the Brasileira

is nowhere to be found, not at the bar, not on the dance floor . . .
At the last minute I find her in the arms of a black man who is moving
her around as if they were of the same race, one of her legs between
his, a hand on his back, the other around his neck, spinning as if she
were a marionette, she so completely fascinated by he who moves
the strings that she is willing to let him do anything he wants with
her. They spin and spin and there it is: the white shirt, the hair
smoothed back with pomade, the watch on his wrist, the backpack at
his shoulder with books on Afro-Cuban art, spinning and spinning,
and now he has the Brasileira's throat in his mouth and his eyes
are focused on me. They smile when they see me (both of them).
The Brasileira shouts over the music, shouts both my name and
his: Cohiba. The man gives me a kiss, his mouth so close to mine
the edges of our lips brush against each other. Before we separate,
he whispers *hola* in my ear. His greeting me this way is worse than
anything that has come before, his greeting turns us into accomplices.

The Brasileira opens the tap in the bathroom and sticks her head
under the water. From the mirror I notice a man's two feet
peeking out from underneath one of the closed doors. Two small,
girl's hands are grabbing his ankles, above high violet heels with
worn-out soles. A man's grunts can be heard coming from inside.
The Brasileira ties her wet hair in a knot to get it out of her face.
He came from nowhere, she explains. He grabbed her to him as
if they knew each other. Their bodies fitted. Later they began to
talk and everything just fitted. She spouts clichés and the tacky
things of a person infatuated. I tell her what happened in the movie
theatre. *Não pode ser*, she answers. *Não pode ser ele*. I swear to her that
it's him. One of the stall doors opens. The hooker who had walked
down with us comes out. She washes her face and rinses her mouth
with water. A grey-haired man in a floral shirt comes out after her,
rubs his nose, eyes like slits from an excess of everything. The
Brasileira waits for them to leave and looks at me again . . . *Why didn't
you tell me what happened in the movie theatre until now?* She looks

at me suspiciously, as if I might have reasons for making something like that up. *Nem sequer se veste bem.* I told her that he had left as soon as the lights came on, that I never saw the front of his face. *Ele é professor na universidade,* she says (as if that explained everything). *Ele pinta, expôs em Amsterdã três vezes, trabalha como curador.* Three times she repeats that it can't be him. The Hungarian enters the bathroom with red cheeks from the heat. If we don't leave we are going to miss the bus. *Eu vou ficar,* the Brasileira says (addressing her; she won't even look at me). *Conheci um cara que tem um carro. Ele se ofereceu pra me levar à escola mais tarde.* The Hungarian shrugs her shoulders. *Okey-dokey,* she says, *nos vemos mañana.* It's not worth trying to insist; we've suddenly become like strangers.

It's not my job to take care of anyone, I tell myself; she can do what she wants. I walk out of the bathroom and before going back up the stairs, I see Cohiba one last time. He's standing behind a few heads, a smile in his eyes. The anger lasts until the minibus takes off for the road. Fear creeps up in the middle of two coffee plantations. Everyone around me is asleep. A small group comments on the latest Iranian movie which seems to have changed their lives. The Hungarian snores with her head leaning forward and the Basque with his eyes half open. A couple are kissing in the first row, bathed in the light from the seat where the driver's companion sits. He moves his tongue around the contour of her lips so slowly it seems as though he were drawing them.

Outside, the plantations accumulate.

I open my eyes at the doorway to the school, when the minibus stops. Nobody says a word. Tens of sleeping bodies drag themselves off to their rooms, mumbling goodnight. Zombies with eyes that fight to open and arms that hang inert on either side of their bodies. The Basque is one of them, his limp more pronounced than ever. The Hungarian is in the middle and I am the last in the line; a metre's length separates each one of us. The frogs puncture the silence of the night. I squash one of them underfoot and it splatters all the way to my ankle. There's no way to remove the little body from the sole of my shoe. It's stuck there with its legs open, as if it were crushed while it was asleep. *One frog less in the world won't change a thing*, the Hungarian says, laughing. I carry the cadaver all the way to the bathroom. There's no water; they turn it off almost every night. There's no toilet paper (there is no paper on the island, no sheets of paper, no notebooks, schools have gone back to using blackboards but there is no chalk). I peel the pieces of frog off with the edge of a dirty dress, cover the bloody sandal with it and hide the remains in a corner. There are two passport photos stuck to the bathroom mirror (one is mine; the other is of the Brasileira). Outside, the frogs continue their croaking. At one point in the night I can feel him standing over me, watching me sleep. But nobody is there when I open my eyes. I hear moans coming from the other side of the wall.

At dawn I open the window but there is no breeze yet. An oil-blue Chevy with a shattered rear window is parked in front. The Brasileira's bedroom door is closed. There are ashes from a stick of incense on the edge of a picture frame. The backpack full of books on Afro-Cuban art is on the wood table in the living room. Wifredo Lam's *La jungla* decorates a cover. *El paraiso ha muerto,* the title states. Expensive books, full of photos and ribboned dividers. There is a notebook full of commentaries. On the last page, handwritten:

The tour operators sell us with four Ss:

Sun,

Sex,

Sand & Sea

Buy us, enjoy us!

Eat us!

The paper is punctured at the end of the last sentence, as if written with such force the pen broke through the surface. *The chronicles of the conquistadors say that our island was inhabited by cannibals with dogs' heads.* The line is not straight and, observed carefully, one can see a tremble in the hand. *Mestizaje: the best we have to offer.* There is a small pouch of tobacco and rolling paper in one of the pockets. A leather wallet. Cuban pesos, convertible, a few dollars (small denominations), and the photo of a girl around five years old, a mulatta with green eyes. She has the same features as the man but softened by a white mother. A rustling sound from inside the room sends me back over my footsteps in a hurry. On my bed, lying face up and breathing hard, I look at the photo of the young girl in my hand, thinking that somehow, by having brought it with me, perhaps I could save her. It's too late to put it back. I leave it where it is, on the sheet.

When I open my eyes, the sun is shining through the window. A breeze coming in from the countryside rustles the edge of the sheet. The Brasileira is humming contentedly. She walks by my door wrapped in a towel and says good morning in Portuguese. She is holding a glass of milk in her hand. The photo of the young girl is in the same place I left it. But my photo is missing, the one that was stuck to the bathroom mirror. I look for it around the apartment, in the corners of the bathroom. I ask her if she has seen it and she laughs as if it were a joke. *What would I want with your photo?* She doesn't wait for me; she's dying of hunger and doesn't want to miss breakfast. I watch her walk towards the main building through the balcony's acrylic window. She sings as she walks, filling her lungs with air (she's so charming even the school's dogs follow behind her). The man's barefoot prints are still visible on the floor, going from the bathroom to the bedroom, slowly drying until they disappear. Outside everything else is silent; nobody is left on the three floors of the building. One apartment near the entrance door functions as a laundry room. Not even the smell of recently washed clothes can relieve my nausea.

García Márquez is already seated at his desk. *The Argentine woman who arrived late,* he says. *I want today's big idea.* I tell him the story of a student who – for lack of ideas – decides to murder her maestro. He interrupts me immediately (asking for another). There is an exchange of glances. The Brasileira breathes in deeply and explains that she has only a beginning. The maestro smiles: all you need for a story is the beginning. He asks her to speak up, and he zips up his jumpsuit. He's dressed the same way for four days now, always in a jumpsuit. A blue one the first day, orange the second, brown the third. The fourth one is English racing green. The Brasileira brings the microphone to her mouth and tells the story of a woman who falls in love on her third evening in Havana. She knows the man is hiding something, but it doesn't matter to her. She would leave everything behind not to lose him. She continues on until the maestro's snoring interrupts her halfway through a sentence. The worker in charge of taping the workshop presses the pause button. Suddenly, García Márquez opens his eyes, as if the weight of the glances focusing on him were enough to wake him up, and he tells the Brasileira that she has a good beginning. Now she needs an ending.

So no big idea that day. He lets us leave at quarter to one. I spend the next half-hour not being able to leave the bathroom: kneeling at the toilet, vomiting until I'm empty. When I come out, the minibus is taking off for the city, more than a hundred metres down the road. I don't try to run, my legs are too wobbly. The walk back to the apartment seems to be getting longer and longer. The concrete is burning and disfiguring the landscape. By day, the frogs cede their kingdom to the flies. A car advances behind me at walking pace, keeping a few metres back. The Brasileira is waiting in the doorway in front of me, wearing a sky-blue dress and black sunglasses. Her hair is in a long braid and she's holding her shoes in her hands. Her smile isn't directed at me, it's for the Chevy that is coming up behind me. Cohiba smiles back at us from the other side of the windscreen. The Brasileira doesn't notice that I am queasy and trembling. She hugs me and moves me towards the car: she wants me to meet him. She opens the back door for me to get in. Cohiba looks at me through the rear-view mirror. He is about to say something when the Brasileira climbs into the front seat and greets him with a kiss on the lips. *My friend is coming with us.* Cohiba doesn't say a word. He does a U-turn to go back in the direction of the school. All the windows are open. There is no glass in the rear windscreen. When the car pulls out on to the road, the wind zigzags between one window and the other. The Brasileira shouts so that Cohiba can hear her over the wind and the car's engine. She tells him her story, that García Márquez says it lacks an ending. Cohiba smiles as if the problem were already resolved. He switches on the radio, puts in a cassette and turns up the volume. He has it up so high it's impossible to talk.

When we get to San Antonio, the car turns off on to a dirt road and he slows down. He doesn't kill the engine, but neither does he continue advancing. When the Brasileira asks him what he is waiting for, he doesn't respond, captivated by the image in front of his eyes. Three young girls are playing with a hose on the corner. The drops of water shine against the sun. The girls laugh, they jump and shout, drenched. They practise a dance step, rustle each other's hair, shake their hips and shoulders. The music playing on the cassette seems as though it were invented just for them. They are hypnotic, and for a while we watch them dance in silence until one of the girls glances over and catches sight of the car parked at the corner. It's the mulatto girl with the green eyes in the photo, but a few years older. She comes closer to the car but stops at a safe distance, as if she knows better than to continue forward. Cohiba moves the car a few metres closer to her, until the girl is right next to us. She looks at us. She's the same as he is, but in lighter colours. The man looks for something in his pocket. An envelope. He is about to hand it to her when a black woman leans out of a house. She must be around forty years old but already looks like an old woman. When she sees the car, she calls to the girl using a strange name: Ixé. It takes a while for the girl to pull herself away from the man's gaze, at first only moving a few steps backwards until a second shout comes, when she finally turns and runs towards the house. The man gets out of the car to meet up with the woman. She speaks quickly, with a closed, nearly incomprehensible accent. *With the foreigners whatever you want, but not with your daughter.* That's the only thing I can understand. She repeats it many times (*not with your daughter*) before taking the envelope. The girl spies on us from the window. If she had the choice, she would go with him. Something in the way the two of them look at each other is reminiscent of two lovers separated by force.

We said goodbye two days later, the last day of the workshop. Without ever finding García Márquez's big idea. Today I received an email from the Brasileira's mailbox. It's written by her older brother; they are gathering information from the last people to see her. She left the school with a man who drove an oil-blue Chevy. She never made it to the airport. They found her body fifty kilometres outside Havana. ∎

GRANTA

STARS AND STRIPES

Santiago Roncagliolo

TRANSLATED BY EDITH GROSSMAN

SANTIAGO RONCAGLIOLO
PERU
1975

Roncagliolo was born in Lima, and his family temporarily left
Peru for political reasons in 1977. His novel *Pudor* (2005) was made
into a film and his political thriller *Abril rojo* received the Alfaguara
Prize in 2006 and is published in English as *Red April* (2010).
La cuarta espada (2007), his non-fiction novel, delves into the mind
of the most dangerous terrorist in the history of the Americas:
Abimael Guzmán of Sendero Luminoso. *Memorias de una dama*
(2009), tracing the origins of the Mafia in Cuba, was censored and its
publication is prohibited throughout the entire world. His new novel,
Tan cerca de la vida, is a thriller set in the sex market of Tokyo.
His work has been translated into thirteen languages.
'Stars and Stripes' is a new story.

Carlitos loved the United States. He papered the walls of his room with American flags and tourist posters from odd places, like 'Idaho, Home of the Potato'. He said all the words he could in English, for example 'Hershey's' or 'Chuck Norris', and when he did, he chewed on the syllables until they sounded the way they did in movies. I suppose he pronounced the language really well, because nobody understood anything. People had to ask him several times what exactly he had said.

It isn't that Carlitos was trying to take anyone in. Just the opposite. I never knew anyone as authentic. He was incapable of pretending anything he didn't really think, though he really didn't think about too many things. If we became friends, it was because neither of us had more ideas than were strictly necessary. That brings people together.

Carlitos's father, an extremely fat man, was an officer in the Peruvian navy. He had studied in Panama, in the School of the Americas, and then somewhere in the United States in a place whose name I've forgotten, something like Naples. In the outside world, he moved around preceded by an escort car, dressed in a black uniform and a white visored hat, which helped to hide his bulk. But indoors he was always in his shorts and undershirt. Seeing his enormous belly about to burst through the undershirt, no one would have imagined he was so important.

Carlitos's mother spent her days reminding him about the time they had spent in North America, recalling it with enthusiasm. Her way of indicating that she liked something a good deal was to say it was 'like up there'. Carlitos's older brother did the same thing, always talking about the clothes you could get 'up there'. When he travelled, he would come back with gleaming sneakers, like the ones astronauts wore, or red jackets covered with zippers in the style of Michael Jackson. Carlitos was too young to have memories of 'up there'. But he loved going to Disney. He had been there four times since he was very little.

Whenever Carlitos talked about Disney, I would go home to my father and say: 'I want to go to Disney.'

'Why? I've taken you to Ecuador.'

'The only thing I remember about Ecuador is that there were banana trees and I got diarrhoea.'

'You can get diarrhoea at Disney too.'

I'd stamp my feet and whine, but my father wouldn't yield. In fact, he didn't even bother to answer me. At the time Carlitos and I began to hang out together, his principal occupation was cheating on my mother. Mama taught at a secondary school outside Lima and would get home when it was almost dark. In the afternoons Papa often came home with a woman when he thought I had gone out to play. Her name was Betsy and he'd take her into his room.

All those times – or nearly all of them, I suppose – I was in the house. I almost never went out to play. The neighbourhood kids played soccer, and I didn't like soccer. I'd stay in the house with Carlitos, who didn't play soccer either because they didn't play it in the United States. We spent the afternoons looking at the baseball cards his father would bring back for him from his trips up North. We didn't understand baseball, so Carlitos and I didn't have anything to say to each other. We would look at the cards in silence, and who knows what we were thinking? This was why Papa never heard us on those afternoons.

On several occasions though, maybe a dozen times, Carlitos did hear my father and his girlfriend. But he never said a word. Not to me and not to his family. Probably because he spoke English with his family and didn't know how to say these things in that language. In any case, when Papa came home with the woman and went to his room to the sound of giggles and whispers, Carlitos would only bend his head and silently pass me another card with the picture of some pitcher or catcher. I was very grateful to him for his silences, and I think this was when I began to value his companionship as I never had anyone else's.

I had the chance to return the favour, but that was a few years later, when we were about thirteen. By then my parents had divorced and I had begun trying to go out with girls. There was one, Mily, who had already kissed the entire neighbourhood, at least the boys who played soccer, who always had priority in these matters. When Mily set aside her final defence, nobody wanted to go out with her any more because it made a bad impression.

I was in no way concerned by Mily's résumé. On the contrary, I thought that, given her record, it would be easier to kiss her. And since she had done it so many times, she could teach me to be a good kisser. For weeks I appeared at all the parties she attended. I was inexperienced and thought that to kiss somebody you had to feel profound things. And so I forced myself to fall in love with her. With practice, I succeeded in thinking about her automatically, until the really complicated issue was forgetting about her and concentrating on my studies and exams.

Finally, after several parties and dancing to a good number of slow songs, I tried to give her a kiss in the kitchen of a friend's house. But she refused.

'Don't come near me,' she said.

'Why not? You've kissed everybody else.'

'That's why. I don't want people to think I'm easy.'

'What's easy about it? I've spent weeks trying to do this.'

'I'll tell you what we can do. Every afternoon I take my dog for a walk in the park. If you come and keep me company, maybe we'll kiss one day. But don't imagine anything else, OK?'

For the whole summer I showed up like a slave to join her on her walks through the park, but she never let me touch her. Her dog, a basset hound with a melancholy face, seemed to laugh at me when I appeared. To humiliate me even more, Mily always asked about Carlitos. She wanted to know what he liked. What games he played. If we saw each other a lot. If I could bring him to the park sometime. I did all I could to ignore what she was trying to tell me, but finally I had to admit that she liked my imbecile neighbour.

It had its own logic. I haven't said so until now, but Carlitos was very far from being handsome. He was enormous and soft, his teeth were crooked, and he had never shown any interest in girls. That's probably why Mily liked him, because he was the only boy who never tried to take any liberties with her.

Though Carlitos wasn't to blame for anything, I was furious with him. Simply put, his company reminded me of my failure with Mily. I stopped seeing him. I didn't want him to interfere with my difficult progress towards a first kiss. Apparently this served only to make Carlitos want to see me more than ever. He rang my bell six days in a row. He asked my parents about me. He telephoned me at midnight. I never responded. It wouldn't take me long to regret that. Mily's kiss never came, but at the end of the summer, I learned from other neighbours about the tragedy that had struck Carlitos's family while I was ignoring him.

That year his parents had sent his older brother to study in the United States. Manuel – that was his brother's name – had begun to travel back and forth very frequently, too frequently, but no one thought it strange. After all, Carlitos's father had been promoted to the rank of admiral. His house was filled with armed bodyguards, and in all probability he earned a great deal of money. Sending the boy back and forth wouldn't represent a huge expenditure for him.

What did surprise everyone was that the police arrested Manuel at the airport, when he was about to leave on one of his trips. This time Manuel had spent barely forty-eight hours in Lima, going out to discotheques at night and sleeping during the day. His family hardly saw him, and even though they were beginning to suspect what was going on, nobody felt like asking questions. They were probably confident an admiral's son would not be arrested.

At first, no one believed that Manuel's detention would last too long. It had to be a mistake. Or the admiral would make certain it was a mistake. But it seems Manuel was carrying too much cocaine for the matter to be ignored, or even for him to be given a light sentence. And apparently his father didn't tolerate that kind of behaviour in his family. He used all his connections to get him a decent cell in a maximum-security prison, but he couldn't or wouldn't do more.

Another boy in the neighbourhood told me all this, and when I heard about it, I felt guilty for having ignored Carlitos's phone calls. I went to see him right away. His mother received me with a sombre expression that I didn't want to interpret as a reproach for my absence. His father didn't even know who I was.

I found Carlitos with his GI Joes, which were beginning to seem anachronistic in a boy his age, and his American footballs, which he never used because nobody knew how to play the game. I didn't know what to say and sat down on his bed. He didn't say anything either. His room smelled strange, but it always smelled strange.

After a time spent in silence, the clock struck five, the time when Mily walked her dog, and it occurred to me that I could do something to make up for my bad behaviour. I took him to the park and tried to organize some lively talk between the three of us. When I thought everything was off to a good start, I pretended I had to go to the dentist and left them alone. I never found out more, and Carlitos never talked about it.

Some six or seven years later, I ran into Mily at a discotheque. We danced, laughed and recalled the old days. In the end we spent the night together. It was fun, and a little nostalgic. Before I fell asleep, I remembered the episode in the park and asked: 'Listen, do you remember the afternoon when I left you with Carlitos? Did you do anything? Even just a kiss?'

'Nothing,' she said. 'I tried, that afternoon and many other afternoons, but he only wanted to show me his baseball cards.'

I never knew Carlitos to have a girlfriend. Neither did anyone else, as far as I know. As my interest in women increased and his remained at zero, we began to grow apart.

Of course, from time to time we'd run into each other on the street and exchange a few words, but increasingly they sounded empty, merely the inevitable formulas of courtesy. He would recount the entire plot of the latest movie he had seen, or the most recent matches in some sport I didn't understand, and actually it was all the same to him whether I listened or not. He recited the complete event, second by second, telling me each point in detail, and if I interrupted him, he would let me speak for a few seconds and then return to his monologue.

Given his general autistic state, people in the neighbourhood speculated about the possibility that Carlitos was gay, which was what they said about any unusual person. But the rumour died almost as quickly as it had started. In reality, Carlitos didn't seem capable of any kind of sexual behaviour.

When we had all stopped growing, he continued to lengthen and soon became too big to climb comfortably into the spacious 4x4 vans into which his bodyguards would cram him. The urgent need for security – by now his father was an admiral of the fleet – prevented him from joining us for a swim at the beach or simply wandering around with us, so that as he grew his entire body turned into a flabby, shapeless mass, like a mutant jellyfish. But all that physical growth was not accompanied by any hormonal development. Carlitos had no facial hair, his voice was unpleasantly high-pitched and shrill, and in summer his hairless legs looked like those of a gigantic baby in imported sneakers.

When all of us in the neighbourhood matriculated at the university, Carlitos definitively left our orbit. We didn't even know whether he had tried to go to the university. We knew only that he was working as a cashier and usher at a movie theatre in a nearby mall. He didn't learn to drive either; every day he came out in his pink mall uniform and got into a van filled with bodyguards. I imagine the same thing happened when he went home.

Carlitos's life seemed a peaceful one, but peaceful or not it was about to take an unexpected turn. During those years his family suffered a second misfortune worse than the one involving his brother.

It happened on one of his father's trips to the United States.

Recently, the fleet admiral's career had stagnated, which meant that the number of his bodyguards had been stable for several years. It was rumoured that he was about to retire, and for a few years he hadn't travelled to Naples-or-whatever-it's-called, or gone on any diplomatic military missions. And in these circumstances he took it into his head to visit his school one last time before his retirement.

Perhaps Carlitos's father wanted to be on record as a distinguished former student. Or probably he simply felt nostalgic. The fact is that, taking advantage of his last vacation, the fleet admiral travelled to Miami to board a domestic flight to his school. He had followed that route hundreds of times. He had an American visa good for ten years. But on this occasion something went wrong.

In the immigration office, when he gave his information, something unusual appeared on the officer's computer screen. At that time, the Americans weren't yet taking your picture and fingerprinting you when you came in, but they did ask if you wanted to kill the president or if you had participated in the Nazi genocide, and apparently they had digital files containing all that data.

In any event, they had the admiral pass into a separate little room. He was pleased to agree. Apparently he thought they had prepared an official reception for him. And in a way they had. Two officers questioned him for a long time, but none of the interrogation details became part of neighbourhood gossip. One can suppose he provided the names of important people he knew, at his school and at other military institutions. He must have suggested that they request references for him. While they consulted his file, the officers left him waiting in the little room. Carlitos's father spent hours there and was still there many hours after missing his connection.

As I've said, Carlitos's father was a very fat man. I suppose that between his nerves and the Miami heat, he perspired a good deal during those hours. And his tension exploded. Or perhaps one of his kidneys failed. The neighbourhood gossip didn't offer many medical details either. The fact is that when the officers returned to the room, they found him dead, clutching his briefcase. Inside the briefcase he carried only his diploma from the military school and his visored hat. That's why it took them several days to inform the family of his death.

Before graduating from the university, I moved out of my house to live on my own and left the neighbourhood. Long after it happened, I reconstructed the story of Carlitos's father on the basis of fragments of conversation with old mutual friends. But even when I heard the story for the first time, Carlitos and his mother had not been in the neighbourhood for a long while. They had disappeared without trace.

In time I married, divorced, married again and divorced again. I had no children, and perhaps that was the reason for my two failures. But I'm not sorry. Though I must confess that the first few weeks of sleeping alone after spending years with a woman are hell.

After my second divorce, I decided to get out of Lima and travel. At least I'd forget more quickly that way. A cousin of mine lived in Los Angeles, and I spent a few days with him, but then I grew bored, rented a car and spent my time touring California. Though perhaps the correct phrase is wandering aimlessly. I wasn't able to look at anything or talk to anyone. The only thing that made me feel good was driving for hours on empty highways.

One afternoon in Oakland I stopped at a cafe for something to eat. A train passed right over the cafe, and I had the feeling it was about to crash into something, just like me. Suddenly I saw Carlitos at a table, eating a cheeseburger.

His baseball cards passed in front of my eyes. The strange odour in his room. Mily. Echoes of a world that was never ordered again.

I can't say we greeted each other with emotion, like two old comrades. Rather, I think we were curious. I don't know how much I had changed, but Carlitos still looked like an oversized version of his cheeseburger. And I would swear his face still didn't harbour a single hair.

'I'm a cameraman,' he told me. 'For a programme of local shows. There aren't many shows in Oakland, but it's OK.'

'And your mother?'

'She lives here with me.'

'You live with your mother? And what do you do when you want to get laid? Do you send her to her room?'

I laughed. But he didn't laugh. He hesitated for a moment, as if he really were examining that possibility, before answering: 'No . . . we get along fine. Everything's OK.'

'Sure.'

We were silent. I didn't know how long he'd been out of the country, and I thought he'd ask me something about my life, or about Lima. But instead, after dipping his French fries in the last drop of ketchup, he asked: 'Have you seen *The Bounty Hunter*?'

His pronunciation brought to mind his painstaking American English, though after so many years, in a country where it attracted no attention to speak the language, his English no longer seemed to display good diction. It was just dense and chewed over.

I shook my head, and he continued.

'Jennifer Aniston has an ex-husband who's looking for her so he can turn her over to the police. When he finds her, he puts her in the trunk of his car, but then she escapes, and he has to handcuff her, and then . . .'

A long explanation of the movie followed, almost scene by scene, which lasted as long as it took the sun to set. Then he talked to me about ice hockey, showing with detailed gestures how the players split heads open.

'But this is Oakland,' he concluded, 'and there's no ice here.'

'I understand.'

I looked at my watch. I had thought about ordering another beer but changed my mind. He was scratching his ear. I began to wonder how to say goodbye without sounding unpleasant. Another train passed, making the restaurant tremble.

'Do you know what Manuel always used to say?' he asked suddenly.

I hadn't dared ask about his brother, and now that he had brought up the subject, I didn't dare ask why he spoke of him in the past tense.

'What did Manuel always used to say?'

'That everything that happened to him was fair payment for the good time he'd had. That the only thing he cared about was enjoying himself, and he had, big time.'

'It sounds like a good philosophy,' I said, just to say something.

'It is. I believe that too. You have to enjoy life to the hilt, right?'

'Absolutely. Absolutely.'

Without knowing why, I couldn't get up. Neither could he. We remained sitting there, in silence, until the waitress began to place the chairs on the tables. If it had been up to me, we would have stayed longer. ■

AFTER EFFECTS

Oliverio Coelho

TRANSLATED BY ANNE MCLEAN

OLIVERIO COELHO
ARGENTINA
1977

Coelho is the author of the novels *Tierra de vigilia* (2000), *Los invertebrables* (2003), *Borneo* (2004), *Promesas naturales* (2006), *Ida* (2008) and *Parte doméstico* (2009), and has been a resident writer in Mexico and South Korea. He has edited *Ji-do* (2009), an anthology of contemporary Korean narrative. He has received the Edmundo Valadés Latin American Prize in Mexico and the National Initiation Prize in Argentina. He methodically squandered the prize money on trips through Latin America, Europe and Asia, where he began a diary that continues today in his house in Buenos Aires. Currently, he writes about the latest books for the magazine *Inrockuptibles* and on his blog www.conejillodeindias.blogspot.com. 'After Effects' is an excerpt from his forthcoming novel *Un hombre llamado Lobo*.

A dilapidated bus, which thirty years earlier had probably been a luxurious long-distance vehicle with reclining seats, pulled up to the stand. A handwritten piece of paper taped to the inside of the windscreen said 'Balcarce'. Iván hurried up the steps and stretched out on the back seat. He turned his head and observed a luminous burr, a sun enlarged or deformed by the dirty rear window. His heart beat loudly, his throat contracted, he felt as if he hadn't slept for days and would never be able to fall asleep again. A sudden certainty calmed him: if he found his father, perhaps some woman would be able to love him in the future; perhaps he'd lose what his grandmother attributed to a curse but was simply an orphan's foreboding shyness. He felt the kind of momentary relief some prisoners on death row must get by cherishing the hope that their sentence will be reprieved at the last moment.

And so, wooed by faith, he slept until the bus arrived at San Manuel. He woke up automatically and walked up the aisle to the driver. The main street of the town was full of speed bumps and he hit his head on the handrail a couple of times.

'Is this San Manuel?' he asked, looking out of the window at the old-fashioned buildings of a ghost town beside the railway tracks.

'This is it.'

'Where's the centre?'

'It's nothing but centre . . . San Manuel ends at the end of the boulevard, where the tracks are. I turn round here. Where are you going?' and he began turning the bus around.

'I don't know, I'm looking for someone . . .' and he immediately thought how simple his adventure would be if he hadn't lost his father's address.

'Then get out here and ask in the bar.'

Iván got out at the door of a typical British-built railway building with a brickwork front. It was midday and, according to his calculations, the trip had taken just over an hour. The bar's metal blinds were pulled halfway down, in spite of which men were going in and coming out. In the large window a sign said 'Chicho's Bar'.

Behind the window, silhouettes of men gathered around a table. The door creaked and Iván's terror at entering made it sound unearthly. Then, when he took his first step inside the bar, one of the pine floorboards, which had probably been bearing the first anxious and last drunken step of thousands of townsfolk for a century, groaned and he wanted to hide or retreat, but the anachronistic decoration of the place held him spellbound: on the high, peeling walls advertisements survived from another era, notices announcing bullfights, Boca pennants and a poster of the championship-winning squad in the National Stadium in 1976. No one turned; nobody noticed a stranger had come in. At one table, near the window, six men absorbed in that atmosphere were playing *truco* and drinking gin. He heard one of them grumbling, 'That's for sure, there's nothing like women's devotion.'

Iván tried not to keep still. He played at thinking that if he didn't move he'd stay frozen forever in these townsfolk's halo of nostalgia. There was a lady behind the wooden counter. He walked over, slowly, so he wouldn't limp, avoiding the pool table with its torn felt, convinced that this feminine figure, as characteristic of the bar as the photos and posters covering the walls, might know something about his father. The lady looked at him, unsurprised. With a Spanish accent and a maternal tone she said: 'If you're looking for work, there isn't any here.' Iván turned round. He quickly observed the landscape of scattered gamblers just before lunch, in a room attached to the main room of the bar. As if taking a shot at reading the stranger's thoughts, she spoke again: 'They don't stay all day. At one they all go off for lunch and come back after their siesta. If you're looking for someone, this is where you're going to find him.'

Iván was horrified by the idea that his father might be among those present and would have seen him come limping in. This new defect, so unbecoming, embarrassed him and was the first thing he'd have to explain. He'd mention a fall, omitting, of course, the adventure that had preceded his arrival in San Manuel, and he'd tell him that Estela had died. Then he'd say that he hadn't come to demand explanations, that he knew – because a man called Marcusse had come to see him and told him everything – that he'd loved Estela and had done everything he could to find them when she ran away for reasons that even after her death still remained mysterious.

Iván looked at the faces, trying to recognize someone who resembled him. The excess of light and dust kept him from distinguishing any features in detail. The faces were as empty as masks. The voices were guttural, distant and very imprecise, as if they were coming out of a phonograph. The wide, cold space, the raised wooden floor, gave such a strange echo that all these men with cards in their hands seemed to be in purgatory, haggling over the price of a ticket to paradise.

'I'm looking for Silvio Lobo.'

'Silvio Lobo? Let's see . . .' and instead of looking at those who were there she closed her eyes to try to remember. 'Medina, Lobo just left, didn't he?'

A man with a thick moustache, wearing a beret and with his sleeves rolled up, the same one who'd said 'there's nothing like women's devotion', turned round immediately and, without putting down his cards or speaking, pointed towards the adjoining room.

'Do you want me to call him?' the woman asked.

'No, please,' Iván almost begged. 'Show me which one he is and I'll approach him.'

'Let's see, I'll tell you.' She leaned over the bar as if leaning out of a window. 'There, see that man in the grey sweater and glasses, at the back . . . that's Lobo.'

Iván looked through the particles of light that hung in the air and fixed his eyes on that man as if he wanted to soak up his appearance. Lobo, like any person who unconsciously senses he's being observed, glanced over towards him out of the corner of his eye for a fleeting instant, then turned his attention back to the game being played at the table. He didn't seem to be playing, but he was watching how the others played with a concentration that could have been confused with the resigned self-exclusion of a born loser.

Iván told himself it wouldn't make sense to burst into that situation out of nowhere. If he limped over and introduced himself as his son, he might embarrass him and provoke taunts from the other gamblers that his father would not later forgive. The bastard son of Lobo, they'd say. The woman who owned the bar, now that she knew he was here looking for a ghost and not a job, was watching over the situation with a view to future gossip that might brighten up her afternoon. Iván leaned his elbow on the bar, found a clear line of vision and followed every one of his father's movements: he didn't make a lot of gestures, he had sunken cheeks, deep lines in his forehead and alongside his mouth, a receding hairline and thin lips that he moistened every few minutes with the tip of his tongue and, automatically, as if he had some sort of tic, dried with the back of his hand. His eye colour was indiscernible because the light glinted off the greenish lenses of his enormous old-fashioned glasses. Iván could distinguish, though, the reverent gesture with which he lowered his gaze when one of the players asked for counting beans to score with. When he showed signs of smiling, dimples appeared, immediately after which the smile retreated. The sallow skin of his face glistened, as did that of almost all those present in the harsh sunlight shining in through the dirty windows. To look at his mouth, to check to see if he had all his teeth, for example, or his hands to compare them to his own – he'd heard that fathers and sons shared bone structure more often than appearance – he'd have to get closer. From here, at this distance, he couldn't see any resemblance except very general attributes, like being ungainly and five foot seven. He felt, however, that as soon as he moved from the inconspicuous position beside the counter that he'd taken with the woman's consent, everyone would turn simultaneously towards him for at least five eternal seconds to study the fact that he was an outsider.

He decided to wait until something broke the spell of the place. Someone would stand up to go to the men's room or home for lunch, and then perhaps he could seize the opportunity to take a seat at a nearby table and study his father's features in silence. He looked at the clock on the wall: it was five minutes to one. He'd been in the same position for almost half an hour. He turned towards the owner, who was still awaiting developments. Before he could say anything, she said: 'Come here . . . They'll be going soon. Where do you know Lobo from?'

'I don't know him.'

'So . . . ?'

'I've come to meet him –' He stopped short, the phrase sounded dangerous and incriminating, as if he'd actually said, 'I've come to kill him.' To change the subject and to settle a concern that had been bothering him since he came into the bar, he asked her if she knew what Lobo did for a living and if he had any children. The woman whispered that what he did was kill time, like everyone else in town, and added: 'Do you want some advice? Go away. He's a poor, sick man. If it's about some debt, speak to the Ventura sisters, he doesn't have any children, but they look after his shop, they've been running everything for years, they live with him, do his cooking, ironing, feed the animals . . . They're like nurses. A couple of saints . . . So much devotion for a guy nobody knows anything about. He was involved in something strange; nobody buries himself away in a town like San Manuel for a better life. My husband, may he rest in peace, always said Lobo had the kind of fear etched on his face of someone who'd lived through something terrible.'

The sound of chairs scraping against the floor broke the spell and interrupted her monologue. The bar immediately darkened with the passage of bodies, coughs and gruff voices. Some approached the bar to pay. Others left calling out what they'd had to drink so she could note it down in her credit book. Silvio Lobo was one of the last to leave. He gathered up the counting beans, stacked the cards neatly on the table, adjusted his heavy spectacles on the dark dent they'd carved into the bridge of his nose, and got ready to leave the place like almost everybody else, calling out at the counter what he'd had.

Iván, a metre away, was about to approach him, would just need to stretch out an arm and touch his shoulder to stop him, but his throat contracted and a shiver ran across his skin.

The woman was following the scene with discreet expectation and did not intervene only because just then someone came over to pay his week's bill. Iván took advantage of the moment to leave on his father's heels. He saw him turn a corner. He walked. He flexed his right leg. The pain had almost disappeared. He raised his head: a desolate landscape. Those men, who'd seemed like hundreds in the bar, were diminished outside and had dispersed in such a way that, looking in all directions, he couldn't make out more than ten solitary figures, neutral dots moving away against the crystal-clear background of nothing.

Ever since the woman behind the bar had confided that Lobo kept some animals, Iván had developed the idea that his father must be an honourable man. Someone who looks after animals without killing them and without eating them could not be a swindler or a traitor. He'd always believed that those who raised animals as if they were children were incurably good people who, nevertheless, perhaps due to that same goodness, might not have the words with which to get close to people.

He followed him for several blocks, at a prudent distance, along the boulevard that was the town's backbone. Lobo walked slowly in the bright sunshine. Suddenly, as if he sensed a strange presence in the air, he stopped at a corner. He didn't turn round. He sat down on a bench, in the shade, with his head between his hands. From about twenty metres away, standing still, Iván tried to guess what his father would be thinking about. He wondered if he was aware of his presence, if he'd recognized him when the owner of the bar had asked if he'd left, and if he wasn't calming his nerves on the bench, waiting for his son to take the first step. In an irrational impulse, Iván decided to keep walking, passing in front of the bench. If his father called him, he'd turn to answer him; if he didn't call him that would mean he hadn't recognized him in the bar and wasn't nursing suspicions, and he'd turn round, walk over and sit down beside him.

In a matter of seconds, he was nearer to his father than he'd ever been and he felt an unexpected withdrawal, different from the shyness he knew so well. As if all the ancestral forces that dwell in a man, suddenly and at once, immersed him in a criminal introversion, he clenched his teeth and quickened his pace to overcome the panic. He walked for a block, without turning round, in direct sunlight. The only idea in his head was to disappear. He abruptly wondered where he was going. He couldn't get back to Tandil on foot, much less Buenos Aires. At that moment, when he heard the horn of the same bus that had brought him and the driver waved to him as if they'd known each other forever, he realized that the only way to go on living was to join his father. He had nowhere to go back to, but he did have somewhere to go. ∎

GRANTA

THE COMING FLOOD

Andrés Barba

TRANSLATED BY LISA DILLMAN

ANDRÉS BARBA
SPAIN
1975

Barba has worked as a teacher of Spanish to foreigners at Complutense University in Madrid and now gives writing workshops. He established his reputation with the novel *La hermana de Katia* (2001, made into a film by Mijke de Jong), the book of novellas *La recta intención* (2002), and the novels *Ahora tocad música de baile* (2004), *Versiones de Teresa* (2006, awarded the Torrente Ballester Prize), *Las manos pequeñas* (2008), *Agosto, octubre* (2010) and *Muerte de un caballo* (2010, awarded the Juan March Prize). In collaboration with Javier Montes, he received the Anagrama Essay Prize for *La ceremonia del porno* (2007). His writing has been translated into eight languages. 'The Coming Flood' is a new story.

First her ears hear; they open. Then her eyes can see; they open. Her face, a revolving door, swings open and shut, open and shut. She no longer sleeps at night; it's too hard to breathe after four breast-implant operations. She drops, like rain down a window, collapsing in fatigue, breathing through her mouth, and even exhaustion seems miraculous. Then during the daytime, tiredness and lack of sleep bring on momentary, frenzied fits of rage. She'll walk into a shop and, if no one rushes to help her, she screams and causes chaos. The people around her turn to look. Mónica can see their faces – they're disgusted, they're shocked – she feels their eyes look her up and down, feels them on her, climbing her legs, hanging from her hips, her breasts, their eyes. When she walks out into the street, their eyes tinkle like little bells jingling from her flesh and that brings back her smile; for days now there's been something new in the world: her body bathed in their looks, but, like acid, something has coursed through her and eaten away the sweetness. Even the house has changed; it's been all chopped up. There are times when she wants to go to the bathroom and ends up in the kitchen, and vice versa.

'It's because I'm not sleeping,' she thinks.

But not sleeping is as familiar as the pen marking the page in her operation diary, suspended there, like a thought containing everything. Who is that, walking at night? Who makes that noise, those footsteps that are suddenly beside her bed and then stop? It's as though someone were really sitting there; she feels their weight, in the middle of the night, and thinks, 'Now they're going to touch me.' And she plays with that touch, she whets it. She changes position again, opens her mouth again, as wide as she can. Inhales. Even the air is weightless now, no longer dense enough to fill her lungs, to oxygenate her blood, as it used to. Her breasts hover on either side of her body, she's suffocating. She tries sitting up and then lies back down. She thrashes around, loses consciousness for three hours and then suddenly regains it, flails her white arms, startled.

'Tomorrow I have a film shoot,' she says aloud.

Immediately she wonders if she really said it aloud or only thought the words. She wants to say them aloud, and so touches her fingertips to her lips to make sure they're moving this time.

'Tomorrow I have a film shoot,' she repeats.

They moved. And thus pass months, and shoots, and naked actors like sinewy tree trunks. Unintentionally, she begins to forsake certain things: clothes, meals. She'll suddenly look in the mirror and think, 'I'm filthy,' and take a shower, scrubbing until it hurts.

'You shooting up, Mónica?'

'Me?'

'You're on something, I can tell. No junkies on my set.'

'I'm not on anything, I swear.'

And then, one day, they stop calling. And intimacy retreats just a little more, into the Internet, into chat rooms, and she barely leaves home. She feels, when she does, that things have become boundless and elastic. One day, sitting in a park, one hand resting on top of the other, she has a strange thought: a horn. 'My face with a horn,' she thinks. She touches her hand to her forehead. Not a big one, she thinks, a little horn, just one, in the middle of her forehead, almost domestic. The image is disturbingly beautiful and startles her, as if she's hit upon a mystery, a sacred thing of almost sinister simplicity. 'My face with a horn, my smile with a horn.' When she gets home, she opens her operation diary and makes note of it.

'Next operation: My face with a horn.'

The idea has a life of its own. She closes her eyes, overcome, feeling something sweet, sharp, finally full of harmony: the safety of the bone. Operations in the past: lips once, breasts four times, ribs removed, cheekbones done, and in her diary, sometimes, between one operation and the next, she'd write: 'I'm a monster.' Other times she'd write: 'For my next operation . . .' Her writing now is perky, vibrant. She doesn't sleep that night either. Little by little the unrest subsides, but come dawn, it's back. Now the house, a dank place, befits her large body. Because the body secretes feelings, but you've got to be close enough to perceive them. And one day she leaves home and lets out a low moan she'd have liked to make last. Who could say why she walks there when what she wants is to avoid the place? But she holds on to the railing at the entrance and then, as if thrust forcefully, takes one step and then another with the trusty tick-tock of a clock. 'My face with a horn, my smile with a horn, my arms and legs and tits and cunt with a horn.' She needs the vulgarity of those words, but there's no more money. There are no more calls, no more film shoots.

Recklessly, she places a personal ad. 'Mónica. 37. UNBELIEVABLE porn star. Waiting naked. BJs, no rubber. €100, the works.' She attaches a photo from when she was twenty-three and had just started, blocks out her face, and adds in minuscule font: 'real photo'.

The horn will cost €2,000 in an illegal clinic – she had to explain what she wanted three times before they got it. Then, scandalized, they told her it would be impossible for under two thousand. So there she sits, calm, clad in a robe, one hand resting on top of the other, waiting for people to come about the ad. Calls start to come in. Men come. Little men, almost always friendly, fast, sometimes ashamed, other times brutal. One time it's a kid, and when he sees her he backs up.

'You just don't do it for me, sorry.'

Someone slips her two phoney bills. Someone else slaps her. Mónica is surprised how little it hurts and she stares at the man, unblinking, taking in his fatigue and his fear, his smell, his skin, until she feels she's penetrated him. For the first time, she senses the trembling of his lower lip, and not only *notices* the trembling but deciphers it, sees how each muscle fibre criss-crosses, how it tugs his frail gelatinous lip upward, how one by one the fibres retract into infrared body cavities through tangled masses of nerves, and then slip inside his brain to the man's eye socket and then she sees his eye *from behind*, the thick optic nerve covered in tiny blue-and-red veins, and she discovers that the man is afraid because she's inside of him.

The park is where she most often sleeps, off in a secluded spot, watching the tree trunks' nervous volutes. One day, while she's asleep, she accidentally wets herself, and feels the warmth of her urine, and then the cold, and then the smell. When she gets home, she showers, and goes back to her diary, writes in it, again: 'My face with a horn.' With each passing day the image becomes clearer, more concrete. At first it was just an abstract horn, on her forehead, sometimes striated, other times smooth, an enormous horn, the size of her face, jutting upward; other times a diminutive, docile horn, almost just a bump, a protuberance. Now with increasing frequency she pictures it three centimetres long, conical, emerging from the middle of her forehead. And when that image comes to her, Mónica embraces it, and feels it's close, getting closer.

At times, the prospect frightens her. As if something inside her might stop being human after the horn. The hard horn, inside her head, like a clenched fist, like the seed of an impossible flower. She isn't sure what it is or what it wants to be but she concentrates on copying the horn's serious appearance, trying to imitate its cruelty and its tenderness. More and more, she searches the Internet for images of animals, make-believe monsters, fish from abyssal depths. Spellbound by their shapes, as if to understand better, as if some part of her had to master a monster's strange delicacy, at least a bit; she spends hours at a time gazing at the images until she feels embodied within them, feels she's taken a great step forward. And when she goes out sometimes, she doesn't know where to go, or has unsettling moments of panic. Gaping and silent, she'll range from corner to corner, hiding. Other times, she suddenly finds herself in the neighbourhood she grew up in, without knowing how she got there or why she came.

The men keep coming, the days pass. She gets beaten up again, this time it's brutal. A teenager, a kid almost, handsome and fragile-looking. She'd been scared of him from the start and yet she let him in. And when he leaves, she's lying on the floor surrounded by glass. She puts her hands to her face. She has a vague recollection of having covered her face, just her face, so it wouldn't get bruised, and since it seems he hasn't left marks, she falls asleep on the floor, out of sheer and simple exhaustion, imagining she's a dog, licking her hands with her little tongue.

Imagining she's a dog, imagining she's a horse, she's a mermaid, a naiad, an insect. The horn is set somewhere between her eyes. Some nights she goes out and prowls the streets: a form of wringing her hands. Dressed for a party: earrings, lipstick, eyeliner. She prowls the streets, trying to incite danger, and sometimes on her way out a thought flashes through her mind: 'I hope I get killed.' A thought with no pity, delicate, like the horn; she thinks, 'I hope I get killed,' the same way she thinks, 'I hope I can sleep.' She's read in the paper that some thugs had set a homeless man on fire a few blocks away and she walks there, not sure what she hopes to see or find. What would the thugs do to her? What she wants is rougher and harder than being burned alive. She's fearless, mad, like a dog. But no. She doesn't want to die. Not really. What she wants is the horn. So she fishes a knife out of the kitchen and when she goes on her nocturnal walks and sees someone, she sets off after them with determination. One time it's a man, about fifty, and when he sees the knife he runs away. One time it's a girl. Mónica heads her off, takes out the knife and says: 'Your money.'

But the girl's got almost no money. All she's got is a book, a scarf and seven euros in change that Mónica simply takes and slips into her purse, her heart racing, but only slightly, surprised at how awkward the whole encounter is, surprised at how ugly the girl is, how ugly her reactions are. She thinks, 'Now I'm a thief.'

At moments when she least expects it, the world turns real again. She goes out one afternoon and, passing by the entrance to a school, a group of teenagers laughs at her. Or she walks into a shop to buy some food and a boy is scared of her. Then she feels cold. She shivers in her clothes. She runs back home and wolfs down food like a centaur, her head bent over the plate, her hair falling into the food, and then she feels so dizzy she almost faints. The sofa stinks, the house stinks. With her head in her hands she dozes off and then wakes up, the weight of her breasts smothering her. She thinks she has so much to do: she has to clean, she has to shower, she has to do something about that painting that got broken the other day, she has to buy toothpaste. But these obligations swirl around in a cloud of smoke that makes them onerous; she's amazed she's lived so long, all her life, doing those things so effortlessly. 'How did I . . . ?' Now everything is muffled, it's intact but mysterious, and the house, like a body, slithers. And when she can't think what to do, she counts the money she keeps hidden beneath the bottle with the picture, *Hanging Houses of Cuenca*.

How much time has passed? A year? The men keep coming, the money keeps piling up: she's got almost enough now. And the closer she gets, the more exasperated she becomes. Sometimes she blanks out for long stretches. Then suddenly she becomes aware of herself again and she's in the middle of the street, or in the bathroom. She wonders: 'How did I get here?' Then, like a memory: 'The horn.' And when she says that, the house seems like another house, the sun silhouettes each object as if it were a charcoal print on the table, on the wall, as if she herself were a natural distillation of this space.

She becomes hypnotized by an image she finds on the Internet: a Canadian man who's had five silicone balls implanted under the skin on his face. She stares at him doggedly, for hours, as if from her fascination would spring meaning, and that would help her, would make the fear subside. Because she still feels fear. She doesn't wonder: 'What will become of me with the horn?' She wonders something else, something more frightening: 'What will I become with the horn?' There are five photos of the Canadian man: lying in a hammock; in his kitchen; in a yard with a swing in the back; in a car; standing beside a roadside sign announcing the name of his town. With serious expressions, fierce, as if they'd been siblings for some time, they stare at each other. The man's name is Jason Stone. Mónica learns his name the way you learn that of a lover. She writes it in her diary: 'Jason Stone'. Then she slips into his skin: she feels the silicone dressing on his flesh, stares at his swollen face in the mirror, runs her fingers slowly over the bumps and feels their coarse, secret texture. And she thinks of a mysterious sentence: 'I am the wound and the knife.' When she writes it in her diary, under 'Jason Stone', it seems so clean and round she has no need to explain it. Two days later, she rereads it and finds it incomprehensible. 'I am the wound and the knife.' And yet she knows she wrote it consciously, in a lucid moment, and that after writing it, she felt no need to add anything more; so profound was the sense of having hit a nerve, a soft and fleshy form, a heart.

The men come again. The fear of the horn, now that it's close, makes her love them in an odd way, devoid of her usual perfunctoriness. Not all of them, just some. But when it happens, she gets the feeling that the men, for her, are a way to cling to life. For a moment, she forgets everything. For a moment, she runs her eyes over the bodies of some of the men who come and thinks, 'I could fall in love with you.' And she becomes gentler. She sees their white skin so close, sees each hair follicle, and how each hair plunges its root into their skin and how at the base of each hair the skin sinks down suddenly and their hair enters it like a tiny extraction needle. And she can see their mouths, like gaping wounds, open scars, and their teeth, and their tongues, blanketed with thousands of tiny taste buds, each with its own unique function. And she can see the miraculous mechanics of their joints: shoulders, elbows, knees, hips; she makes herself tiny enough to touch the membrane that joins the bone to the flesh and skin. She is awed by their erections and thinks, 'How beautiful,' as if her feelings could only be superficial. When they come, she concentrates on the slight slackening of their eyes, their mouths. Their cheekbones seem to sink slightly then, their skin to regain its flaccidity; she revels in their sweat, imagines the miracle of each pore like a little cup overflowing with salt water, and she makes herself as small as her fears and travels each pore as if she had to plant a flag in each one.

There's even a man who inexplicably falls in love with her. His name is Antonio but everyone calls him Toño.

'My name is Antonio but everyone calls me Toño,' he says.

He sends her text messages, dirty messages, in the middle of the night, almost always monosyllabic: 'Come.' 'Cock.' Anxious messages. He himself is big and anxious, he sweats a lot, tells jokes Mónica doesn't understand, laughs a lot. And after he tells them, he waits a second, distraught as a boy in his Sunday best, his arms restrained, sheer expectation, and then abruptly laughs a thunderous laugh. Mónica attaches herself to him for a few weeks, but the attachment seems a betrayal of the truth, the horn. She doesn't say anything. She simply watches what happens. Then Toño stops paying. But he keeps coming. Mónica doesn't know how to tell him to go; she finds it harder and harder to speak. As if she's forgotten how to pronounce certain words, certain sentences. She opens her mouth, she wants to say, 'Toño, I don't want you to keep coming,' but nothing comes out. With Toño her body expands one last time, like a rubber band that's been stretched insufferably but doesn't break and then suddenly is released, becomes flaccid. Toño talks and talks. He's oafish and inoffensive, and at times even unexpectedly sweet.

One day he says: 'It's time to clean your house.'

And he cleans for half an hour before he gets bored. The effect, in the end, is doubly damning: the cleanliness of one half of the house makes the dirtiness of the other much more obvious. The same is true of her body. It's falling apart but only in certain spots. The bags under her eyes are almost purple some days, her nails are filthy and need to be cleaned, one of her nipples has darkened more than the other, the corners of her mouth have drooped, sloping down slightly, her eyelids are swollen in the mornings, her left knee hurts, she's got indigestion, as if somehow the missing ribs put unnatural pressure on her intestines. With no warning of any sort, everything takes on the thick stench of rotting flesh and Mónica thinks it's coming off her own body but can't get rid of it no matter how often she showers. Because for the past two days, ever since Toño started showing up at will, Mónica has felt constantly filthy. One day she simply doesn't open the door. He pounds furiously, then seems to feel ashamed and leaves. His texts keep coming for over a week, until slowly they, too, stop. He'll send a cheap shot, and then, two minutes later, an apology. Three hours later, another cheap shot. His final messages are simply sad. And yet, Mónica doesn't want them to stop; she looks forward to them, as if the texts contained a final link to something, as if Toño's body, a body she was never attracted to, the one she can only remember certain specific parts of, were a great loss.

Then comes the silence. Striking silence, there where the ground should be. And suddenly this painful, inexistent place: the horn. She lets the days slip by, no longer accepting clients. She gets from Monday to Sunday, each day an attempt to eliminate a thought. Every imaginable being inside her body has finally left. It seems that somewhere, they're singing of her.

She stripped slowly, leaving her clothes primly folded, the way some people do before committing suicide, before jumping out of a window. In the waiting-room mirror, she looked at herself for the last time. Looked beneath the trembling ripples of skin, bones, flesh, intestines. She'd have liked to take a picture, then, in exactly that pose, in the mirror. She'd have written on the back, in her careful, round hand: 'Me, before.' Softly. Wistfully. Like someone who knows it's time to leave a place they'll never see again: her hair hanging to the left, her right hand trembling slightly, her skinny knees, things that would never again be. More, much more. To take that image in her hands and renounce it. Renounce the memory. She'd got there almost an hour early and they'd left her in a small room with a few magazines. An hour later a woman had walked in and asked her to take off her clothes.

'Well, then. Ready?'

'Yes.'

She had a moment's hesitation. Then she whispered to herself: 'My face with a horn,' a mantra; the nurse had made her lose her confidence. That was when the horn began to emerge, slowly, very slowly, when she began to feel it actually grow, and she felt fear. Its presence wasn't much different to a simple headache. They gave her a blue paper gown, open at the back, and paper slippers, and took her to the operating room. The table was cold. She liked the way it felt, the cold. Then they put a mask on her. The plastic surgeon appeared.

'Just breathe normally.'

'What is this?'

'Anaesthetic.'

But she knew it was anaesthetic, that wasn't what she was asking. She thought: 'They'll stick me in a kettle and I'll come out all flushed and red, with a horn.' And as the anaesthetic took effect, she had the feeling that her body was fossilizing like a calcareous substance, creating a hard shell comprised of hundreds of thousands of substances all superimposed.

The dream she had under anaesthesia was wild. It started in her stomach. The dream began sweetly, alighting like a tiny hunger pang. She saw images, almost abstract images, and little by little they began taking shape and they became faces, but not entirely human faces. Their features were like those of any face and yet, there was something that made them totally different. They opened their mouths and out came long, slender tongues that licked the length of whatever surface they were on, as if that was how they fed. She tried opening her mouth, too, and out came a similar tongue, even finer than theirs, like a long pink thread. She could feel everything she touched with her tongue. Her tongue was the only place she could feel.

There was a sort of primordial joy, demoniacal almost, about the whole thing, as if it had all gone further than she'd imagined, as if for the first time she'd found a polar opposite. But she knew it was a dream, and that she was under anaesthesia, this had happened in her other operations too. She awoke, bloated, delirious. She asked if she was dead.

'No. The operation was a success,' the nurse said.

She was awake. Had she woken up or was this still a dream? She remembered getting up, like a statue, from the operating table, greeting the doctor. A hand had very gently removed her IV drip, recommended she bend her arm back and forth so it wouldn't leave a mark, and she'd done that; another hand helped her get dressed in her old human clothes. They were using her name, which suddenly sounded strange and melodious. She vaguely recalled having been named that. She saw their human faces from the outside and they looked ugly – ridiculously, almost heart-rendingly ugly. Then she remembered having left. Was that the street? Yes, go straight ahead. Call that: 'straight'; call that: 'street'; call that: 'ahead'. The others watched without seeing; she named things. She recalled having put her hands to her forehead, trembling, having touched the bandage, removing it awkwardly, hurting herself slightly. The doctor had said before she left: 'You'll need to leave that on for the next two days.'

She had understood each individual word, but not the meaning of the sentence. As with the faces, her syntax had crumbled. She took off the bandage right in front of him, deposited it in his hand, and left.

Outside, in the open air, the light hit the horn for the first time, and when she touched it with her fingertips she felt an electric jolt course through her entire body. She felt the need to vomit, and in her vomit, finally, she expelled all that she no longer needed, leaning up against a tree, tasting the acid taste of what she no longer was. As if she wanted to forgive, as if an unstoppable urge to forgive were flooding through her, she forgave the vomit, and the tree, and its irritating constancy – the last things. Then something seemed to fit, all across the land, as if the bowels of the earth had produced a minuscule movement that had finally made every immense piece of the universe fit. She looked down at her hands: there were hands there. She walked, searching for a mirror, a reflection, a surface of any kind that would let her see herself and finally see the horn. She found it. ■

Join
The Royal Society
of **Literature**

WINTER SPEAKERS INCLUDE:

Philip Hensher
Susan Hill
Sean O'Brien
Don Paterson
Fiona Sampson
Anthony Thwaite
Sarah Waters

Membership of The Royal Society of Literature is open to all.

For full information about the benefits of membership and how to join:
Telephone 020 7845 4677
Email rachel@rslit.org
Website www.rslit.org

GRANTA

THE PLACE OF LOSSES

Rodrigo Hasbún

TRANSLATED BY CAROLINA DE ROBERTIS

RODRIGO HASBÚN
BOLIVIA
1981

Born in Cochabamba, Hasbún has published the book of short stories *Cinco* (2006) and the novel *El lugar del cuerpo* (2007). Awarded the Latin Union Prize for the Most Original Spanish American Short Fiction, he was part of the issue that *Zoetrope: All-Story* dedicated to emerging Latin American fiction. His writing has been included in various anthologies and two of his stories have been made into films, for which he also co-wrote the screenplays. He lives in Ithaca, New York. In 2011, Duomo Ediciones will publish *Los días más felices*, his second collection of short stories. 'The Place of Losses' is a new story.

Take your shit with you, all your memories, I wanted to say before she stood up, but then, when I started to stammer it, when I finally got up the courage to say it, it was too late, she had turned around, she was already walking out of the cafe, out of my life, to the street, into someone else's life. Take your name with you, bitch, thief, woman, I wanted to say, to wound her, to return some of the pain she was causing me. Take everything with you and please don't come back (because Valeria always comes back after leaving). And please don't come back this time, Valeria, I wanted to say to her, that's what I ask above all, that you leave forever and take your memories and your scent. And, if it's easier for you, think that you're leaving because I want you to leave, like in the bolero song, like in so many other lives (but I only want you to leave after you've left). Take yourself with you, the ghost you summon. Take your body. And don't come back, I wanted to say, this time don't even think of coming back. Please, if you've really stopped loving me, don't come back.

But one week later, we were there again, at the only table by the window. It had to seem as though we'd run into each other by chance and it had to seem as though I hadn't found anything out or that I'd already put away the hurt. So I took the photos out of my backpack without saying anything, without reproach, and I left them on the table, next to the coffees that had just been served and were still steaming. Valeria looked at them for a good while.

She didn't understand because she hadn't gone to the last session of the workshop, to which, in spite of everything, I'd only gone to find her. One of them took place in a train carriage. An old man appeared looking slightly lost, possibly he'd got on the wrong train or perhaps he'd forgotten where to disembark. Perhaps he was still stuck in some war, escaping fire and bullets. In the other photo, still alive, or not, covered entirely by a white sheet, a man appeared in a hospital bed.

They were strange photos. One couldn't really tell whether they were assembled, staged, or whether they'd come directly from reality. From the reality in which I told Valeria that she should choose one and write a story from it for the next session. Did you pick them? It was at random, you know how Madeiros is. Which one do you like best? The one with the train, I said. Well, she said, in that case I'll take the other one. Why didn't you come the other day? Because I didn't feel like dealing with all that foolishness.

Her tone and cruelty hurt me, and at the same time I liked them. Bitch, I wanted to say to her as I remembered what had happened the week before and sought her gaze and sipped my coffee. Thief, I wanted to say, woman. And I put the cup back on the table and reached my hand out to take hers. Madeiros's exercises are less and less interesting to me, she said, far away from everything I might be feeling. I don't know what he's trying to accomplish, I've stopped seeing them as necessary. The old man knows what he's doing, I said, trying to defend him, although in truth I'd lately thought the same thing. Also, writers should invent themselves on their own, added Valeria, who for months had been the most enthusiastic participant in the workshop. My hand was still over hers but they were dead hands, hands that no longer belonged to us. Will you stop going? I asked, afraid. She answered by making a face I didn't understand and then we were silent again.

It was four o'clock on a Friday afternoon like any other, and I realized in that moment that I would write my story about those hours. We, the characters, would talk about the photos while we slowly destroyed ourselves, while we grew into our betrayal, our oscillations and sex and coffee, our useless words. And the most certain thing is that Madeiros would detest it. He'd be bothered by its self-referential nature, the absence of a clear plot, the absence of local colour, the sentimentality or what hovered too close to it. This damn exercise was supposed to do the exact opposite! he'd surely shout a few days later, with that voice destroyed by cigarettes, to make you tell me about what you saw in the photos, to take you out of yourselves! And he'd get too worked up to speak and spit in a corner before finishing off his beer.

Are you all right? asked Valeria, bringing me back to us, to the tiny cafe.

Yes, fine, I replied. She was there. As were the long calm hours in which we'd have a good screw, the hours in which I'd forgive her again.

I smiled and she smiled and we separated our hands and downed the rest of our coffee.

Then we paid the bill and left.

II

each time you think of me pinch your hand. each time you think of me, valeria said, jump three times or start dancing. it'll be fun to imagine you that way.

a night on the piss with madeiros. i accompanied him. when we got to his house, he lay down in the front doorway, saying he wanted to sleep there. i told him he'd get sick. he said he needed to know how vagrants felt, with no place to return to.

idea. an artist turns on a camera, puts it on a tripod, opens the window, squeezes eyes shut and jumps. the apartment is on the fourth floor, the fall only manages to break a few ribs. months later, another attempt. this time the camera is positioned on the ground, to record the moment in which the body hits cement. the damage is worse but the artist doesn't die. the artist sells the tapes to an important museum and becomes relatively well known in the city.

she asked me to suck her toes and also wanted me to spit in her face. she had seen it in a movie the night before.

these notebooks are my place, here i learn, here i lose. (what i mean to say is that to know how things work you must destroy them first ...)

her tongue, when she smiles. and her breath. and her hands and ankles. her broken tooth. the small scars on her knees.

what we need: lemons in our mouths, to lie in the sun. a precipice or a war. to kill fifteen ants and feel no guilt, to tear the wings from six flies and smile.

what we need: a fight in the middle of the night that keeps us from sleeping. to look out of the window and find violence or the simulation of violence beyond the glass. a tremor. subtler revenges. to say yes or no or more or less to the same things, to be ridiculous in a similar way. for her to be good and never leave. love or the simulation of love.

to be together forever. never to let go of each other's hands. that's what i said. she said: every time you think of me, start clapping. seven times in a row. hard.

Estranged Lives

Lies would have been sweeter, not to have known, to have known less. Lies, perhaps, could have saved us. We could have cancelled them out after a while, become used to them, believed in them only later to plunge them into that silence of days and months and life. To be capable of smiling every once in a while without remorse or guilt. Without this shit. But it's also because of the dog and because of Dad, the world isn't just her any more. With lies the world might have continued being only her. With lies we might have been able to invent a less sad story, she'd still be here and the dog would never have gotten sick, although one thing is not related to the other in any way, and we wouldn't be killing the dog and Dad wouldn't have to hide his need to cry from us. The dog can't move any more, he watches the world for maybe the last time. These are the decisive minutes that all of us will have to face one day. Dad can't bear the sight any more, he lets Juan go, undoes the embrace and joins in, he throws himself to the floor, strokes the dog, kisses his snout, his ears. Mario says something to him but it's no use, he doesn't even respond. He approaches and tries to pick him up. He can't, the old man pushes him away, insisting on saying goodbye in this manner. As if searching for instructions, confused, he looks at us (the only one who seems to have kept some remnant of childhood is Mario, with his still-vigorous body, ready and willing, cheeks closely shaved). Neither Juan nor I say anything. Meanwhile, the animal's breathing slows down. I'm sorry, Dad murmurs, I'm sorry, little one, but he refuses to cry. A quiet afternoon, three brothers together after long separation, the father of the three lying next to a dog that may already be dead. Juan looks at me. I suddenly realize that behind the bags under his eyes, his unkempt beard, behind his silence . . . I want to talk to you, he says.

I'm getting a divorce, I'm considering a divorce, I think I want a divorce. We're in the car, the dog in a bag on the back seat. I stay silent, again, thinking that he hasn't chosen the best moment to announce this. Why? I ask. The relationship isn't working any more, we don't love each other much any more. His hesitation, the awkward oscillations of his voice, and the almost imperceptible quiver of his chin, which hasn't been visible in years, make me suspect that he isn't telling me everything, that he's hiding his true motives. I think of those streets, of that city, of the cafes she could be entering. I recall the way she smokes. You two, who loved each other so much, I say. Yes, us. It starts to get dark, I accelerate. Do you know the place well? Yes, we're close. Juan won't ask about her because he doesn't know anything, because I never told him much, he thinks she was just one more in my life, toward the end of the list. I look at the bag on the back seat through the rear-view mirror, it seems to be moving. I turn on to a dirt road and slow the car. Is there something you're not telling me? I want to be able to hear him think, to hear the thoughts of everyone around me. It would be terrible, almost as terrible as reading the emails your girlfriend's lover writes to her, but I still wanted to. I still want to. The lies, having made me forget, would have . . . Nothing, says Juan, the relationship is worn out and neither of us is prepared to force the issue. The same old story, he says, don't look for anything sophisticated in it. I stop the car and turn the engine off, there's very little light left. We go out, take the shovels, and start to dig.

Nobody says anything at dinner. Alone, irrevocably alone, and even more so when we remember or imagine or dream, or when we love from afar, without saying so. Juan will not mention his imminent divorce. Mario has already exhausted all his resources and is also slightly drunk. Dad was never much of a talker.

> *i don't like that ending. (i never know where to stop. that is to say: i'm not a good writer . . .) i don't like a narrator who is so hard to see. i'm going to rewrite the whole story. tomorrow or later on today, directly on the machine.*

> *but i read it to her anyway. she said she was proud of me. then she yawned. and smiled. and said: bet you don't know how to do this. and she made herself cross-eyed for several seconds. i missed her already even though she was half a metre away. i told her i wanted to read her new stories. she said: i ate them all. i seasoned them with olive oil and ate them.*

> *i try to move a coin with my mind. i try for ten minutes.*

> *girlfriends leave, pets die, uncles rape their maids. the maids have a good time, the maids ask for more the next day. (this notebook and*

all the rest of them will one day go to the garbage . . .)

the lasagne she made. i almost couldn't swallow it. but when she asked how it was i said it was incredible and a little later i even asked for more.

an elderly lady told me this, the other day, in the hair salon. her husband was a drunk who disappeared every once in a while. then he'd call and make up stories and ask to borrow money to pay off debts that had accumulated in bars or while gambling, debts that kept him from coming home. this lasted for decades, until she got tired of it and didn't want to give him anything any more. one day he was truly in urgent need of money. in his desperation, the only solution that occurred to him was to ask a friend to call his wife and tell her he'd been run over and had died in a nearby city and money was needed to transfer him out of the morgue. it was a terrible night for her. he, as if it were nothing, showed up the next day, sure his wife would be glad to see him back from the dead. after slapping him extremely hard, she burst into tears. they lived together for fourteen more years, until he died in earnest, but she never spoke a single word to him again.

madeiros said that we're the two most talented writers in the group. he was drunk when he said it. valeria believes he's said the same thing to everyone else.

still afternoons. to have seen her vomit (and then i kissed her . . .) to have seen her cry (and then i kissed her . . .) to have heard her saying over and over, a thousand times, that she doesn't want to age. i don't like to spit in her face. i don't like to suck her toes . . .

sometimes she falls asleep. from one moment to the next. she's saying something and she falls asleep. without any guilt, it's what she most likes to do.

she dreams that she is air. she said: i was air. she said: i need to be invisible. she smoked. to see her smoke. to hear how she leaps from one place to the next. her places. she grows by my side. there are things we've done together for the first time in our lives. this connects us.

is it hard to be you? is it nice to be you? how does it feel to be you?

sometimes she repeats the same word for a long time, eighty or a hundred times. she acts crazy sometimes. i tell her to stop and she does it with even more passion.

call me a fucking whore, she asks between gasps, call me a disgusting dog. it's hard for me to say it but i say it and come two seconds later. she embraces me.

Final Weeks

He hid bottles in bathroom trash cans, submerged in the pool, hanging from trees in the garden. Later, in the days that followed, he didn't leave a single one unemptied, always listening to those old records and sometimes wondering aloud, to throw Mom off course, when Mom was near, about how he'd get his hands on new bottles and where he'd hide them, whether in the laundry hamper or buried in places that he wouldn't easily forget. Or in the wardrobe in my bedroom, which was all right with me. It didn't bother me that Dad got drunk all the time, I was used to seeing him that way, dancing in the living room (in the best moments), grumbling and crying (in the worst), I was already used to lectures that could last several hours.

I have at least three hundred dead people, he suddenly said that afternoon, haughtily, as if something like that could make him proud. I'll count them for you one by one, mister. Three hundred at least. Or four hundred. We can bet if you want.

I have four, I said. And I had to think of my grandfathers and my uncle, but above all of Mastrono, whom we had to kill right there, in the garden in which Dad now buried his bottles.

This one you see here is a survivor, he went on. One of the luckiest. I'm surrounded by the dead, but I'm still here. Three hundred or four hundred dead, my boy, maybe more, all the people who were important, and me still here, talking to you. Did I ever tell you about your Uncle Eduardo?

I knew his stories by heart. They touched me, they moved me, they gave me joy. I loved Dad and I liked what he'd accomplished in his life, including making that woman fall in love with him, a brave woman who held an important post at an important bank and who allowed us to live a certain kind of life. He was forbidden to leave the house and he obeyed as long as he had his bottles, which were also forbidden. I got them for him and Mom knew. The thing was that I was about to begin my studies, meaning these were my final weeks in the city, my final weeks at home. I had promised to return often, at least once a month, but I also understood well that there is nothing easier to break than promises. I wouldn't fail Dad, I kept telling myself in those final weeks, forcing myself to enjoy the most inconsequential details. I wouldn't leave him to feel even more alone or abandoned.

Have I told you that one or not?

I don't think so.

He liked women of ill repute. At that time they were very cheap, so a week didn't go by without him getting laid. He knew them all. They even greeted him by name. With affection, because he was a good man.

He'd interrupt himself to drink. Singani brandy with lots of ice and a splash of lemon. While he emptied the glass and prepared another one, I looked out of the window. At the ruined garden, at the stagnant water of the pool. At the trees and the sky, which was losing its intensity as night approached.

The problem was that he fell in love. And he left his family to go live with the little whore, whom I believe was called Miriam or Mariam.

People never change. Not even for love. That's what your poor Uncle Eduardo never understood and what I need you to understand now, so you don't suffer in vain. You'll be far away and you'll need to be strong and not forget for a single moment that people never change. Later he resigned himself, your uncle. But underneath, sadness kept growing, and shame . . . I'm not sure you're ready for what comes next. It's something hard.

He shot her, I said, feigning an unsure tone, as though I were suggesting a radical possibility just to prove that I wasn't so innocent any more.

Yes! Dad said, surprised that I'd hit the mark. Exactly! But it's not just that. Afterward, Eduardito did something even worse . . .

He shot himself? I asked, feigning even more doubt.

Yes, he assented, less effusive this time. I saw his body, I saw his head open, his scattered brains. I saw him without life, next to Miriam or Mariam or whatever the fuck she was called. She was a voluptuous dark-skinned woman and she did it so delicious, forgive me for saying it crudely, but at the end there your uncle had pussy to spare, getting into it with half the world, the more to share with us. There were no illnesses back then, my boy, now you've got to take care of yourself, act the pimp.

He stared at me steadily for a few seconds as he said this. I held his gaze with effort, there was something frightening about it, perhaps I saw for a second my future reflection, what I too would become, and then he stood up, tottering, and walked to the sink. He threw out the remaining ice cubes and washed his glass. He picked up the bottle, silent, as if he were alone, making his son disappear while he thought of his brother, remembering him, attempting to be with him again, and then he went out. I stayed still, watching him through the window. Two or three minutes passed that way, suspended, and at that moment Mom walked in. She said hello and asked about Dad at the very moment that he entered the kitchen through the other door, his hands covered in dirt.

It's possible that even in that state he'd embrace her. It's also possible that she wouldn't complain, nor mention the smell of alcohol, the red eyes, the evident sadness.

Before they could say anything I offered to take them out to dinner. They looked at me and asked where and whether I had money with which to do it, sensitive as they were to my imminent departure, which would be the beginning of something but at the same time the end of something, of what we had been until then.

Of course I have it, I said. How does pasta sound?

Fantastic, they said, it sounds fantastic.

may the little monsters not play at staining themselves. may they never turn their backs on each other. may they not say to each other that they no longer love each other if indeed one day they stop loving each other.

sometimes she leaves without paying. sometimes she takes tips left on cafe tables by other customers. sometimes she tells me terrible things. later, at the end, she always says the same thing: i don't know why i'm telling you this.

the university doesn't matter. the future doesn't matter.

sometimes we play at being blind. she or i. we cover our eyes and let the other one guide us, keep us from falling. the noises of the city, to walk without seeing. to caress without seeing, to feel without seeing. to keep being ourselves without seeing.

that the other day she was seen having a drink with a professor, that they were dying of laughter, that valeria looked happy. i waited half a week for her to say something, she said nothing. betrayals have stopped being beautiful. our new pact: you make the wound, i'll bare my skin.

what we need the most: clouds that look like things. for things to

*go very badly for our friends, to set fire to the neighbours' house. to
have a horrible dream and wake from it. (i don't write here to tell
myself the truth. i write here to lie to myself . . .)*

*we spend a while in the cafe. my inability to tell her what i was
feeling, her ease at bending me. we spend some time in her bed. she
likes me to come inside her, it doesn't worry her. nor does it worry
me. it's been a horrendous week.*

*the people i hate, she said. the clothes i hate, the gestures i hate,
the memories i hate. it shouldn't be so easy to hate.*

III

I cry in the shower. I'm not sure why, but I cry and the tears get
confused with the water and then I dry myself off and it's done.

I return to the room. I don't find him and for two seconds I think
he's left, I panic for two seconds as I imagine him running back to
the cafe or to his home, running anywhere, but then I think he must
be reading in the kitchen, that he's prepared a *mate* and he's reading
in there, because he likes reading in there very much. Pablo? I ask, in
a strong voice, just in case, and he doesn't respond and I don't insist.
I sit down on the bed. It still smells of us and that scent we make
together is my favourite scent in the world, but I erase it with the
cream I put on my body. I look for something to wear. White panties,
a yellow skirt, a blue blouse. Then I go in search of Pablo. But he's not
in the kitchen and I feel desperate for another two seconds and want
to understand and don't understand and I look out of the window
just to have somewhere to look, and there he is, sitting on the
landlord's daughter's swing. I smile and he doesn't see me and I keep
smiling. It's unusual for him not to be reading. It's extremely unusual
in fact, because Pablo doesn't waste a single free second that he could
spend reading.

He looks thoughtful. He's thoughtful, or he seems so. This

scares me. But then I realize that he's got his notebook open and I smile again and the fear leaves, and that's it. Perhaps he started writing the story for the workshop. That's how he is, obsessive. I'm not even sure where I left the photo he gave me. We still have the whole week and I'm not going to think about that right now. I go out and approach him and he doesn't say anything and I don't say anything and I sit on his lap. It's hot and the swing creaks a little from holding both our weights. I embrace him and he still smells of us and there's an incredibly long silence that doesn't feel too long because Pablo closes the red notebook and lets it fall on the grass and places his hand on my hip. He doesn't let me read his notebooks, I sometimes read them when he's asleep. They're lovely notes. They're sentimental, tender. And it's idiotic to mention this, but I know that one day I'll recall afternoons like this one with unbearable sadness. That's what I think sometimes when I read them and that's what I think now, as I sit on his lap. I'll be living far away, in another country, and before I turn thirty, at work or in some bar or wherever, I'll meet a man who'll fall in love with me, and we'll get married and I'll give him children. Nothing will be as special as this, right now, and we'll know it and it won't matter and the worst thing will be for it not to matter and I can't imagine how or why we'll grow apart, but now, on the patio, embracing him, I'm sure that it will happen. I love you, I say then, partly to defend myself from the future, to defend us both from the future, and I kiss him on the mouth with fury. I love you, Pablo, I say into his ear, I need you to know that I love you with all the love in the world. And he is sad or seems to be so, sometimes sex makes him this way, despite my words, or perhaps he'd turned himself over to what he was writing, surely the beginning of his story for the next workshop session, or what happened last week, which in reality is nothing, absolutely nothing, and his response is to lean his head on my breast. One of the swing chains gives way in that moment and we fall. Laughing helplessly, we embrace. ∎

CONDITIONS FOR THE REVOLUTION

Pola Oloixarac

TRANSLATED BY MARA FAYE LETHEM

POLA OLOIXARAC
ARGENTINA
1977

A writer and translator, Oloixarac's first novel, *Las teorías salvajes*, was
published in Argentina (2008), Spain (2010) and Peru (2010), and
will soon be translated into French, Dutch and Portuguese. In 2010
she was awarded the Argentinian National Endowment for the Arts
and is currently in residence at the International Writing Program
at the University of Iowa. She has a philosophy degree from the
University of Buenos Aires and has written on culture and technology
for various magazines. She has been writing since she was a child and
likes taking bubble baths. Her blog is www.melpomenemag.
blogspot.com. 'Conditions for the Revolution' is a new story.

I

That morning, Mara went by her mother's house to get some clean clothes. She slid between the armchairs in the living room and the coffee tables overflowing with magazines; she didn't want to run into her. On the modular shelving in the library, flanked by books by Eduardo Galeano and Gabriel García Márquez, the computer screen showed an unfinished game of solitaire. Mother Cris wasn't there. She'd been a little depressed because Quique, her current lover, had way too much time on his hands. At first he wandered around Cris's house, leaving his toothbrush there, and then kindly (suspiciously) offering to cook, until one day she gave him a hard stare and said, look, I think that, these days, the most important thing in a relationship is respecting each other's space, but if you need to, please let me finish, if you really need to, you can stay here. Quique was of medium height and had brown eyes and a disorientated air about him, but he seemed stripped of everything that makes disorientation an attractive or romantic trait.

'You don't recognize me because I let my grey come in and now I have a ponytail.' He had brought his snout closer.

Cris would have preferred that he didn't make such direct mention of the ponytail; she was enough of an adult – and alone, not getting any younger – to know she could stand the sight of the ponytail, but not talking about it. Quique wasn't intimidated by Cris's sideways glances, the deliberate nature of some of her absent and distracted moments. He read it as a display of parameters, a female logic lubricating its own version of the conquest seconds before launching, insatiable, into mating. The sweetness of desperation was an inalienable asset in middle-aged ladies for whom casual sex would soon be a piece of Grandma's jewellery that nobody would want to touch. Quique was an optimistic guy. He narrowed his eyes, fulfilling his civic role of mensch playing at seducer:

'In those days I already had you in my sights, but you were with somebody else.'

Cris pursed her lips, trying mentally to distance herself from the scene: for the moment, being the recipient of Quique's attentions was far from flattering. But 'somebody else' awoke Cris's interest (vanity disguised as interest) from its lethargy and, overcome with complicity, she used the opportunity to laugh hysterically. And yes, she was always with somebody or other. Quique felt as if the fat men of the Metal Workers' Union were urging him on, gesturing at him with full arms as if he were in a car and wanted to park; you go ahead, he thought, as he slipped his thumb cautiously through the loop of Cris's jeans. With a quick glance, Cris detected his hand hanging close to her proud ass, her personal PR agent; unable to renounce her chance at playing the coquette, Cris commented: Hmm . . . dangerous. I'm the type that falls in love, so if I were you, I'd think twice. If Quique had been twenty years younger, he would have made a bet with himself as to how long it would take him to penetrate her anally; now, mature and serene, he stuck out his tongue slightly before touching her lips.

Then he told her about when he set off for Spain, in '73. She looked at him with her eyes open very wide, and then exclaimed in a shocked tone: But that was our brightest moment! Our whole generation, all the young people, like never before, in the streets! You couldn't have left in '73! She was exaggerating her enthusiasm a bit, aware that widening her eyes and raising her voice was part of the display of politics and passion and, therefore, part of Cris herself: the small groups of demonstrators talking nearby noticed her fiery presence, her dynamic and battle-hardened style, and she immediately felt younger. And when we freed the prisoners! And when we took over the Student Centre and made them kick out all the right-wing staff! And when – in a tender shift that exasperated Cris – Quique interrupted her, taking her sweetly by the chin.

'I felt that something wasn't going right, Cris. The maximalist prerogatives were pushing things to a crossroads. Besides, I had an aunt who was moving right then, all her things were on the boat, and I got on.' Cris pursed her lips again; her attention was becoming erratic. He tried to get her to come to her senses. 'Cris, the bases had shifted. The logic of the situation was headed down the pan. I abandoned Peronism when I realized that violence was the only path left for me to go down. I've always been political, but I've always considered myself more Gramscian than Peronist. Trotskyist too. Strictly speaking, for a while I was methodologically Marxist but officially Peronist.'

She wasn't convinced, but at least he had managed to confuse her somewhat. The context helped. The democratic disillusionment with the fall of de la Rúa's government translated into the semantic realm as 'urgency', 'change' and plans for society's future. Carefully, Quique dropped a few names while checking out the effect they had on his prospective lover's face. It was some sort of encoded game of Battleship, where the breadth of his combat itinerary sought out correspondence with some emotional oasis in Cris's swampy sentimental structure. Certain facial expressions maintain bi-univocal relationships with a group of data; the expressions are stimulated by the data; Quique's objective was to provide nuggets of information to stimulate those elusive mental objects that typically nest beneath the female skin and make a man 'interesting'. Testing out the coordinates of the grid, Quique's attack on the female fantasy included comrade experiences, youthful rebellious spirit, true commitment to the bases, active participation in the armed struggle (sunk!). Quique smiled, savouring very similar words, reliving an old tactic applied in Barcelona and Paris on Spanish women, Uruguayans and luscious recently arrived Argentinians. Political commitment fuelled a strong fusion with other lives. In exile, Quique had discovered that the traumatic arithmetic that melded a past and a moustache could function as proof of a set of privileged experiences, as shared as they were private, in the light of whose mysterious shadow the true socialist homeland would always exist, in the hearts of comrades and lovers, as stated in Walt Whitman's dedication to his readers in *Leaves of Grass*.

Cris sighed, somewhat nervous; this guy must be a coward, a rookie, the kind of low-ranking guerrilla that doesn't even carry a gun. She ran her eyes over the gathering of the Neighbourhood Assembly; a slight drop in the electricity threw her briefly into shadow. Quique was moving his mouth; he must have been saying something. Cris parted her lips, leaving her gaze suspended between her recollection and the fine hairs that surrounded the Adam's apple across from her. Between symbol and memory, Cris managed to take refuge in the abstract idea of a man, from which she planned to resist the annihilation of her libido by that particular one, who reeked of failure. She slowly uttered, 'They were very tough times, very tough, you know, for those of us who stayed here.' He pulled her towards him with as much virility as he could; he understood her perfectly. From the pocket of Cris's jeans hung a key ring in the shape of a heart. Quique had a fierce erection. He wanted to hold it up against her so she could feel it, thinking that maybe it would make her happy, and just then they put on a song by César 'Banana' Pueyrredón.

Now the party's gettin' started, said Eduardo, who came over swaying with a tray of fritters and quince pie. They'd been made by Comrade Irma, an unemployed cook, for the new swap club that was starting that day. It was customary to put on a bit of music, because it stimulated cohesion. Everyone brought home-made liqueurs, whiskey, grenadine or whatever they had in the house; they listened to songs by 'Nano' Serrat, Celia Cruz, Juan Luis Guerra and the occasional Internationale. The fifty-something men paced back and forth, with their little plastic cups and their foreheads creased with thoughts of hope for change; the women waggled to the beat of an image of themselves that was decidedly different from the one they shared with the rest of humanity, making an effort to show that they could be, if not women, at least antidotes to depression.

After a few meetings, one could identify the single women, the separated ones, those inclined towards the pure old in-out, and the stuck-up ones who liked to play hard to get, at least for a while, like Mara's mother.

But now the neighbourhood assemblies were dwindling and the swap club founded by Eduardo and Quique was about to shut down.

The revival of the little things in life, that had so benefited him, was proving to be a short-lived paradise; Quique was losing credibility. The re-establishment of political calm kicked him from that Eden where he'd survived with so little, spiritually and economically. Quique's monetary and professional failure, which in those golden assemblies was read as proof of his honesty, had used up his aliquot of opportunity cost; it was no longer as profitable as before, nor could it easily be reconverted into honesty capital. For the moment, he had no doubt that Cris would let him live at her house. It was probably unlikely they'd give him a compensation settlement for exile, he had certainly never been officially active in any political organization; but Cris believed that Quique was expectantly awaiting the arrival of recognition from the state, and he announced that he would take Mara's room to set up his study, even though he slept all day long.

Or at least that was the impression Mara got, when she went into her old room and found him splayed out on her ex-bed, with a book by Levinas open on his chest like a dead bird. The creaking of the closet door woke him up.

'Oh, Mara, what a way to find me.' Quique flashed a combination of cigarette stains and saliva, grabbing the book. 'You see how these French guys are. Sometimes they just knock you out cold.'

Mara turned her back on him and started stuffing T-shirts into a bag. Quique put a bookmark into the book and checked out her ass. It was different from her mother's, but not that different. He adjusted his glasses.

He could smell the aroma of Mara's body; she smelled different, different from all the others. Quique remained on the bed. Isn't imagination something? thought Quique. Everything is there and not there at the same time, *todo paasa y tooodo queeda, pero lo nuestro es pasar, pasar haciendo caminos, caminos sobre la maaar.* Suddenly something in Quique darkened, as if storm clouds were reflecting on the brown waters of his understanding: what a proletarian organ, the ass, the organ you sit on, and even though it seems to work and have working-class awareness, it's really just waiting to die. I should say something, he said to himself, I should say something so it doesn't look like we're alone.

'Hey, Marita, did your mom tell you that Rodrigazo and I went to the same high school?'

Like in a soap opera by Manuel Puig, Mara folds a piece of clothing and lifts a face devoid of expression. Her mind is filled with images and memories that she could have lived, or not: in the mental films we call thought, memory and imagination are usually the same operation. Rodrigazo must be Silvia's ex. Silvia was a friend of Cris's from college who was kidnapped in Campo de Mayo and now lived in Spain. Mara had never met her, she only knew her as another chapter in her mother's never-ending story: Imagine, poor thing, they had killed her lover, her comrade in the struggle, and she was locked up there, they only took off her hood to stick some crap into her mouth or so she could kiss him – him and only him. She was a lovely girl, a cute little blonde, not very tall, but very pretty. Well, what happened was that Jaguar Gómez took her for his lover and, well, you can imagine, there was no way out of it. He was a dark, ugly guy, very hairy, with one of those Andean faces that make you just want to run away the minute you see them, but that Jaguar, he was fierce, you'd shit your pants just looking at him. Besides, he was the big boss of the task forces, so you can imagine how powerful he was. And with him all gung-ho, you couldn't say no to him; you had to do everything he said. Believe me, Mara, if I had had to sleep with a guy like that to save you and your brother, I would have done it, don't you doubt it for a second.

Mara closed the bag with a tug, frightening away images.

---

* From 'Cantares', a song by Joan Manuel Serrat, based on a poem by Antonio Machado. This first verse says, 'Everything goes and everything stays, but our lot is to go, making paths as we go, paths through the sea.'

Meanwhile, Quique hovered over her with two expectant arms, like a goalkeeper waiting for a penalty kick.

It would have been easy for Mara to get rid of that walking, trouser-wearing symptom of her mother's depression. Cris would never have tolerated him making a move on her daughter like that; spite would have swept her up in waves of fury that Quique (half drowned, adrift) would be unable to surf; wipe him out, make him disappear forever, John Doe, *kaput*. But Mara didn't feel like doing her mother any favours; she didn't want to get that close to her. Her most recent Oedipal pretext, Horacio, was a journalist friend of her mother's. Horacio had written for the magazine *Fierro* for a while; with the return of democracy he got a post as Inspector of Potholes and devoted himself to investigative journalism. One night in her room, after having sex with him, Mara made a brusque movement and kicked him out of bed, literally. The guy ended up on his knees in front of her, exposed and vulnerable. Mara sat up calmly, without looking at him, and lit a cigarette.

'Why did you do that?' he asked.

'Because I felt like it,' she answered.

He gave her a slap that sent her cigarette flying, and she stood up furious, her nostrils defiantly flared. He slapped her again; then she ran into the master bathroom and pulled the bolt across. She curled up beside the bidet and waited. She was waiting for him to come looking for her, to kick down the door amid hissing threats; when she sat on the cold floor she realized she was all wet. Then she heard the elevator grille open and close.

That episode with Horacio was a few days before the pot-banging protests started. Mara remembered it perfectly. Her mother had come into the apartment like a whirlwind, her eyes ablaze (the way her friend's eyes, the one imprisoned in Rawson, got when she described the FAR leader with a shotgun in his hand and that incredible thing shining in his eyes, when he came to free her as she waited curled up and trembling in her cell). Turn on the TV, Mara, the uprising is here, everyone's out in the streets (you heard it from your mother first).

Fifteen floors below, a brightly coloured, flattened animal came in and out of focus against the asphalt. From the windows of nearby buildings, where other people were sticking their heads out, came metallic flashes that climbed the walls and made the street throb. Mara went back into her mother's room, where she was now pulling clothes from the closet and spreading them on the bed. Where are you going? Should I be packing too? No, Mara, how could we leave now? We have to be here to support the people who are out there expressing themselves. Fleeing is for cowards. All this time enduring and enduring and suddenly the will of the people prepares for battle and lifts its fist in the air. What do you think? I can't decide between the denim skirt or should I go with the linen pants, more sober? It was nine at night; the news of the looting in Greater Buenos Aires alternated with updates of avenues blocked by indignant citizens throughout the capital, contorted faces breaking shop windows and Chinese supermarket owners trying to defend themselves. The city was synchronized in a single rhythmic pulse; finally, Cris went for jeans and sneakers.

'Cos when you start fucking with the middle class, there's no turning back, reflected Mara's mother as she banged on her stainless-steel saucepan along Avenida Coronel Díaz. Her political analyses mingled with those of other 'girls she knew', women her age with whom she had coincided at the dry-cleaner's some time or another, without the slightest interaction. Mara went beside her; walking where the cars usually go reminded her of the '90 World Cup held in Italy, and of her father waving a blue-and-white flag. All around you could see peaceful crowds walking in the same direction, some with their dogs, who barked excitedly or shat placidly in flower beds. People chatted with those beside them, keeping the melody of the pot banging. The street vendors' kiosks were open; looking up, you could see more windows ablaze with people waving their metal conductors of political heat. Mara was worried some crazy bus driver would take the opportunity to 'express himself' and kill hundreds of people. There were no police on the streets.

Columns of demonstrators headed to the Congress and the Plaza de Mayo along the city's main boulevards. At Santa Fe and Riobamba, Mara met up with a schoolmate, Lucía. They hadn't seen each other in a long time; Mara forced the encounter by heading towards her – fearing that, if she didn't, Lucía would do everything possible to avoid her. Lucía told her that she had just come back from Bolivia, where 'the rural situation is at a tipping point'. She worked taking pictures for an independent journalism NGO. The photographer she worked with came up again and again in the story, it was clear that Lucía could talk about him for hours. Mara listened to her eagerly; she had always had a delightful way of explaining events and falling in love with people. Lucía checked her watch; there were people waiting for her. Mara exaggerated her meekness when she said she wanted to go with her, quickly explaining that she had to get away from her mother, so the decision to walk together became more a question of Lucía's altruism than of Mara's desire, and Lucía agreed. They walked through shouts, drumming, columns, security fences; when they got to the Congress, Lucía closed her hand around Mara's arm: Careful, said Lucía, it's a death trap.

II

The high point of Mara and Lucía's relationship took place one summer in Buenos Aires. They got together every day in Lucía's house with another friend, Liti, a very pale, tall girl with dark hair who looked like some kind of punk Marilyn Monroe. At six, when Lucía's mother came home from work and the light that fell on things tinged violet, they would split up. They talked the entire time; they had so many things to tell each other! They shared information on the pressing universe that hovered, lying in wait for the right moment to pounce on them. Everything seemed to indicate that: at the age of twelve, they had entered the piss-filled waters of a summer camp swimming pool where the boys were playing shark, trying to reach them beneath the water so they could then emerge to the triumphant shout of 'I touched it.' Questions such as: When is it OK to touch their balls? What is the perineum, and where exactly is it located? held their attention. Gradually, the speed of their phrasing changed, and the theories about sex were mixed with stories of fear.

Liti's parents were in the ERP, the People's Revolutionary Army; Liti kept a mental image of her mom, pregnant, running across a field beneath bullets in Ezeiza. Her father never confirmed it, but she was sure, something told her that he'd 'shot down a few'. Lucía's parents met as activists in the Christian Youth movement, in a slum where they taught the catechism; they never entered the armed struggle but accepted the responsibility of housing various guerrilla friends who later died or fled. Most of the kids in her high school were children of former militants; in some cases their parents had been enemies, for belonging to the Peronist Youth movement (Lucía's boyfriend's father) that sent others (Mara's future boyfriends or their fathers) to the front. Or parents that negotiated with leaders (army leaders or guerrilla leaders), leaving the rest unprotected, like the notorious father whose wife was freed in exchange for a list of comrades-in-arms (alleged parents of classmates). Lucía had gone to a Catholic elementary school in Belgrano, where there were a lot of daughters of military men; she had a friend, Mariu, who had been raised by her grandparents, an army colonel and his wife. Mariu said that her parents had died in a car accident, but the rumoured version was that her mother, the colonel's daughter, had fallen in love with a guerrilla. Knowing they were in danger, they handed over their two little girls to their grandparents for safe keeping; later the couple was kidnapped. Her grandfather had told Mariu that her parents considered themselves soldiers, that his daughter had told him that after stealing his weapons and the military uniform he kept at home. 'I wanted to protect them and they didn't let me.' The grandfather was ashamed and in torment. Even with all that, what Mariu most liked to do as a child was ride around in a tank, but you couldn't mention it without people feeling sorry for her or insulting her grandparents, either behind her back or to her face. Every detail was a coherent beam of light that fell in with others, like lasers of love and brutality that allowed them to attend the torrid scenes of their own births. They were the bookish daughters of a strange literary country, populated by monsters of serious prose and Gothic *Facundo*s illuminated beneath an overcast sky. Just as tragedy brightens Antigone's moral beauty, those stories exalted the miracle of their very presence; it made them stand out as pure and individual beings, born of a national aristocracy of fire and bravery; like girls smearing their faces with mud to scare each other, they watched in fascination how cruelty transformed into astonishment on their own mouths and expressions.

Mara still missed that summer. In fact, she wanted to hug Lucía and tell her that she looked beautiful; but the crowd pushed them towards a narrow corner, on a street adjacent to the Congress, and she saw that Lucía was getting paranoid. Mara felt like she was bursting with joy: at least they were together in a riot!

'No, not this way,' Lucía had said. In the presence of danger, she had touched her. 'With this many people, it's a death trap.'

In the mobbed streets, everything was black with bodies. They could barely make out facial expressions; noisy shadows surrounded them, setting their muscles in a state of alert. Mara stood on tiptoe to see further; they were hundreds, in every direction, hundreds followed by thousands. She prayed for the cavalry to come and chase them; she would take Lucía by the hand and they would escape. Lucía's expression was tense and expectant; she still had Mara by the arm. They were both afraid and excited.

Around them there were expressions of anguish, with peaks of euphoria and excitement. Old ladies shouted curses at the politicians leaving their offices, out of step with the general melody; those contributions were quickly syncopated, levelled out by the force of the whole. Teenagers in scruffy T-shirts pogo-danced through the crowd. Others just followed the beat happily and chatted with those beside them; youthful anxiety cast them into the front rows, curious about the possibility of a police confrontation. The atmosphere was glorious, and there was no shortage of remarks such as: 'Look how many of us there are, more than a hundred thousand. If just a third of us took up arms, we could take over the country.'

Mara spotted the troupe of stencillers made up of Powa, Toni and two blond guys who were pretty cute. They were surrounded by female satellites with crew cuts and May of '68-style berets. After midnight, spirits were running high and the throng crowded against the railings that surrounded the Congress building. The girls climbed up on the shoulders of Powa and one of the cute blond guys; in that moment they pulled out their mini DV cameras and started filming each other participating in the social protest. The girls were shouting and raising their fists, saying things like 'Hey ho, let's go', 'Charge' and other phrases of celebratory slang usually associated with football; the boys were holding them up and looking at the camera. Then Toni got on another friend's shoulders and kissed one of the girls against the background of popular struggle. It was a pretty postcard; as she looked at them jutting out over the people, Mara remembered that Toni longed for another catastrophe, with the backdrop retouched: his dream was to swing from vine to vine over a Jurassic Buenos Aires of tropical forests and rusted iron structures, destroy this corrupt capitalist system for once and for all, go back to being animals, Mara, hang from the trees!

Toni's Neanderthal utopia maintained a little Marxist heart, with a streak of the ecological anti-globalization vogue used in Europe to while away the dull hours; Mara was too much of a snob to tolerate it. Lucía watched them, somewhat distant, without making any rash comments that could cloud the purity of popular expression.

That was when Mara spotted her mother. She was chatting with Jerom, one of Powa's cronies, tall, dark-haired and attractive, with a slight reputation for filming girls he slept with. Cris was laughing too much, her mouth increasingly closer and more open. Mara knew what that meant, in the same way a moon rock is attached to its heavenly body before being hacked out violently. The recently arrived hordes pushed her; they were teenagers pogoing to the shouts, and a couple of columns of the MAS. Mara squeezed Lucía's hand tightly and closed her eyes, imagining horses in the distance bucking in place, held back by the firm arm of the law mounted on their backs; they could let loose the reins at any moment; Mara couldn't wait.

Her mother and Jerom saw each other again at the Palermo popular assembly; Jerom had gone to check it out because he lived nearby. Cris came along with him to paint some stencils; she held up the plate and Jerom pressed the aerosol. The operation destroyed her nails but it didn't matter, she was delirious. Mara did her best to avoid finding out more details about her mother's new hobbies – but certainty is a frisky little bunny that persists in being captured – and it wasn't long before they were all three having breakfast together in the kitchen. Jerom presided over the table buck naked, because it was hot; his lack of hygiene exalted his masculinity. Somewhat convulsive due to her happiness, Cris heated up the kettle, anxious.

Mara sat at the table in silence. Jerom immediately read the scene and sprawled himself out in his chair, winking an eye at Cris; any comment he made would be an explanation; he didn't owe anyone explanations.

'We were painting some stencils with Cris.'

'You should have seen them, so beautiful!' Cris's voice sounded more shrill than usual. 'They're so much better, more detailed.' She paused; the idea had come out half-baked. 'Than graffiti, I mean.'

Cris immediately served Mara some *mate*. Mara restrained herself from touching it, afraid of replicating her mother's agitated psychomotor state.

'If you're interested,' and Jerom seemed interested, 'you could come with us. We have commandos covering different areas of the city; Powa and the guys organize them. Sometimes we're in dicey spots, other times it's quieter. Always at night, when there's better cover and it's more obscured. We go out in groups of three or four per car. We do the stencil, document the scene with photos and in mini DV, and then we get all the material together at the Cyborga, that's Powa and the guys' lair.'

'Aha. And what kind of things do you paint?' Mara already knew; they had slept together a few months ago, but he had clearly forgotten that.

'Things against Bush, against imperialism, war, capitalism, all that,' answered Jerom, who hadn't forgotten for a minute.

'It's incredible how everything comes back around again, isn't it?' Cris rested her elbows on the table, looking at both of them. She felt more secure when repeating familiar phrases. 'I mean, a few years back, we were fighting for the same things. Look at them now, the kids of the new generation, in an all-out popular rebellion, backing the demos, struggling to make a more just world. Kinda blows my mind, you know?'

'The protest now is pacifist and yours wasn't. There's a world of difference. Besides, this demo is pure bourgeois self-defence,' said Mara.

'That has nothing to do with it,' Cris said angrily, shifting her hair a little bit, attentive to Jerom's actions. 'Every era has its own discourse, but the important thing is the essence, which is breaking with individualism and working for a better world, or are you going to disagree with that too? Everything came real easy for you because you were born here, not a care in the world, and I could pay for you to have an education, a fitting social environment, but there are other people who never had what you had, you understand?'

'And what does that have to do with it?'

'All I'm saying is that if you had fought for other people's right to study, eat, work and other things, then you'd understand there's a big difference between living so comfortably and selfishly, and trying by any means necessary to help others, in any way you can, with weapons or with your teeth, if need be, if that's what the historical moment asks of you.'

ENJOYING YOURSELF?

**SUBSCRIBE NOW
FOR YOURSELF OR A FRIEND
RECEIVE FOUR ISSUES
A YEAR
SAVE £22**

UK
£34.95
(£29.95 Direct Debit)

Europe
£39.95

Rest of the world★
£45.95

Subscribe now at Granta.com/UK113
or by Freephone 0500 004 033
(Ref: UK113)

★Excluding USA, Canada and Latin America

GRANTA.COM/UK113

Cris sipped her *mate*. In the end she had raised her voice a bit; it's true, but what could she do? She was dynamic, passionate, she told herself. Her speech, however, didn't appear to have convinced Jerom. While Mara grumbled that all fascisms promoted the highest ideals to justify violence (Bush brandished values of freedom and democracy), Cris noticed that Jerom seemed to be nodding his head in agreement. Cris prepared another *mate* and took it over to Jerom. Jerom brought his mouth to the straw, without looking at her.

Bitterly, Cris remembered that course on Emotional Capital and Neuro-Linguistic Programming she took in '99. Tone, micro-rhythm and blinking speed served as empathy's transmission tubes, the means of contagion of shared ideas; later, these ideas grow until they become 'life perspectives'. Was she becoming unable to give and receive? She remembered her teacher, Sami Wasskam, and how he'd controlled her empathy once by using those biorhythms. Sami had been a jackass, too. She never would have screwed him if it weren't for him controlling her biorhythms that way. Ugly, that's what he was; ugly and beneath her. Out of control, Cris's smile faded for a few seconds; disappointed, she realized that it no longer mattered what she had to say; to quote Sami, the what didn't matter any more, only the how. The technique for navigating modern certainties eluded her; Jerom was no longer talking to her; in fact, he didn't even seem to register her presence.

On the opening day of the swap club, Jerom arrived at the neighbourhood assembly with a Japanese girl who had pink hair and – surprise, surprise – tits, which are rare in Orientals. Cris had seen her hanging around the stencil commandos: she laughed frequently, but also knew how to keep quiet and open her slanty eyes wide when spoken to, as if the words entered better through her eyes than her ears. Jerom's self-satisfied behaviour bore witness to the fact that getting her into bed hadn't been difficult for him; the little Chink must be photogenic. While Quique and his cronies passed out the quince pie, which Jerom and that Chink hadn't even wanted to try, Cris realized that her romance with the new guerrilla modalities was over, without much fanfare.

Among other disappointments that summer, the dreaded Cavalry Regiment and their praetorian guards never arrived. A few nights would pass before they condescended to wield the incandescent beam of brute force, tossing tear gas and flaunting their hunger for innocent people, machine guns at the ready. The marches in December weren't as much fun as before; dissolved into the crowd, the magic of her encounter with Lucía soon faded away. Mara made mental plans to go look for her at the Workers' Party meetings, at the headquarters in Balvanera where that photographer she was into went, but never actually did it. ∎

THE HOTEL LIFE

Javier Montes

TRANSLATED BY MARGARET JULL COSTA

JAVIER MONTES
SPAIN
1976

Montes is a writer, translator and art critic. Though he always ends up back home in Madrid, he has lived for extended periods in Equatorial Guinea, Paris, Lisbon, Rio de Janeiro and Buenos Aires. In 2007, he received the José María Pereda Prize for his first novel, *Los penúltimos*, and has just published another, *Segunda parte*. Together with Andrés Barba, he received the Anagrama Essay Prize for the book *La ceremonia del porno* (2007). They also co-edited the anthology of short stories *After Henry James* (2009). As a translator he has focused on critical publication and research into the works of Shakespeare: he has published versions of *Cymbeline*, *King Lear* and *Coriolanus*, as well as the essay 'Shakespeare y la música' (2009). 'The Hotel Life' is an excerpt from his novel in progress.

I took only one light suitcase with me, although it was such a short journey that I could easily have taken more and heavier luggage if I'd wanted. Ten blocks, or 1.132km according to the electronic receipt from the taxi. There was so much traffic, though, that it took me twenty minutes. No one said goodbye to me or closed the apartment door behind me, no one came with me, still less followed in my tracks. I was, however, expected at my destination, and the room where I was to spend the night had been reserved in my name.

I live so close to the hotel that it really would have been quicker to walk, but I decided to hail a taxi so as to get the journey off to a good start. However short, it was still a journey, and I wanted to show that I was taking it seriously (but then I've always taken both my work and my journeys seriously; they do, after all, come to more or less the same thing).

Or perhaps the opposite was true, perhaps it was a matter of being capable of a certain playfulness too, when required. I've spent half my life moving from hotel to hotel, but this was the first time I would sleep in one in my own city. That's why I finally agreed to do it when the newspaper called and suggested the Imperial. I think we were all surprised when I did.

'They've finished the refurbishment now and have just sent us their new publicity pack.'

Initially, I refused. They know I never write about new hotels.

'But this isn't a new hotel. It's the same old Imperial. They've just given it a facelift.'

I don't like new hotels: the smell of paint, the piped music. And I distrust the refurbished variety. Any 'facelift' destroys the prestige and character which, in older establishments, are the hotel equivalent of good sense and even sentiment, or, at least, of memory. I don't know that I'm much of a sentimentalist myself, but I do have a good memory. And I've noticed that, after a certain age, sentiment and memory tend to merge, which is probably why I prefer hotels that know how to remember.

I long ago agreed my terms with the newspaper. I choose the hotel of the week, and they pay. Cheap or expensive, near or far, undiscovered or famous, and usually just for one night, but sometimes two. No skimping (they skimp quite enough on my fee) and no favours either. I never accept invitations in exchange for a review.

Not even if it's a bad review, as some either very stupid or very astute PR guy once asked me over the phone.

People in the hotel world know my views, but an awful lot of invitations still get sent to me at the office (I won't allow the paper to give anyone my home address). I suppose the PR companies send them just in case I do, one day, take the bait, just in case I relent and end up accepting and going to the hotel, where they will treat me like royalty and give me the very best room, so that I will then write a five-star review, which they will frame and hang up in reception or post on their website, and which will bring in money from guests or, even if it doesn't and even if they don't need it, will doubtless bring them other things that are sometimes worth as much or more than money: the approval of fellow hoteliers, the warm glow of vanity confirmed, the certainty that they are, as a hotel, on the right track.

My column, I have to say, continues to be a success. And although the people at the newspaper never say as much, so that I don't get big-headed, I know that hotels, airlines and travel agencies are queuing up to put a half-page advertisement in my section: 'The Hotel Life'.

That success is, of course, relative, as is any success in newspapers and in print. Every now and then, someone suggests I start a blog with my reviews. Even the people at the newspaper do so occasionally. It might be fouling our own nest, they say, but if you started a blog and got some advertising on it, you'd make a mint.

I think they're exaggerating.

'Besides, you only live around the corner. All you'd have to do is spend a couple of hours there one afternoon to check out what they've done.'

Again I refused. They know perfectly well that I don't write about hotels I haven't slept in. It would be like writing a restaurant review having only sniffed the plates as the waiters brought them out (of course, my colleague on the next page sometimes does exactly that in his column: 'Dinner is Served'. He said to me when we met once, 'I can tell by the smell alone what's cooking.' I didn't take to him, and the feeling, I imagine, was mutual).

'Well, if that's what's bothering you, spend the night there.'

They may have been joking, but I took them at their word. I rather liked the idea of sleeping in a hotel room from which I could almost, you might say, see the windows of my own empty apartment and bedroom. A night of novelty might buck me up a bit. I've grown rather jaded with the years; well, I've been doing the same job for a long time now. My choice, of course. And I do it reasonably well, I think, possibly better than anyone, to judge by the emails I sometimes get from readers and even the occasional letter written the old-fashioned way, with pen and paper, envelope and stamp, and which the newspaper also forwards to me.

The letters always arrive opened. Apparently it's a security thing, but it seems a bit over the top: I might be somewhat harsh in my comments at times, but not enough to merit a letter bomb. Then again, I don't mind if the people at the office read them, always assuming they do, because at least the editors will see that I do still have a public.

On the other hand, there's nothing so very amazing about being better than anyone else at a job for which there's scarcely any competition. There aren't many of us hotel reviewers left, not at least in the newspaper world. The Internet is another matter, there everyone wants to give his and her opinion and to analyse their journey down to the last detail and even write as if they were real reviewers (I think some of them copy my style and my adjectives). There's nothing wrong with that, I suppose. On the other hand, the reviews are never somehow right either: they're nearly always ill-intentioned, ill-considered and ill-written by venomous individuals or by just plain weirdos: I mean, I like my work, but I certainly wouldn't do it for free.

In the end, I gave in, which is presumably what the people at the Imperial were counting on when they tried their luck. The editors were thrilled, so I guess they had some advertising deal going on as well. As usual, they made the reservation in my name. My real name, of course, not the pseudonym I use for my column. The surname on my ID card throws even the sharpest manager or receptionist off the scent and means that I can be just like any other hotel guest. That's also why I won't allow my photograph to appear alongside my name, and why I never go to conventions or meetings with colleagues. That's no great sacrifice, mind: they're doubtless as dull as the reviews they write. Having no face makes my job much easier and – why deny it? – more amusing too. That way, the whole thing has something of the double agent or the undercover spy about it. A double double agent, because in hotels, no one is ever who they say they are, and who doesn't take advantage of a stay in a hotel to play detective, however unwittingly?

After all these years of only using my real name to check in, it now seems to me falser than my false name; apart from the people on the newspaper, few people know it, and still fewer – almost no one, in fact – uses it.

At midday on the dot, just as the taxi drew up beside me, it started to rain. I wasn't wearing a coat and had no umbrella. I must have been the only one not expecting rain, because within seconds, the street was awash with cars. I didn't mind. In fact, I would have been happy if the journey had taken longer, even though I was paying for it, not the newspaper (I'm very particular about that).

At this stage in my life, taxi journeys are the only ones that mean much to me. I have no qualification in the career or, rather, pursuit I chose for my journey through life, and I've long ceased to think of it in those terms, although I suppose I got off to a pretty good start. In the end, though, I lost sight of my fellow runners, the ones you're so conscious of at first, when you're in your twenties or thirties and keep glancing out of the corner of your eye at those behind, intent (or so you believe) on overtaking you, meanwhile calculating how big a lead the runners ahead have over you and conserving your energies as you imagine the best way of getting past them for the final sprint.

But there are no sprints, and certainly no final sprints. Indeed, I stopped running a long time ago. There's no point. Just walk at the pace that suits your feet and you'll end up arriving at the place you set out for. Or else keep quite still: lately, I've had the feeling that it's simply a matter of sitting and waiting, that it isn't us who do the walking, but the things around us, and they won't fail us; they never do, because nothing ever fails and everything ends up happening anyway.

Certainly through the taxi windows things continued to happen (and in their proper order too): the familiar streets, the doorways in single file, the treacherous glare of light as we turned a particular corner. Even when we were stuck in a jam, life continued to happen, like in those black-and-white taxis you see in gangster films: the interior of the cars as still and steady as a house you could live in forever, despite the pretend bumps and jolts created by the brawnier assistants on the set. The actors would sit against the backdrop of a screen on to which were projected dripping street lamps and blurred pavements and the ancient shadows of pedestrians. Fortunately, at night, they always drove with the interior light turned on. It wasn't exactly hard to spot that the landscapes in those films were fake. Perhaps they were so sure of themselves then that they deliberately made it obvious. The driver would turn the wheel regardless of the fact that there was no bend visible in the perspective to the rear; or else, beyond the silhouetted windows, the backdrop would merely vibrate and shake and be pierced by occasional beams of light. As if the person in charge of special effects had simply given up all attempt at pretence.

It was the same with the cartoons which, when I was a child, always preceded the grown-up feature: the talkative bear or the cat in the hat would run and run. And behind them, a repeated parade of trees and buildings would speed past. It saved work, because that way they only needed to produce a single backdrop for the one fleeing figure. In fact, nothing and no one moved during those thrilling scenes. As a small boy, I soon caught on to that use of loops; I became expert at detecting them even before I could come up with a proper explanation.

On the way to the hotel, it occurred to me that I was escaping in that unnecessary taxi. Or playing at escaping, like those pretend cops and gangsters. Only a man trying to give someone the slip would get into a taxi carrying virtually no luggage in order to stay at a hotel ten blocks away. And if anyone did that and someone did actually follow him, it would look most suspicious. He would give the impression that he was trying to cover his tracks, as they did and still do in old films.

But no one was going to follow me or say, 'Follow that cab.' On the way to the hotel, the driver didn't even express surprise at the shortness of the journey, in a car that felt to me like a hotel room where I could find bed and board for a night and imagine I was in hiding from my pursuers. Pure invention, of course. If it wasn't for the articles about the various hotels that I sent to the newspaper, they would long since have lost track of me.

Twelve twenty on a random Tuesday afternoon in March: the bored porter who failed to open the taxi door for me and to pick up my one small case did, however, accompany me to the revolving door beneath a vast umbrella. Given the hotel's large, pretentious canopy, the umbrella was clearly more for decoration than anything else; at most, a baton to set the right note for the rest of the hotel.

The two receptionists in the deserted foyer were bored too; indeed, the whole hotel was bored at that deadest of hours in all hotel foyers, when no one healthy or in a healthy state of mind is still in his room, when it's too late to leave and too early to check in, and when the tide of visitors who have gone or are about to arrive has fallen silent.

Seen from closer to, the receptionists seemed very young, and not exactly thrilled to see me. Perhaps the last thing they expected to have to do in that job was check in a guest. They both became absorbed in the screen showing reservations. At their age, disdain and confusion are hard to distinguish.

I hadn't visited the Imperial since I was a child. I've often passed by its facade, which is as grandiose as its name, and seen its two corner towers from many balconies. The towers still look like new arrivals, even though they've spent the last hundred years helping to locate the centre and orienting visitors viewing the city from afar (assuming they know where to look). The towers were intended as beacons of the country's cosmopolitanism but right from the start, they seemed somehow antiquated, as did the hotel itself, which was home to gatherings of bullfighting aficionados and had the air of a provincial social club, with a lot of people arriving for pre-supper drinks but, rarely, it seemed, any actual guests.

The deadly silence of the foyer was composed of various sounds: the distant clink of glasses, the galumphing roar of vacuum cleaners on the other side of the world, and a sinuous, tenuous, techno stream of piped music that slithered past the legs of the furniture before coiling around your ankles and up your body in order to go in one ear and out the other. The music fitted in well with the new designer decor, so familiar from the publicity packs forwarded to me by the newspaper that I still don't know whether I liked it or not. I probably never will know either, because that's how it is in such cases, knowing or not knowing doesn't much matter.

They say that the previous owners sold the whole place for next to nothing, but renovating it must have cost a pretty penny. The brochures I read were rife with clichés along the lines of: a refuge for the experienced nomad; an operations base for the world traveller.

The kind of superhero jargon that comes down to little more than a few flashy, but rather dim lamps. Bright enough, though, for you to be able to guess that the armchairs and rugs in the lobby won't feel as good as they look. In the entrance to the hotel, there were no longer the wax flowers beneath glass domes that I seem vaguely to remember, no, not vaguely, but with a nightmare clarity within an otherwise fuzzy recollection. Instead, they had skimped on real flowers and overdone the air freshener – without success, for even in the broad light of day there still hovered in the foyer the ghost of the aficionados' cigars.

The ghosts of the bulls were there too, for on the wall behind the reception desk the new owners, as if in jest, had left the stuffed heads of bulls who had once known fiercer days. A Sobrero, an Embajador and a Ventoso, who gaze upon everything now in stupefaction. For a moment, it seemed to me that I recognized their faces. Or that their small glass eyes glinted when they recognized me. I almost saw myself as a child again, holding someone's hand, surrounded by adults busily talking about their own affairs, while I stared at those same large heads in the old foyer, with their modest tongues poking out from the cheap stuffing. I don't know if I invented the memory or if I really did feel at the time, as I did a while ago, the same twinge of solidarity.

Yet another hotel that acts as a maquette or mascot of the whole country, as both doll's house and scale model of the real house, and which has the bad taste to put it on display in the main living room or just to leave it to gather dust in the attic. This renovated Hotel Imperial has watered down its rather tainted quaintness, gone to a lot of trouble to exchange some of its old rough edges for newer ones, and ended up with a precarious kind of 'luxury' held together with pins. Its touch, however, is still uncertain when it comes to creating and providing genuine luxury.

The whisperings and tappings of the two receptionists had been going on for ages. I considered getting out my notebook, which rarely fails as a last resort: taking notes always attracts attention. Then the machine finally spat out the smart card for my room. The receptionist didn't bother to summon anyone to carry my bag, and I could have sworn that they both held out the card to me simultaneously. Or perhaps that was simply the effect created by their disconcertingly double smile.

The corridor on my floor was empty and silent, as if it were five in the morning. Or as if it were precisely the time it was, because hotels are often very noisy at five in the morning. No employees, no guests. The thick, gluey smell of new carpets. I reached my room door and it took me a while to work out how to put the card in the slot. Finally, the little red light blinked, then turned green. The door gave a kind of wheeze and reluctantly opened a couple of centimetres. Beyond lay a dark area, one of those spaces in hotel rooms that serve as a kind of no-man's-land and provide the luxury of a square metre with no furniture, no name and no other purpose than that of isolating the bedroom, at least in theory, from any noise out in the corridor.

To my right, the door of the bedroom stood slightly ajar, letting in just enough light for me to see that the door to the bathroom stood wide open. A gleaming tap dripped in the darkness. Before I had a chance to close the main door to the corridor, I heard a voice inside. Like a thief taken by surprise, I instinctively froze, an instinct I had no idea I possessed and which was, besides, entirely misplaced. To my left, in the full-length mirror in the vestibule, something moved. In the reflection, I could make out the inside of the room that the door was preventing me from seeing. I saw a double bed with a beige counterpane that matched the grey light coming in through a window invisible to me.

A girl was sitting on the edge, towards the head of the bed. She was pretty, despite the ridiculous amount of make-up she was wearing. She looked very young. She had on only a bra and panties. Her hair and skin were the colour of the bedspread. Her hands were resting on her lap, and she was staring down at them with a look of utter boredom on her face. She was blowing out her cheeks a little, drumming lightly on the carpet with her feet and sighing scornfully, exaggerating these signs of tedium, like a child pretending to be bored.

Out of the corner of her eye she was watching something happening on the part of the bed not reflected in the mirror. She wasn't alone. The mattress creaked without her having moved a muscle and someone – a man, of course – panted once, twice, three times.

I didn't know whether to go back out into the corridor or to walk straight in and demand an explanation. Since they clearly couldn't see me, I took another step forward, my eyes still fixed on the mirror. The girl's reflection disappeared. On the other side of the bed, with his back to the headboard and to her, I saw a naked boy. He was probably slightly younger than the girl and much darker skinned too. I couldn't see his face because his head was bent contritely over his chest: I could see only a tense forehead, the beginning of a frown. He was still breathing like someone about to make some great physical effort, and was running his hand over his chest with a strangely insentient, robotic gesture. Then the girl spoke.

'Get on with it, will you?'

The boy jumped and looked at her as if he had forgotten she was there.

'All right, all right.'

He again focused on his hand and let it slide slowly down his chest to his navel. He placed it, without much conviction, on his flaccid penis, which he shook a couple of times, like a rattle. Then suddenly a shiver ran through him.

'It's too bloody cold in here.'

'Yeah, yeah.'

The girl's 'yeah, yeah' sounded resigned, as if she had said it a thousand times before, as if she had spent her whole life in that room, sitting there in her underpants, listening to people complaining about the cold. I imagined her arching her eyebrows and nodding in mock solemnity, but to check that I was right, I would have had to stop seeing the boy's face. She must have liked the woman-of-the-world air that her 'yeah, yeah' gave her, because she repeated it.

'Yeah, yeah.'

The boy started breathing hard again as he went about his business without success. The girl joined in his next out-breath.

'What's wrong?'

'I don't know. Can't you help?'

'No, I can't, I've told you already. You have to do it on your own. Then we can fuck.'

'I can't get it up.'

'Well, watch the film then.'

The girl had suddenly adopted the tone of an older sister.

'Wait, I'll turn up the volume.'

I heard her feeling for something next to the bed and heard things falling on to the carpet. I didn't dare change my position in order to be able to see her face again. I was beginning to feel afraid they would discover me there. The idea of marching into the bedroom, pretending to be surprised and asserting my rights had vanished of its own accord. I should have gone down to reception. The truth is, I don't know if I stayed there because I was afraid of making a noise as I left or because I wanted to see and hear more. It seemed to me that I could safely wait a while longer: if the boy or the girl got up, I would still have time to step out into the corridor and close the door before they saw me.

'Where's the remote gone?'

The boy said nothing. He was kneading his penis with both hands now. He did it in a careless, oddly clumsy way, as if he had never touched it before. Suddenly a chorus of moans blared out above the unmistakably inane soundtrack of a porn flick.

'Yes, yes. Just there. Just there. Oh.'

I realized that I was standing in the vestibule, smiling. A solitary smile is never a proper smile. I was probably just trying to quell both my nerves and my unease about the whole situation: given the stimuli available, I wasn't surprised that the boy was finding it hard to get an erection.

'Turn it down.'

'OK, OK.'

The groans and the music abated just as a hoarse, rather unconvincing voice joined the chorus.

'Yes. That's it. Just there. Yes.'

The boy was staring at the screen. He must have been immediately behind the door to the vestibule, and for a moment, I had the impression that he was looking straight at me through the wood: my heart was pounding hard now. But what the boy was looking at through the crack was his own image reflected in the vestibule mirror. This was apparently more arousing than the mechanical heavy breathing on-screen. His apathetic penis began to show signs of life. He turned slightly and looked at his reflection full on. I thought then, this boy is seeing exactly what I'm seeing and is excited by the very thing that I can see without feeling any excitement: the image of himself reflected back at him by the mirror in this small, dark space; the image that would be replaced by my own reflection, the wrinkled back of my jacket, if I were to take one step forward.

Standing just half a metre from the mirror, in the gloom of that tiny vestibule, which was neither corridor nor bedroom, I felt almost as if I were in the boy's presence. The rectangle of light framing his reflected body blocked my path like a concrete wall: I couldn't go into the bedroom without pushing open the door and interrupting the scene inside, but neither could I retreat into the corridor without coming between the boy and his double. After a few interminable seconds – during which I barely dared to breathe – I again heard the dripping tap in the bath, I became aware of the handle of my bag digging into my shoulder and of how tired I was from standing. Perhaps a still more ridiculous parenthesis of tedium was about to open inside that senseless anxiety. I was aware of the dark space, the terrifying paralysis one experiences in ghostly dreams or during childhood games. I noticed, above all, that the knot in my throat had been growing gradually tighter and looked set to become a black, childish panic.

The boy was masturbating energetically now. For a second or two I had been watching everything but seeing nothing, and he and I both jumped at the same time when we suddenly heard the voice of another man.

'No, no. That's fine, but don't turn away. Keep looking over here.'

There was someone else in the room. The boy looked round and away from the mirror. I breathed again (and realized that I had been forgetting to do so for some time now).

'That's better. You know, it really is cold in here. I'm going to close the door, but you carry on.'

And I probably shouldn't have breathed, because the new air made me drop my guard. The panic gathered momentum and went straight to my head: I felt its hands gripping my shoulders hard and brushing my neck and pressing into the corners of my eyes before giving me a silent slap around the face. It had understood before I did what those words meant. The owner of the voice would approach the vestibule door and find me standing there and that would be terrible. I stood with my back against the wall. I could see nothing in the mirror now. Anyone in that room or, indeed, in the whole hotel, would have been able to hear my heart pounding. On the other side of that half-open door, I heard footsteps walking across the carpet towards the door – I doubtless imagined them or felt them on the soles of my own feet or in the deepest recesses of my ears, because that carpet would have been capable of muffling the noise of a whole army on the march. I saw myself from outside – from above to be exact – and it seemed to me that I had all of eternity in which to calculate what was probably going to happen (and what was probably not going to happen), the various emotions provoked by my collision with the owner of the voice: anger – Where the hell did you spring from?; surprise – What are you doing here?; ominous malice and feigned amusement – Well, well, look who's here!; and worse, our absurd shared astonishment – Oh!

Only now, as I'm writing this, do I realize that the one thought in my head at the time was that this room was, after all, mine, and that the law, if you like, was on my side. Of course it was, but at that moment, the room was outside almost everything, certainly outside the law.

Then the door closed. Someone pushed it shut from inside, that was all. I saw nothing, no hand, not even a shadow. I felt a sense of relief tinged with a feeling of stunned disappointment. On the other side of the door, the footsteps belonging to the owner of the voice moved off. I heard him say:

'There was a bit of a draught coming in.'

I heard nothing more: not the voices of the girl or the boy, nor the soundtrack of the porn movie. I breathed deeply again and that was when the accumulated panic overflowed. For another eternal second, my feet seemed soldered to the floor. I would never escape from that vestibule, which, now that the mirror had been reduced to a blank, black surface, was pitch dark. Then suddenly, in two miraculous strides, I was out in the corridor and very slowly closing the door to the room. The corridor was still deserted.

Only then did I notice the red 'Do Not Disturb' sign hanging from the handle, and I even pretended to be angry with myself: Honestly, fancy not noticing that, I almost said out loud. My heart was slowing and I felt the euphoria I always used to feel as a small boy, after pulling off one of my rather discreet pranks. I realize now that I was still thinking in childish terms: I was all right, I was safe and well and alive. They – the baddies, the grown-ups – hadn't caught me.

Then the adult in me resumed his post, brushed off his sleeves, and relegated to a dark corner the boastful, fearful boy who had taken command for a moment or so. After all, I thought, I hadn't done or indeed seen anything very wrong. It had been a curious scene, though. Hard to interpret, odd.

I couldn't face getting in the lift and so I took the emergency stairs. No carpet, no air freshener, no piped music. It was cold and my steps echoed above the dull machine throb coming from the bottom of the bottomless well of the stairs.

'No, not odd, weird.'

This, I believe, I said out loud as I raced down the stairs. I took them two at a time until I reached the basement, only to have to climb them again, one by one. ∎

GRANTA

GIGANTOMACHY

Pablo Gutiérrez

TRANSLATED BY ANNA KUSHNER

PABLO GUTIÉRREZ
SPAIN
1978

Gutiérrez won the Tormenta en un vaso Prize for the best new author in Spanish for his first novel, *Rosas, restos de alas* (2008). In 2001, he was a finalist for the Miguel Romero Esteo Prize for Playwriting with a play that never made it to the stage. He studied journalism in Seville but soon left the profession. Currently a teacher of literature at a secondary school in Cadiz, he lives in peace and tranquillity, very close to the sea. 'Gigantomachy' is a new story.

As cadets, we rubbed Coca-Cola on our soles so we wouldn't crack open our heads while playing outside. The dew soaked the concrete and we glided on the court like an aeroplane when it rains, our hands hidden in our fists, the pavement greasy beneath Saturday's frost and, just at the mouth of the airport, eleven pale giants fastened to the seats like packages, the pilot narrows his eyes so that the nose meets the blue lines, the wind, the rain, all of the gods' lightning illuminating our enormous jaws. On those winter courts, how we broadsided those boys from the Salesian school, there go the boys having taken communion – we used to say – there go the boys parading their embroidered crests, no one breathes until the aeroplane rushes on the runway and the pilot releases the brakes. A pitch-dark night: the sky falls in pieces over Treviso, it always rains in Treviso, what does it matter if from here to the hotel and from the hotel to the field we're watched by the guard dog, oh, how we bit as cadets, how we rushed at anyone, and one Saturday they came to see me from La Caja and they shook my hand like a gentleman, they said, aren't your parents home? Damn, you can really hit it, how would you like to try spending some time with us? La Caja! With Izquierdo and Lafuente and that tower of curls who was shooting at just fifteen years old, a trunk with elephant ankles who moved slooooowly like a mimic, but when he got it down court, oh, La Caja. My folks said fine, but only if you go on with school, and there was Mom, crying as if I were going off to Antarctica, don't cry, Mommy, I'll come home every weekend, all those hours on the bus that brings back the San Fernando recruits, heads shaved and bone-thin as lepers, sad and gloomy-faced with their backpacks hanging at their shoulders, their noses covered in pimples. Two breakfasts, meat at lunchtime, fish for supper, piles of vegetables on tin trays: we also made up an army, an army of gigantean kids with sharpened hands, prominent Adam's apples and the shadow of a moustache. We followed orders, we had leaders, punishments and uniforms, La Caja's uniform is so pretty, with gold borders, a name and number on the back, it was the first time I saw my name printed on a shirt, like an idiot I stared at it like someone who stares at the picture of his girlfriend, I would have slept in it if my room-mate hadn't laughed, serious as a monk and stretched-out and dry, he spent his time reading and he could throw well but didn't run much, and there you had to run like a deer, run and bust a gut during training so during games you could fly like Son Goku when he took his weights off, we hit any one of them with a hell of a lot of blows, it would be great if you could still play that way now, if it were that easy to glide right past your rivals like an aeroplane on the runway, jump that way, hit that way, laugh and always win that way, but everything now is fight and surround and bite down on your protector so they don't break your teeth, like here in Treviso when they ripped one of my molars out during the first charge, minute one and boom, down to the floor like a sparring, of course I wasn't even twenty years old then and I would be shaking as I came on to that court that had the appearance of a gym and the fans shake you from the minute you step on the sporting ring and Perotti the winger ripped my tooth out with a full contact blow of his elbow, I went running to the clinic so they could sew up the hole because I wouldn't stop haemorrhaging and there was a monsoon-like rain falling, imagine, a guy as big as a castle all covered in blood asking for a doctor, the nurse nearly fell right over at the sight of me, how the Italians shake you in Treviso or Bologna, each point is an Olympic battle, they grab on to your neck like Medusas, I don't have the heart or the patience any more but there's nothing else I know how to do, after what happened at the Forum, who would trust me, I thought I would end up training kids for a modest salary, I don't want a Nordic house on the peak of some mountain or yachts or cars that I can't park but after what happened at the Forum who would dare put me in a locker room with kids if all I'm good for is being moody and putting on weight, although I've also been quite refined and elegant and have kept some of that, like when we were up against Baskonia, down by two, and Otis had gotten the whistle in the fifth and in the last play, they set a trap for the skinny guy and I threw that rock that I thought would end up outside the pavilion but goddamn, it went in like Larry Bird hit them, the stands went wild, in *Giants,* they did a retrospective on me, I appeared in all the television news programmes, well, if this isn't going to be my day – I thought – but then what happened at the Forum came, and because of that I understand quite clearly that before the year is up, they're going to kick me out, if it would at least stop raining, if only I could take off this tracksuit and button up a real coat and escape from this hotel without telling anyone, just looking left and right in case the guard dog is making his rounds as if we were juniors, if only I could rip off this ridiculous smock that's hurled down on you from a fifth floor when you're over thirty years old, I'm fed up with being a walking adman for AGR Insurance and Univision Optics, if only I could slip away from this remote hotel dropped down on a traffic circle with decorated roundabouts and carpet-covered hallways and brass banisters, a forlorn, tiny receptionist who looks at me with round eyes from deep inside her cardboard uniform as if I were a sulphuric giant banging the counter asking for the Yellow Pages, the classifieds from the newspaper, for a taxi to take me to the city: to walk wildly, feeling splendid and lazy, sit down at a cafe and invite a blonde girl to join me, ask for a cream puff, wolf it down in one bite, make a call like in the last century from a telephone booth, talk to Luisa about the weather in Treviso, ask her if the little one is asleep already, no, not yet, she's cheating me in Parcheesi, tell her to get on the line, you're-so-far-away-I-have-a-burn-mark-on-my-finger-I've-already-got-two-up-on-her, if I could, I would care very little about what happened at the Forum, but it's raining like in the Great Flood and I've become a prisoner of this room watched over by the guard dog, inside this walking adman costume, sharing a room with this little acrobat boy who thinks he is Vince Carter and who has been playing video games for two hours already, imprisoned as if I were at camp training a pony and riding zip-lines while Mom and Dad go off to Paris for a week to see if they can kiss each other there like they don't here, and even though I could escape and strip and get into that taxi, I would still be moving this mountain-like body crowned with the face of a chased aboriginal. On that peak, my forehead like a movie screen would stand out like the lamp of a lighthouse: the little blonde would squeeze her knees together like a girl who is peeing herself, there wouldn't be any cream puffs left at the pastry shop, in this century, there's no finding a telephone booth with anything more than an amputated cable hanging like a terrible extremity.

Gigantomachy. Humans against giants. All of those midgets spitting at me from the stands, hanging strips of toilet paper from my ears, urinating on my towel, calling me hair-raising things, the word repeated from their rounded mouths that sounds the same in every language, even syllables and fricatives and different I-don't-know-whats always sound like the same thing.

The little one will already be asleep in her small bed, Luisa will have already clothed and tucked in her soft little body with her thin fingers, left on the hallway light, sat down in front of the television set like an Indian, she won't be able to sleep and will pick up a book from the shelf, she'll read until day breaks, will make coffee and dress the girl, don't forget your coat, she'll have to leave the car double-parked, she'll get out with her in her arms and will run back because the horns are already honking and later at home she'll go back to bed and sleep until noon, incorrigible Luisa, you never listen to me, you can't live on that birdseed, your ankles are becoming bird-like, bird-like hands, your bird-like fingers and eyelids and empty stare like the rabbit-kid from the Forum.

In the mirror over the sink, my face is reflected like a death mask, a wax mould that says who I once was, where my nose and my cheeks were, where my twisted mouth was, how many lines on my forehead. I hear the tap-tap of the mini Vince Carter with his little game; I want at least to look good when I show up on his camera lens tomorrow. They take pictures of me, they hate me and they take my picture, they shake their fists and focus their telephones on me; the same thing happens in Belgrade and in Lyon. They're happy, they hate me and they're happy because there's nothing like the relief of concentrating that electric vector on a single focus, I carry out such a valuable social service that the government should subsidize me for life, I keep them from thinking of banks and bureaucrats, I am the favourite villain, they gather their anger and disgust all week long then spit it out on me, I play my role of public enemy better than a paedophile, better than a coup leader, better than a corrupt politician, the tyrant of an exotic country, you should rot in a jail cell no matter how much you swear it was an accident, a mishap, an incident, a misfortune, a series of movements, the video so oft-repeated, your large, heavy hand like granite falling over the rabbit's neck, poor, poor, telegenic kid, the frozen scene of your pressed jaw while you shake that single blow, the audience's silence that allows you to hear the doctor's steps on the parquet, the towel over the kid twisting and convulsing, your expression, your gaze fixed on the body that is no longer the kid who ran after you on the court and mocked you – old geezer – but just a shadow of him beneath a towel advertising Univision Optics, the game called off, the question, the slowness with which you cross the sporting ring. What does it matter if they say we regret this shameful act, he's so emotional that he can't talk about it, a fatal accident, a damned coincidence, how could one even suggest it was on purpose, how could you say file a complaint and get a judge, condolences to the family, he still doesn't feel capable of talking about it, the razor gliding, the tap-tap of the little Martians, you never listen to me, Luisa-bird, you have to sleep and eat and get some sun, you're a bat, the girl so white, so thin, but instead of sitting with her in the park, you take refuge in the house and play like kittens or make cathedrals out of plastic blocks, rickets, you even forget about dinner and snacks, children need snacks and to run under the sun, run until they get asthmatic, vitamin D, you never listen to me, at least put on a good face tomorrow, offer up cheeks smoothed with the sacrifice of his saliva, they said it's better you stay at home, rest for a while, but what home, what while, what hole, no – I lied – I need to keep going to not get stuck on the image of poor-rabbit-kid, so that anxiety and guilt don't ensnare me, and by contrast, so that the healthy, beneficial routine that cures all evil, the rail, normality, go after you on the court, they said, they're going to go after you, they said, people only understand that horrible thing, it was you, it's absurd, how could you – my cheeks polished like a shield.

Ever since then the feet are so quick, the feel of the leather is almost as soft as when I was a cadet, sometimes I think I am still just a child and that I haven't learned anything from anything, now they make space for me and I sit, agile, liquid, it must be that the faggots don't dare, I struggle, I jump, it must be that the rabbit-kid was reabsorbed within me, but it's Treviso and it's raining like the devil and tomorrow the film is done, tomorrow they're going to damn me, they're going to jump at my throat tomorrow, revenge for their compatriot, they said it would be better for you not to come, there will be a row, but they shouldn't blame me or chase me, and that's the reason for the poker face and the tap-tap of the video game. There should be a video game of poorkids against me, me executing poorkids with blows to knock a rabbit's head off in revenge for all the old geezers dragging themselves on the court like Moses Malone, sneakers with wheels for us, retirement with Admiral's honours for us, a regular life with a wife and regular children who aren't conspiring against you or telling you you're inconvenient or ugly, it would be better if the two of us lived alone without you, of course I still love you, it's something else, something else.

In Treviso. The streets. The taxi. It can't be that hard to find a pharmacy. ∎

AFTER HELENA

Andrés Neuman

TRANSLATED BY RICHARD GWYN

ANDRÉS NEUMAN
ARGENTINA
1977

Neuman, the son of emigrant musicians, grew up in Buenos Aires and Granada. He has been a teacher of Latin American literature at the University of Granada. At the age of twenty-two he published his first novel, *Bariloche* (1999), followed by *La vida en las ventanas* (2002), *Una vez Argentina* (2003) and *El viajero del siglo*, which won the 2009 Alfaguara Prize and the Critics' Prize in Spain and is translated in ten languages. He is also the author of the short-story collections *El que espera* (2000), *El ultimo minuto* (2001) and *Alumbramiento* (2006); the collection of aphorisms *El equilibrista* (2005); the Latin American travel book *Cómo viajar sin ver* (2010); and *Década* (2008), his collected poems. He has been awarded the Hiperión Prize for Poetry. His website is www.andresneuman.com. 'After Helena' is a new story.

After the death of Helena, I decided to forgive all my enemies. We like to think that big decisions are taken step by step, that they are nurtured over time. But time doesn't nurture anything. It only corrodes, subtracts, wears things out.

I tidied the house, cleared away her things, cleaned her study from top to bottom. A week later I donated all her clothes to a charity. I didn't take any comfort from this act of goodwill: I did it for me, not for the needy.

I had always imagined that to lose the person one loved would be like entering an interminable emptiness, ushering in a permanent sense of deprivation. When I lost Helena, quite the opposite seemed to happen. I felt closed down. Without objectives, without desires, without fears. As if every day of my life were an extension of something that, in reality, had already ended.

I carried on going to the university, but not to cling to my routine, or my salary. With the savings we had, plus the life-insurance money, I could have requested an extended leave of absence. I continued with my classes only to see whether, with the youthful evidence of the new students, I could manage to convince myself that time kept flowing, that the future existed.

One stagnant evening as I was going over my list of contacts in search of some name that it might please me to utter, I took two simultaneous decisions: to take up smoking and to announce to my enemies that I forgave them. Burning cigarettes was an attempt to prove to myself that, although Helena was no longer there, I was still alive. To show to myself that I could survive each and every cigarette. As for my enemies, there was no plan. It was not done out of goodness. I perceived it as something inevitable, preordained. I simply saw the names Melchor, Ariel, Rubén and Nuria in my diary. At first I tried to drop the idea. But, with each match that I lit (I have always preferred the slowness of matches to the immediacy of lighters), I was thinking: Melchor, Ariel, Rubén, Nuria.

Melchor hated me because we were alike. Two people with similar ambitions are each continually reminded of their own pettiness. I'd hated him too from the start. Although I also admired him, a sentiment I doubt he shared. Not because he was worse than me, but because of my own vanity: what I admired in him was everything that, in some way, made me proud of myself. And it disgusted me that Melchor did not recognize those things in me also. Over a period of time I fooled myself into thinking I was more virtuous than he was. With the passage of academic years and at departmental meetings, I ended up understanding that this non-reciprocated admiration was based on a brutal consistency on Melchor's part. For him, if we were enemies, that was how it would be.

What I considered most despicable about him was his pose of disinterest. I couldn't stand the way he had of coveting everything with such a humble air. Such fraudulence – which for me was as obvious as wearing shades in a darkened room – brought him many followers. Melchor had more than half the department on his side, and his acolytes would religiously repeat the refrain that he was an upright man, incorruptible and aloof from the wheeling and dealing to which all the rest of us descended. It was this, rather than his recognition as a scholar, that most exasperated me. Early on – I don't know whether out of weakness or strategy – I had made an attempt at rapprochement. But he showed himself to be unbending, rejecting me without an iota of tact, and made two things clear: that he would never stoop to diplomacy with me and that in his heart of hearts he was as afraid of me as I was of him.

In recent years hardly a word had passed between us, apart from the occasional sardonically courteous greeting at some conference or other. On these occasions, if he noticed I was nearby, Melchor hastened to gather his lackeys around him and made an effort to appear nonchalant. My tactics were different: I hung around, talking with his minions, conversing with them in the most cordial manner, and on taking my leave enjoyed the sensation that I had sowed the seeds of doubt among his little band.

My enmity with Ariel was quite different. Perhaps it was more violent, although for that very reason it turned out to be more inoffensive. Ariel was, let's say, a classically envious person. And, like all classically envious people, his fury clashed with his own interests, robbing him of the little happiness available to him. Since he was able to provoke in me a certain uncharacteristic aggressiveness, many supposed I considered him my worst enemy. Nevertheless, I found something purifying in my unpredictable outbursts of wrath against Ariel, and I sensed, beneath my own hostility, a small, shadowy glimmer of compassion. Tortured beings have that advantage: they extract from us – whether justly or unjustly – a greater benevolence than those others who keep intact their capacity for pleasure. The gratuitous suffering of the first type will never offend us as much as the others' well-earned happiness.

While Ariel was below us on the academic ladder, he made life impossible for me and three or four other colleagues. When he finally received tenure, he seemed to calm down and he forged among us that attitude of false camaraderie that I have learned to carry off so effectively myself. Of course, I never lowered my guard. I continued to monitor his movements and made an effort to keep him at least nominally on side whenever there was a dispute in the department. I am absolutely certain that he did the same. I know that it was he who, years ago, was responsible for bringing to Helena's attention the rumour that I was sleeping with a student. Since I was able to sort it all out with Helena (communication between us was our treasure, our miracle), I never let on to Ariel that I knew about his machinations. I let the matter pass, and spent my time instead contemplating with satisfaction and pity how, forever single, forever failing in love, he carried on being consumed with envy. When he telephoned me to offer his condolences, the last phrase that Ariel uttered stuck in the craw: 'I can't even imagine what it must be like to lose a woman like Helena.' I still don't know whether it was an expression of moving honesty, or the cruellest shot he could have fired at me.

What can I say of my enmity with Rubén? It was without passion, cold, devoid of insults. More than an act of war, loathing each other had almost become habit. There was something inexplicable and fascinating in the way in which, from the start, we recognized each other as adversaries. Helena insisted on introducing us one winter's morning, with that cheerful, irresistible enthusiasm of hers. Rubén and I shook hands, looked each other in the eye and knew that we would never be friends. Rubén played his cards, and I mine. He pulled a face, as was his habit, and I smiled at him with my most exemplary hypocrisy.

Although from that day onward we never left off wishing each other ill, I think it is fair to add that neither one of us lifted a finger against the other. We were like two tightrope walkers advancing along parallel ropes, waiting to see who would be the first to fall. At Helena's invitation we even ate together, quite frequently. It goes without saying that Rubén always wanted to go to bed with Helena, if he didn't in fact succeed in doing so. For that reason, because I knew how much he desired her, I am certain that when he came to my house to offer his condolences, his sadness was genuine.

I couldn't avoid including Nuria on my list of enemies. I believe that, by and large, I have been a man who has got along well with women. That is, I have known how to listen to them, enjoyed their company (and not only in bed) and intuited what kind of things wound their dignity. At least that is what Helena – who always considered me a better man than I in fact was – used to tell me. But with Nuria none of these supposed qualities seemed to do me any good. Having committed the error of sleeping with her for a spell, when we were both students, I was forced to do battle with her intelligent phantom for the rest of my life. Nuria reappeared once or twice a year, apparently discreet and secretly resentful. Taking the role of an accomplice, she would tell me that someone had been speaking ill of me. She would remind me, as if by the way, of the long-distant treachery of an ex-partner. Laughing, she would recite some anecdote in which I had behaved in a reprehensible manner. She used to ask after Helena with an ambiguous expression. She lamented that she had loved me a great deal, whereas I had loved her only a little. And then she would disappear for a while.

I would remain plunged in a state of vague anxiety and, when I had almost succeeded in forgetting her, Nuria would send me a postcard, write me an email informing me of some intimate catastrophe, or phone me in order to tell me about her latest lover. I remember how Helena – who, as a rule, didn't seriously dislike anyone – felt queasy simply having to say hello to her. She said that Nuria would click her tongue or grind her teeth as they brushed cheeks in greeting.

At this stage, I know that a shameful question needs to be asked: Why did I not turn Nuria away? Why, instead of passively keeping up our remote and youthful friendship, did I not dare to expel her from my life? There are several reasons, and none of them exonerates me. On the one hand, guilt worked in me like a sordid halter. I had once hurt her, and that memory weighed on me. Very deep down, I feared damaging my image still further before a potentially vengeful person like her. Helena would reproach me for my compassion towards Nuria. In this she was mistaken. Guilt is incapable of pity, because the one who feels it only seeks relief in dealing with the other person.

On the other hand, there was something defenceless about Nuria, which, in an involuntary and, I suppose, arrogant way, impelled me to offer my help every time she asked for it. I have always tried to avoid patronising behaviour. Helena never tolerated it. But Nuria, I don't know how, managed to awaken it in me. And finally, I acknowledge that, in spite of everything, I continued to desire Nuria, to desire her bitterly. Her behaviour incensed me and her presence excited me. There are people who possess the virtue of making us more luminous, like Helena. And others who have the sinister faculty of reminding us what shady beings we really are.

The day that I took the decision to forgive them, I didn't think twice. And, lighting one match after another, I set about telephoning Melchor, Ariel, Rubén, Nuria.

Nothing appeared to me more logical than their initial incredulity. I would have been even more distrustful of them than they were of me. Perhaps the loss of Helena contributed towards their believing me. Awareness of death makes us touchingly disposed towards a Yes, and melancholically timorous of a No. So my enemies felt sorry for me, however much they hated me. This demonstrated how relative hatred is, and how inevitable is empathy.

As soon as she heard my voice, Nuria asked me if I would continue to live on my own. I closed my eyes, took a deep breath and answered yes, that I only needed to talk. At first she was on the defensive, as if in fear of some crushing reproach. But when we met up in a cafe, it didn't take her more than two hours to confess, tearfully, what she had kept shut away for twenty years. All I had to do was talk openly about some of my mistakes, acknowledging that I had not been honest with her and explaining how much she had made me suffer. That's all it took for Nuria to launch herself into an admirable and at times savage display of self-criticism. I don't know which of us felt more surprised. In the end, rather than put ourselves at risk by prolonging the meeting, we cautiously said our goodbyes just before dinner time.

Of my other enemies, Ariel was the most receptive, perhaps because behind every classically envious person lurks a frustrated admirer. Rubén, at first, didn't show too much understanding, nor was he inclined to confidences. But my arguments were so simple and lacking in subterfuge that he could not avoid betraying some emotion as he left, however much he tried to hide it from me, right up to the sober embrace with which we parted. The conversation with Melchor was more tortuous, until I began to think that, with him, my efforts would fall on deaf ears. If I had to select a few words from among all that I told him during our meeting, perhaps I would choose these: 'I am telling you the truth, precisely because I have hated you more than anyone.' Melchor understood that such a declaration of hostility could only proceed from a sincere intention.

I manoeuvred all four of my enemies into admitting that they considered me a detestable person. That they had wished the worst for me on numerous occasions. That they had rejoiced in each of my misfortunes. But, above all, I made them see that I understood them, because I had felt exactly the same with respect to them. That I had dreamed they might suffer, lose their jobs or meet with some kind of accident. That I had attempted to excuse myself by judging myself morally superior or motivated by causes more decent than their own. And that it would do us no good to deny all those things or to be ashamed of ourselves for them, because at the end of the day all of us, they and I, we and our worst enemies, were human. That unfortunately all we humans would soon die. And that to live in a state of hatred was far worse than to die in a state of love.

At the end of my conversations with Melchor, Ariel, Rubén and Nuria, I didn't feel happy (happy is not the word after Helena) but I felt as though I had come closer to owning my pain. I had wept at some point on all four occasions. And on each one of them my enemies, apart from Melchor, had joined me in tears. On the other hand, Melchor was the first to take the initiative. A week after our meeting, he came to my office to invite me to lunch. From that moment, I believed I had made progress. I had learned something as an individual, even at the cost of great sadness.

What can damage us more? The blunt honesty of hatred, or the thwarted objective of reconciliation? If one is not prepared to love others, does that mutilated love, that failure to put ourselves right, console or torture us? I could not specify how much time passed before I began to feel bad again, and I decided to arrange that party at my apartment.

It was distressing, and at the same time strangely reassuring, to see, for the first time, Melchor, Ariel, Rubén and Nuria – on account of whom I had suffered so much in the past – together in my apartment, smiling. In the same home where I had loved Helena and, in confiding tones, had spoken badly of them to her. To encourage a friendly atmosphere among my four guests, I made sure there was lively music and an abundance of alcohol. Everyone arrived more or less punctually (Nuria was the last) and they were introduced to one another, with the exception, of course, of Melchor and Ariel, who already knew each other from the university. It was, in all probability, the first time these two had socialized together at night.

Having overcome the first signs of awkwardness, I must say that soon the conversation became enjoyable, and occasionally comical. The night wore on, and we even allowed ourselves to joke about our old quarrels. Melchor was unusually witty and loquacious, to the extent that Ariel underwent some strange jealous fit and anxiously sought out my approval. Rubén kept up his restrained front, but without ceasing to be congenial and courteous. Nuria alternated between phases of pensive silence and outbursts of effusive elation. During one of these she made a move to kiss me, but before I pulled away, she checked herself and planted her lips on my cheek.

Around daybreak, after several more drinks, I demanded my four guests' attention. I raised an arm and declared that I was making a toast to all those who knew each other truly, in other words, without innocence. Amid applause, Melchor, Ariel, Rubén and Nuria seconded my toast. We continued uncorking bottle after bottle. Nuria and Rubén began to dance, holding each other close. Ariel sat down by my side and spoke to me in a low voice. Melchor set about browsing through my books and music collection. I smoked until my throat was raw.

A short while later – I don't remember at what time – I announced that I was going down to buy cigarettes. Nuria came over to me, threw an arm around my neck and, putting on one of her customary pained expressions, asked me to bring another pack for her. I smiled, told her I would. I looked at them all: Melchor, Ariel, Rubén, Nuria. Then I left the apartment and locked the door behind me. ∎

Lukas Prize Project Awards 2011
Honoring the best in non-fiction

ॐ

$30,000 for a Work in Progress
$10,000 for the J. Anthony Lukas Non-Fiction Prize
$10,000 for the Mark Lynton History Prize

www.lukasprize.org

in conjunction with

 Nieman Foundation
for Journalism at Harvard

Columbia Journalism School ♛

GRANTA

EVA AND DIEGO

Alberto Olmos

TRANSLATED BY PETER BUSH

ALBERTO OLMOS
SPAIN
1975

Olmos, born in Segovia, made his literary debut in 1998 with
A bordo del naufragio, a finalist for the Herralde Prize. Since then
he has published the novels *Así de loco te puedes volver* (1999), *Trenes
hacia Tokio* (2006), *El talento de los demás* (2007), *Tatami* (2008)
and *El estatus* (2009). He is also responsible for the volume *Algunas
ideas buenísimas que el mundo se va a perder* (2009), compiled with
texts from the Internet. For three years he lived in Japan, in the
Tochigi Prefecture, where he taught Spanish and English.
His blog is www.hkkmr.blogspot.com. He lives in Madrid.
'Eva and Diego' is the first chapter of his new novel.

Boredom leads to evil, but in the meantime there was an August when I still loved my husband. It went like this.

'Nothing that will involve spending.'

The sentence resounded in the nursery. A boy rushes in crying. Diego bends down, picks him up and hoists him on to his shoulders. He is smiling. He's smiling at me while the boy's tears drip over his head. I take a deep breath, look at my watch and try to kiss him. 'Not here, Eva.'

Nothing that will involve spending, I think.

I leave the nursery and get into my car. I drive in the direction of home. En route I listen to music. I drive up and down a number of times before I find a parking space. Then I go up to our place. I look at my face in the lift mirror. I peer closely at my face in the lift mirror. I'm tired.

I've put my bag on the table and opened it. I've just bought an iPod. I take it out of its packaging and fill a couple of hours with everything an iPod has to offer before it even plays the first song. When I've succeeded in putting thirty-four songs on my iPod, I put my headset on and press the bottom part of the wheel. It's the first song.

I move through our apartment to the first song.

I look through the window to the first song.

I've just stretched out on my bed to the first song.

And when the second starts playing, when I'm all relaxed on the counterpane on our double bed, shoes off, eyes shut, I start touching myself over my panties, I start touching myself under my panties, I start masturbating thinking about a man who isn't Diego.

It went like this.

It all started over a shop. The thought, I mean; the ideas. I explained my ideas to Diego at breakfast. I spend my days managing ideas at the newspaper and if I've an excess of anything, it's ideas.

Shitty ideas.

I told Diego that life's capped. That's what I said, it's capped, and

I put my hands over my cup of coffee in the shape of a small roof. It was Sunday, the paper was on the table and we'd both switched our mobiles on. Diego was wearing a T-shirt that said: A Great Day for Dads.

'Tell me all about it, Eva,' Diego said.

In fact, he didn't say that. Not exactly.

'Tell me all about it, Evita.'

That's exactly what he said.

I found the ideas that brought me to this point in our own street. That's what I told Diego. I suddenly got the sense that our street was just one mutation after another. There was an electrical goods shop in front of the entrance to our block, an old-style electrical goods shop. Toasters, microwave ovens, hairdryers; I bought one of everything there. But one day the business shut, and from then on I kept speculating about the kind of shop that would replace it. The temporarily empty, street-level window allowed me to glimpse an almost amniotic interior. Every day I could see a commercial structure gestating: a table, a counter, a few boxes, variously sized, mysteriously shaped packages. People moved around inside with what might be faces belonging to dentists, plumbers, lawyers, estate agents, florists . . .

Finally, a signboard emerged victorious with the words 'Shoe Shop'.

So it was to be shoes. But you had to be quick, because the shoe shop went bankrupt after three months.

The process of total destruction and the next entrepreneurial pregnancy was repeatedly rehearsed by the front of the store. An ice-cream shop. I groaned. They can't set up anything I don't find tempting.

Six months later, a travel agency.

Four months later, a children's clothes shop.

'Don't you think that's a sign?' said Diego.

'No.'

'I reckon so.'

The worrying clothes shop for children from 0 to 12 years old lasted one month and twenty-two days, but to me the message it preached seemed eternal.

I didn't understand what was wrong with that space. Why none of the options worked in those two hundred square metres, as if passers-by and market opportunity couldn't see eye to eye.

I expect the solution would have been to open another electrical goods shop . . .

I lost interest. And that was because an entire building came to dwarf the failure of a few small traders.

It was a building four blocks from our place that I really wished I could remember. But I can't, because one day the building suddenly vanished.

I would walk past it on a Sunday when I went to buy the newspaper. The Sunday I noticed it was missing (how cute to say several tons of real estate went 'missing'), it was raining. I was wearing a coat with a hood and walked the whole way looking down at the ground and dodging puddles. On the way back, however, I looked up, even though it was still raining just as hard. I wasn't worried about sinking my shoes into the puddles as long as I could avoid seeing my face reflected.

I sank my shoes into a huge puddle and kept them there for ten minutes. I was terrified out of my mind standing opposite an empty plot.

A single thought went round my head the whole time I stood there with my high heels in water: what the hell used to be there?

I'd walked down that street at least once a week for the last five years. I'd looked in the shop windows. I'd drunk coffee in several of the bars along the way. I'd made eyes at the gorgeous man who had usually just bought his left-wing paper as I was about to buy my right-wing paper. I knew that a red-headed girl lived in the blue house. I knew that there was a park with swings and two slides. I took care not to stain my skirt when they painted the benches green. I'd noticed several new rubbish bins. I'd noticed that two public telephone boxes had been removed. I'd occasionally got a whiff of a strange burning smell.

But that day, as I gazed into the huge, misshapen void, as ugly as a missing molar, I couldn't remember how many floors the vanished block had had, the colour of its facade, the shops at street level (if there were any), if people looked over the balconies, if they hung clothes out to dry; if Spaniards or South Americans or ghosts without a homeland lived there; if I'd ever leaned against its walls to adjust my high heels; if Diego had ever mentioned that building in a conversation about someone or something; or at the very least if that building got wet, for Christ's sake, when it rained.

I asked him, as soon as I was back. Diego, did you see they've demolished that building? What used to be there? Can you remember? Diego couldn't remember. Why is it you can't? Why is it I can't?

Life's got a cap.

And I thought, will this building, the new one, the one they'll erect far too quickly after the plot's been covered in rubbish and dog turds and drug addicts' syringes and all kinds of shit, will *it* be the one that won't be demolished one day, that will survive, that, in the end, will no longer watch me walk past to buy the newspaper or sit on a green bench that's been repainted nine times? Will *it* be the building that can't even remember that I looked it straight in the eye hundreds of times and was dumped there, dressed anyhow, with or without handbag, but *alive*?

I am such a plot.

I really don't understand *what* you're talking about, love. I'm sorry.'
'I'll try to explain myself.'

'I'm all ears.'

I told Diego about an experiment we'd just reviewed in the newspaper. It involved putting one person in a room by himself. It's comfortable enough but has no facilities or means with which to communicate with the outside world. There is no window that looks out on life. There's no television to bring in some kind of life. There's nothing, apart from time.

The individuals subjected to the experiment hit levels of psychosis that can only be compared to levels inspired by the spectacle of real horror. When asked about the causes of their stress, grief or (in some cases) anxiety attacks, they all drew the same conclusion: nothing had provoked their anxiety attacks, their grief or their stress. Nothing.

Nothingness was how I read it and I told Diego so. Nothingness is real horror.

I did yoga once; I did aerobics. I did German and a course in another language I don't remember now (not just the words in that language but which language it was). I spent whole evenings watching videos on the Net. Whole evenings searching for pornography. Whole evenings with an old friend, talking about things I can't for the life of me recall now. I routinely went to exhibitions, until I got fed up. To the theatre, until I got fed up. To modern dance, until I got fed up. I did cordon bleu by correspondence. I did things; I do things.

'We do things, Diego.'

But when I immerse myself in a new activity there always comes a moment when I wonder: whatever did I do before I started doing this? And I can never remember. And Diego can't either. Yes.

Do we do things?

The building disappeared, and I couldn't remember it. Now there was an empty plot, a plot that, very shortly, would be capped by another building in the same way that my aerobics classes on Saturdays were immediately capped by my German classes; I didn't remember the building in the same way I can't remember all those hours of aerobics, hours of German or hours of ridiculous languages: only a name that describes their absence.

Because an empty plot, sometimes, demands its own space.

You know what I always do in the cinema, Diego?'

'You whisper: this film is revolting. That's what you always do in the cinema, Evita.'

'Yes, but I also do something else, a kind of prayer.'

'You pray the film's going to be a good one?'

'No, I tell the film, "Get me out of here," Diego. I tell *the film* that.'

And if it's a good film, it does get me out of there. Like a good novel, an evening at the theatre or the 8,500 songs I now have on my iPod.

Like a shop.

Particularly a shopping spree.

In fact, is there anything one can do in this world that doesn't involve spending?

And that's what I said to Diego: 'Isn't there anything one can do in this shitty world that doesn't involve spending?'

'Quiet, please. We're talking.'

'God's Gonna Cut You Down' by Johnny Cash was playing. I remember that because an enormous batch of CDs had just arrived in the editorial room; the release of which the record companies were hoping we would publicize. As usual, the editor-in-chief and I took advantage of our position in the pecking order to ransack that ton of free music before anyone else got near it. I just appropriated a couple of CDs (including the Johnny Cash); Rafael Presa took more than fifty CDs home with him.

Both Rafael Presa and I earned more than anyone else in our section. In fact, I earned more than anyone. We didn't need to 'steal' the CDs and books; or the DVDs and concert tickets that arrived in the Culture section every day. But we did.

The fact that I took less advantage than Rafael Presa of my position wasn't because I was more honest or generous than he was (generous in the sense that everything we stole or enjoyed could be enjoyed, if they were so lucky, by people – editors, interns – who really couldn't allow themselves the weekly luxury of buying CDs or going to concerts or plays): it was down to the fact that I like spending money. I like buying things.

Particularly buying expensive things.

Because cheap things like bread, milk, paper and fruit are useful, the pleasure they give comes from the fact that you use them. The best part of bread is in the eating; the best part of a pencil is doodling in the margins of a newspaper. Besides, there is something moving in the constant company these more humble products provide. We could even say our daily bread is very tender, like a husband.

Nonetheless, expensive things are completely useless and never give more pleasure than when you are buying them. They are passions that perish. Like lovers.

'I'm going to buy an iPod.'

'What on earth is *that?*'

An iPod is an MP3 music player created by Apple in 2001 that has revolutionized the way we understand music. I, personally, no longer understand music.

I had a salary that allowed me to buy approximately fifteen iPods a month. My salary was then fifteen iPods a month, fifteen potential iPods a month, fifteen monthly temptations to buy an iPod.

Consequently, I was one of those people who just *had* to buy an iPod. I simply have to buy whatever they've just invented to be bought. I involve spending.

I bought the iPod out of boredom. But out of fear as well. Spending is about the fear of dying. Everything I've ever bought is a bet I place that I'll keep on living. If I were going to commit suicide I wouldn't buy anything; if I'd set the end of my life for 1 August I wouldn't buy an iPod on 31 July. We buy because we want to be here for a lot longer, because what we acquire needs us alive. Things make claims on us. The meaning of life is simply that everything we buy is meaningless if we are dead.

Spending implies a future.

The day I bought my iPod, forty-five people died in a terrorist attack. When an important piece of news breaks, part of my section collaborates with the 'affected' section (National or International Affairs, usually); additionally, the Culture pages are reduced in number and, as the one in charge, I'm left with almost nothing to do. I'm bored and look out of the window.

The bombs exploded at 8.56 a.m. in a Madrid shopping centre. They were hidden in the changing cubicles on the women's clothes floor. Thirty-two victims were women; twelve were children. Only one man died. Several dozen more were injured, in a similar ratio in terms of sex and age to those who had died.

Responsibility for the attack pointed to Arab terrorist groups.

I saw one photo and refused to look at any more. A dummy clad in human flesh. The bomb had completely wrecked one individual's body and her skin, bones and organs had splattered all over the front half of a dummy.

'We're next.'

Journalism is essentially pessimism. I left the office before lunchtime.

To go spending.

I like buying new technology because it takes me quite a long time to realize it is pointless. I read the instructions, hit the keys, connect a cable here and another there, and feel as if I'm confronting a huge mystery I have to solve. And I enjoy it. Then there is no mystery, only a useless gadget I jettison in any old drawer.

I bought my iPod because the sales assistant was very handsome. The shopping centre was strangely devoid of people (or not so strangely: forty-five dead, after all). I'd decided to use the morning to pay Diego a visit, so I opted for the ground floor rather than the sixth. I take less time to buy a microcomputer or PDA than to buy a pair of shoes and the result is the same.

The sales assistant was very handsome.

I spotted him within five minutes. He was reading a magazine on the counter of his Apple stand. I have thousands and thousands of CDs at home and the last thing I'd have thought of would be to purchase a gadget that would force me to get rid of them all.

I assumed his drive to sell had been deactivated by the lack of customers. The least he could do was offer me a fucking iPod.

I walked past the young man again, much more slowly and nearer this time. He ignored me.

I finally went over to him.

'Hello,' I said.

The young man took off his headset (I'd not noticed it) and smiled.

'I'm sorry,' he said.

His mouth was very sweet.

'How can I be of help, madam?'

'I'd like one of those.'

I pointed to the most expensive iPod on display. Indeed, I pointed at the price tag, not at the gadget itself.

The sales assistant headed over to the display cabinet. I gave him a good look up and down while he unlocked one of the glass doors.

He turned round and stared at me.

'What colour would you like, madam?'

'Red.'

The nursery is in the north of the city, not far from the newspaper's head office, but a long way from the shopping centre where I went that day. It took me almost an hour to get to where Diego works.

It was a blue building, with yellow swings in the playground and children in red and pink dungarees. I'd just looked at a photo of human flesh stuck to a dummy.

'Eva, long time no see.'

'Is Diego around?'

'Yes, of course. Come with me.'

She was young and pretty. I watched her bum as I followed her along the corridors. I don't see why she needs to come to work with children in such tight-fitting gear.

Her name was Laura or something similar.

'Diego, your wife's here.'

I don't think we'll do anything these holidays. Anything at all.'
Diego led me into an empty classroom. We sat on two tiny chairs and talked about the terrorist attack, my latest purchase and the holidays. I didn't understand his comments on the last item.

'Won't do anything? What do you mean? Didn't you want to go to . . . ?'

'It all involves spending, Diego.'

I involve spending.

A child entered the classroom. We stood up and, as if driven by an extraordinary thrust of gravity, the boy immediately rushed at Diego. Diego took the boy in his arms and hoisted him on to his shoulders.

'Nothing that will involve spending, Eva. You just see. Trust me.'

I drove home and couldn't stop thinking about the Apple shop assistant the whole time.

I do trust Diego. ■

GRANTA

THE SURVIVOR

Sònia Hernández

TRANSLATED BY SAMANTHA SCHNEE

SÒNIA HERNÁNDEZ
SPAIN
1976

Born in Terrassa, Hernández grew up in a working-class town with an evocative name: Badia. She works as a literary critic for the *Cultura/s* supplement in *La Vanguardia*. She has always felt drawn to the outskirts, not just the urban, though she never found there the sadness of landscape described by Michael Ende – the writer who made her a reader – or the rawness of the streets of Juan Marsé. She is the author of the poetry books *La casa del mar* (2006) and *Los nombres del tiempo* (2010). Hernández is the coordinator of the literary research magazine *Quaderns de Vallençana*, dedicated to the humanist Juan Ramón Masoliver. 'The Survivor' is from her collection of short stories *Los enfermos erróneos* (2008).

I should have died six years ago. On 16 July 1999. That's what Dr Castro said. A medical doctor. Marisa, my wife, was with me and she stared furiously at the doctor, as if the woman said I *had* been dead for six years. Perhaps that's what she actually said, and I misheard her. My mind went blank. There were a few seconds of silence, like those moments of uncertainty when you awaken in someone else's bed. In a way, I was awakening to a life that wasn't mine.

Dr Castro half smiled. She's a rather unfortunate woman, physically: too skinny, a sharp nose, large but glassy eyes. News like that should come from a more attractive woman, or a man, a corpulent, taciturn physician who would leave no room for doubt. 'What I mean is that you're very fortunate,' she added. I'm very lucky, according to my physician.

After a few more instructions about my upcoming endoscopy and prescribed echocardiogram, we left her office. Marisa began to babble nervously, on the brink of a hysterical outburst, the kind she usually has when things don't go as she's planned. For a moment, I felt guilty; this vague, confusing terrain where Dr Castro had dumped me was a great inconvenience to our life together, a life which had cost us so much effort to build. I supposed that for Marisa it must have been a huge problem, not to know whether or not her husband had died, or worse, not to understand why I hadn't died according to plan on 16 July 1999.

Suddenly, I realized that the logorrhoea, the rhetoric, the flattery and the timid reproaches that poured forth from my wife upon exiting the doctor's office were nothing more than words intended to fill my mind – my immediate memory – to prevent me from dwelling on that strange diagnosis which had made me into a rebellious patient. My other memory – the mediate, or deep, or whatever it's called – was different. There the lights were still off, that sense of strangeness of a hotel bed, the descent into an abyss – they weren't melodramatic but made no sense. Marisa was livid about the doctor's lack of tact, and repeated her rather pragmatic question, 'Why on earth would she tell you that now? The accident and the operation belong to a very difficult chapter in our lives, why would she want to torment us with the possibility of what might have happened?' Few people survive an accident like the one I had and, according to Dr Castro, no one survives an operation with complications like that.

Marisa decided that after the visit with the doctor, I wasn't fit to go to the factory, so we went home and let the day run its normal course. I went to Pepe's bar for a while, spoke with the regulars and put a coin or two into the slot machine, nothing special. I thought about telling everyone what the doctor had told me, to see how they'd react, but I stopped myself because it would have legitimized the joke she made at my expense. It was later that night, as we were watching television, that I began to think about the past six years, a gift of sorts from Providence, God, science, chance or my body. I realized that the whole time, I had been living irresponsibly. It's a fact that after the operation Dr Cabrol, the surgeon, had said the situation was touch and go. And the days in the ICU were nothing but a fog, followed by a convalescence in our apartment in Altea before returning to real life in September. I went back to work against doctors' orders because at the time I was indispensable at the factory. After years of toil and misery, we had finally managed to become one of the main sofa manufacturers, and I couldn't leave everything hanging, especially after my brother Ramón had washed his hands of the business, more concerned with discovering Taoism and the truth of Zen. Returning to work was the first of my mistakes. For some strange reason, my body insisted on continuing to function; in other words, I had been given what's called a new lease on life, and I wasted it among feathers, foams and wooden frames.

Perhaps it was time to admit that Marisa was right and to accept that I'm insensitive and incapable of seeing beyond material things. I hadn't adequately appreciated all the important things that had happened since the accident: the children had grown; they had even provided us with a granddaughter; we had made a new circle of friends; and my party had won and lost a few elections. I'd had a gift of nearly 2,200 days at my disposal, and I had wasted them.

The day after visiting Dr Castro I was certain I was dead. The rhythm of things continued without me: I wasn't going to work, at home my absence and my presence were so immaterial as not to be missed by anyone. There was nothing to motivate me to take part in a routine which had been perfected without my participation. No one, not even Marisa, found it strange that I had taken to my bed. Nothing differentiated night and day; in the dark, being and not being are similar sensations. Suddenly, everything that had endowed my existence with meaning seemed a lie, a joke in poor taste that wouldn't even be used in a bad play. During those days, the past and the future ceased to exist. The past was just a jumble of disjointed scenes. In some, Ramón, Josito, Ángel and I were rolling oranges down the hill by the entrance to Los Pizarrales. While we watched to see whose would reach the bottom first, the little kids from town ran down after them, trying to catch one, so we chased after them and if they caught one, we beat them. In other scenes, which also featured oranges, we went to the plazas where Félix and Arturo were playing the trumpet and stood in front of them, eating the oranges slowly to make their mouths water so much they couldn't play their instruments properly. They watched us with fury and when they finished playing they came looking for us to knock our teeth in. It was all so abstract that I couldn't be sure it had really happened. In my personal fog, time didn't exist, neither the present, nor any of the other things that had happened so long ago. Nothing had any meaning. I had not died six years earlier, but I still could at any moment, and that meant I would never do anything ever again, not breathe, not see, not eat, not speak . . . nothing. When I realized this, the panic attacks began, the ones Marisa learned to quell with a couple of pills she always kept on hand and which she was delighted finally to put to use. She's certain that medication is a great remedy for low spirits, and back then I really was a spirit in some strange purgatory where I was paying for, among many other sins, being alive. What is clear is that, thanks to diazepam and Trankimazin, which became my intimates, or perhaps due only to weariness, I came out of that dark tailspin.

I experienced a kind of resurrection, which is not to say that I stopped being dead. I went back to work, dined with my family on Sundays, saw friends during the week and I even played golf. I was calm and able to control my outbreaks of anxiety, which felt like a huge triumph, but I was waiting, expecting the sign that would announce that the play had ended, once and for all, that someone had discovered that I had cheated destiny on 16 July 1999 and it was finally time for me to return to the fold. This constant expectation made me a more interesting man, I won't deny it. I discovered that the pensive and absent air of those of us who don't hold forth in conversation makes us more attractive, sort of like tortured poets. Some kind of sparkle settled in my eyes and shadowy curtains were drawn there, too, which turned me into one of the most admired and desired members of our circle. I learned to use my sadness to my advantage and, despite the results, I felt no better, because after flirting, I would fall into a profound apathy which prevented me from fanning the fires which I, myself, had kindled.

In my reflective phase, I undertook to review all the events that had taken place over the last six tacked-on years; no matter how insignificant, I examined each in an attempt to reinterpret them. I also wanted to speak to Marisa and my children, to discuss what the fact that I had not died that July meant for them. It wasn't especially fruitful, to be honest. Marisa's eyes filled with tears as soon as she realized I was broaching the topic, and she reproached me for my cruelty, for wanting to return to that painful *thing*. I couldn't figure out exactly what had been so traumatic for her. I didn't fare much better with my children, but I think it was largely my fault because, when I brought it up with Manolo, I made a mess of it; I didn't know how to begin, I stumbled over my words and I felt more ridiculous by the second. 'If I had died in the accident, what would have happened for you?' The boy opened his eyes and couldn't help smiling, but when he saw my face, his fell. 'What are you talking about? That's a pretty idiotic question, Dad. It seems obvious, what would have happened. But what's the point of all these questions?' 'I mean, in the six years since the operation and everything else, have you had any good times with me?' 'What questions! We've had good times, yeah? We've been to football games, Sara's birth, Christmas with the family, the business has grown . . . What do you think? Mum says you're depressed and I think you're being unreasonable, there's no reason for you to act like this. What exactly do you want?' My son was right. With the girl, Soledad, I didn't even try. At the time, she had just landed a couple of shows in some Barcelona galleries, after I had convinced the owners of a few furniture stores to put some of her pictures up. She'll be a great artist one day, no doubt.

It took a long time to make up my mind, but I finally decided to call Isabel to ask her the same question. Our thing had sort of petered out, crushed under its own weight, much as the dying die, little by little, following the path of a tired body, heading slowly towards eternal rest. If there was anything in our past, it was tired bodies, of that you can be sure. We had continued to bump into each other at parties, pleasant encounters, and there was no reason why I should not call her. I found her mobile number in Marisa's phone book and we agreed to meet at a cafe in town; I didn't suggest the back table at Doria, though, she would have misinterpreted that. It was a strange afternoon. I felt a little of the old excitement upon seeing her in this way. She had made herself up exactly as she always did and she was even wearing the same perfume. Perhaps she'd never stopped wearing it. Her make-up was impeccable, as always, although I deduced that she'd had something done to her lips, maybe that's why her smile was different.

It was just as awkward with her as it had been with my son. It took me a while to ask the question, but she handled it gracefully, without even blushing, with the resolve she's always had, which both fascinates and frightens me. 'Look, Mateo, it was a beautiful experience. Very much so. It happened because it happened, and gave us some precious memories. I once said, and I don't mind repeating it, you're the one who's known my body best and the only one who has known to give it what it asked for. That's a lot, it's more than a lot, and that's what I've got to keep. Now, if you ask me whether or not that was love, I don't know. I've discussed it with my analyst ad nauseam and I believe I've found a somewhat logical explanation, but I came to that conclusion alone, after a lot of work and introspection. On the other hand, I don't believe that's what you're looking for an explanation of at this stage. Things are going well with Marisa, no? You achieved what you always wanted: your sofas are in the living rooms of half of Spain. What's the point of this regression to adolescence to analyse what the hell our past means. I got over it, and supposedly I'm the victim; is it that you're feeling guilty? If you want, I can give you the number of a great analyst.' 'And the accident?' 'Of course it could have ended on the operating table, but you made a miraculous recovery. Do you want that number or not?' Her certainty began to overwhelm me; I took down the number of the analyst thinking that perhaps he was her new lover. Judging by the confidence with which she spoke, she certainly had got over me and she'd given me a real lesson in survival too, to me, the fortunate survivor. Nonetheless, after that meeting I felt a strange sense of loss, of defeat and of nostalgia, so I headed to the back table at Doria, by myself.

I was thinking that Isabel had given me a gift that afternoon. She said that no one had known or satisfied her body as well as I had. No one had ever spoken to me about my lovemaking abilities that way. Of course, it's not a question you ask just any old person. Nevertheless, this comment by my old lover raised a question which led me to yet another painful conclusion. In my amorous or sexual relations I had never stopped to think of the other person. I thought you could measure someone else's satisfaction by their caresses, moans, or whispered words; but I realized that the pursuit of my own ecstasy always took precedence in my union with another body.

That was all those extra six years had meant? I forgot about the piece of paper with Isabel's analyst/lover's number on it until it disappeared from my wallet without me ever missing it. My son was more or less content with me, my daughter favoured me with affection from time to time, depending on our conflicts but affection nonetheless, my wife burst into tears when the possibility of my death was mentioned, and my former lover said no one had ever satisfied her as much as I had. In sum, I could consider myself fortunate, as Dr Castro had already said. I maintained a precarious equilibrium – like a trapeze artist with bipolar disorder – and I could consider myself something of a hero, because I was a survivor, no matter how dead I felt.

I founded a new family tradition. We would celebrate 16 July as my second birthday, a far more important date than the dull, worn-out 26 October. My family and some of my friends found the idea a little morbid and chalked it up to my new persona, tortured and tormented for vague reasons that no one understood. The party was a complete disaster. It was right before the holidays and many people had already left Barcelona. Even Marisa would have preferred to be in Altea. So it wasn't a huge party, not even a modest one. Isabel didn't even come. My wife was irritable and annoying all night long and the conversation of my select group of friends bored me no end. My kids didn't show up either. In summary, a spectacular failure, which brought me to the brink of the same dark abyss from which it had been so difficult to extricate myself. Sometime during the night, I don't know why, I started to think about suicide, but in a calm way, without any drama. It couldn't be all that difficult and there was no denying it provided eternal rest. Moreover, it seemed the best way to confront the awful fear of death which I had developed since my last visit to Dr Castro. The idea of no longer existing was tempting. I had lived an extra seven years and I didn't understand the meaning of either the extra time or the fifty-two years prior to the accident.

The following day I called Dr Castro to tell her that I couldn't bear being so fortunate. Now I'm the only man in the whole world who's had three chances, which, no matter how I look at it, seems to me an excessive and unnecessary waste. ■

SCENES FROM A COMFORTABLE LIFE

Andrés Ressia Colino

TRANSLATED BY KATHERINE SILVER

ANDRÉS RESSIA COLINO
URUGUAY
1977

Ressia Colino was born in Montevideo in the middle
of a military dictatorship that would continue until 1985.
With a degree in Biological Science, he currently works at a
pharmaceutical laboratory in Uruguay. He made his literary
debut in 2005 with a short story in *Pimba!* magazine and in 2007
he published his first novel, *Palcante*. In 2008, he received the
Municipal Prize for Fiction for the novel *Parir*.
'Scenes from a Comfortable Life' is a part of a work in progress.

Family Matters

It was on a Sunday afternoon in spring, a family lunch at the house in Carrasco. The servant is clearing up the coffee cups under the watchful gaze of Isabela, Virna's svelte mother. Bruno, her hefty Teutonic father, interrupts the conversation and turns to me: How would you like to drive the Peugeot? It's a little old but . . . I hesitate, am astonished, like a child who's just watched a magic trick he doesn't understand, as Virna smiles at me, made happy, or rather intrigued, by her father's noble gesture, and she tries to encourage me to say yes. Moments later we are in the garden watching as the garage door rises and rolls up slowly. We wait a few seconds until Bruno drives out in a white Land Rover Discovery, parks on the side of the driveway, gets out, smiles at us and returns to the garage. Then he brings out an aqua-blue Mercedes-Benz C250. He parks it next to the Discovery and on his way back to the garage motions enthusiastically for me to come join him. Between the two of us, we bring out a blue Yamaha 1800 jet ski on its own trailer, a Zodiac-style inflatable boat and a heavy old Zündapp scooter. Then we move several bicycles, a lawnmower, a ping-pong table and, finally, There it is, Bruno says. The first car I bought when I came to Uruguay. Now let's see if we can get it started, he adds. It hasn't been moved for about two years.

We push it outside. Don't worry, Bruno says, the battery is dead but we can charge it with the Discovery. It then occurs to Isabela that this is a good opportunity to clean the garage floor, and she calls the servant to do it. In the meantime, Virna is looking through some of the cabinets. She finds hockey sticks, rackets, balls and dozens of objects that remind her of how active and competitive she was when she was a teenager. Let's play tennis one of these days, darling, she shouts to me from the garage. I'm standing next to the Peugeot, trying to be useful in some way while Bruno gets to work on the engine. I look at her and make a gesture that means something like, what a good idea! but she has her back to me, caught up in what she's doing, so for a second I check out her body, I look at her ass, then quickly turn my attention back to Bruno. Just at that point he looks up, intercepting my gaze and producing an awkward moment in which suddenly the idea 'sex with Virna' flashes through my mind, and at the same instant it seems as though Bruno, who is staring at me, can also see that idea. Suddenly, it is as if Virna's voice saying play tennis reverberates between the two of us but as if she had said have sex, and he is the father and it's obvious that we do it, and that's why I am there and why he wants to let me use his car, because I am his daughter's boyfriend, for only three months so far, but for some reason he's taken a liking to me and perhaps that is reason enough. After all, it's so obvious, their lives are not going to change in any substantial way because he lets me use his Peugeot; but making sex so explicit, even though nobody has, in fact, explicitly said anything, is surely uncomfortable, and I feel as though I won't be able to breathe normally until, mercifully, this strange exchange of looks ends. It lasted only a second. I breathe. Bruno turns back to his task, looks at the oil stick and says, in a low voice, How about you open the cap? I'm going to get . . . He points, then returns to the garage, wiping his fingers on a rag. Virna comes running up to me while I struggle to open the cap that isn't budging. Look, she says. She's holding a professional tennis racket and an old ball she bounces next to the car. Let's play later? She prances a few metres over to a green wall that stretches away from the garage, and uses it as a backboard, contributing a rhythmic tapping to the afternoon. Finally I open the cap so we can fill up the oil. Bruno still hasn't returned. When he appears, I am watching Virna run back and forth after the ball. He looks at me, but there are no more strange exchanges. Blank mind. OK, let's fill it, and then we'll hook it up to the Discovery and see if it'll start. Pock, plock; plock, ponk, the sound of the ball Virna's hitting accompanies the stream of oil Bruno is pouring into the dirty, greasy engine. Pock, plock. Bruno! Isabela shouts out from somewhere. He keeps the oil flowing with a steady hand. The ball hits the wall again, I hear the scrape of Virna's shoes on the ground, I picture her sprinting to hit the ball, I imagine her in a short white tennis skirt. I resist. I watch the oil flowing. Bruno, darling! The clacking of Isabela's heels announces her arrival from the house. I look up. She comes up behind Bruno with her lovely breasts and semi-transparent silk dress. I think about Virna's breasts. Darling, I'm going to take the SUV to María Laura's, Isabela says. I expect this to create a conflict, because Bruno needs the Discovery to charge the battery, but I soon realize that Virna's mother is talking about another SUV, the bigger, darker one that is parked on the pavement. Bruno finishes filling up the oil and stands up straight. Kiss, Isabela says, and they kiss each other in front of me, briefly but not without passion. She walks away, clacking her heels and brushing down her dress. Bruno intercepts my gaze . . . He must be thinking about sex now.

The sun is setting by the time we manage to start up the Peugeot and take it out on to the street. Then we put everything back in the garage. Virna went into the house earlier, so we tell her the good news when we come in; by now we're a bit tired. After carefully washing our hands – each in a different bathroom – Bruno offers me whiskey to celebrate, and he stretches out on the sofa to watch the Bundesliga's most important plays of the day on the gigantic screen. Not sure to what extent I should continue to thank Bruno humbly or start to behave like the already consecrated son-in-law, I decide to sit quietly and watch television while Virna holds a long conversation on the telephone at the far end of the room.

Outdoors

The Peugeot was a white 205 Cabriolet from the late eighties, the perfect car to drive around Punta del Este, where what's old becomes vintage and the well-heeled delight in admiring the beauty of simple things from their enormous brand-new cars and expensive collectable models. Their comments amused me, and I made an effort to strike up casual conversations whenever I noticed someone eyeing the car.

One morning, while we were driving to the port along the esplanade, I noticed on my right a man about forty years old in a

BMW M3 sports compact looking at the car. I surreptitiously reduced my speed so we would both stop at the lights. The trick worked and, once alongside him, I glanced over in his direction for a split second, then feigned indifference, like a teenager on the make.

'Yours?' the man asked in a loud voice to get my attention.

'What?' I answered.

'. . . if that's your . . .'

'Oh, yes, yes . . .'

'Awesome, man. Perfect design.'

'It really is; and these engines are cool, *boludo* . . .' I knew there were few things more amusing than hearing a Japanese person say *boludo* in a perfect *porteño* accent.

'How about twenty?'

'Twenty what?'

'Twenty thousand.'

'Oh . . . no, no,' I answered after a short silence, and looked away, a blatant bargaining ploy.

'Twenty-five?'

I turned back, ready with a response, then I suddenly realized that behind those dark glasses the man wasn't, in fact, looking at the car but rather at Virna, who was sitting between the two of us, already a bit tense and staring straight ahead of her, and that his ploy had been the better one, and was for something much more valuable than what we'd been discussing. I looked at Virna, and discovered, as if I'd never seen it before, that her firm, dark nipples were visible through her thin blouse. This time I was the fool. Fortunately the lights turned green and, without another word or gesture, the man stepped on the gas and the BMW pulled several metres in front of me.

'You're a fool,' Virna declared later.

Facing Facts

After he hung up, Jimmy realized that he'd spent the whole day waiting for a phone call, from Virna or anybody else, though it had not occurred to him that if there was one person who would likely be interested in speaking to him right about then, it would be Bruno. Perhaps he was more disorientated than he had thought. He looked around. The cars' headlights drew bright dotted lines along the streets of the narrow peninsula; it looked like a mechanized beehive, a swarm of tourists, excited for some reason that nobody could put a finger on.

He said he'd walk there, and he had no intention of changing his mind. He arrived at the house more than an hour later, somewhat thirsty, definitely tired but indignant about the long stretch where he'd had to walk on the road because in that neighbourhood the ostentatious homes extended their gardens right up to the street. At the entryway he looked towards the pool. He couldn't tell if they'd already done some repairs, or if the darkness was mercifully hiding the evidence of the incident.

'Come in,' Bruno said after opening the door.

Upon seeing him, Jimmy mistook his reserve for composure, and his delight at this first impression made him fail to notice that Bruno had turned his back on him and started walking towards the living room without offering him his hand or committing to any particular form of greeting.

'What will you have?' Bruno asked in a cool voice, without turning around.

'I don't know . . .'

'Vodka?'

'That's fine.'

'Come on. Don't act like . . . ' Bruno seemed to draw a blank. 'Like that,' he specified, almost by way of an apology, looking Jimmy in the eye for the first time.

Jimmy now doubted his first impression of Bruno's mood. He walked over to one of the large sofas and stood there waiting, watching Bruno near the liquor cabinet.

'Have a seat,' Bruno said brusquely, while motioning with the hand that held the bottle.

A few minutes later he came over with two medium-sized glasses in his left hand and an open bottle of vodka in his right. Still standing, he poured a large measure into each glass. Jimmy watched him. He was a burly man, a Germanic type with straight features and watery eyes, who for some reason was capable of pouring vodka in exactly the same way even after consuming an entire bottle and then some. In fact, no matter how hard Jimmy attempted to formulate some idea of Bruno's state of mind by scrutinizing the accuracy of his movements as he poured the liquor, he couldn't tell if he was completely sober or totally drunk.

Jimmy took the glass Bruno held out to him and waited for Bruno to offer a toast. His host, however, put the bottle down on the coffee table, took a long draught from his own glass and fell into a comfortable leather armchair, sighing loudly.

'Why don't you tell me what happened yesterday?' Bruno suggested without beating around the bush.

Jimmy reflected for a second, took a sip of vodka, glanced around the room, hesitated and finally began.

'The truth is we came here –'

'How much had you had?' Bruno interrupted him.

'A lot,' Jimmy hesitated. 'When we go out, we drink, Bruno. To tell you anything else would be –'

'What?' Bruno insisted, interrupting again.

'What do you mean what? Whiskey, beer, champagne, speed –'

'What? Which?' Bruno insisted.

'Which?' Jimmy asked, surprised.

'Yes. Which? Tell me.'

Confused, Jimmy gave up. He clearly understood that all those whichs and whats were not alluding to alcoholic beverages or any combination thereof, but beyond this obvious point he found nothing that helped him discern what drugs Bruno might be referring to:

cocaine, acid, ketamine, ecstasy, or any of the other pills that had passed through his and his friends' hands those last few days. What, exactly, did Bruno know? he wondered.

'Forgive me,' Jimmy said, trying to be honest, 'but I don't understand what you're getting at.'

'Cut the crap,' Bruno replied, irritated, and gulped down the rest of his drink.

'No, no, no, no,' Jimmy said, trying to find his footing. 'I get that you aren't talking about alcohol, but –'

'Blow, snort, coke. Now do you understand?'

Jimmy was taken aback. He definitely didn't expect anything so direct. He looked at his glass. It was empty. Then he remembered, he could almost feel the tiny white envelope stuffed into his trouser pocket. For a split second he wondered if it would be a good idea to go to the bathroom and get rid of it (probably snort it); if there was any chance he'd be searched, things would really get complicated. But going to the bathroom at that moment, so soon after arriving, would be too obvious.

'But . . .' Jimmy stammered.

'Want a little more?' Bruno offered, noticing that Jimmy had looked at his empty glass as a possible and brief refuge. Without waiting for an answer, he picked up the bottle and began to pour the vodka out slowly. 'Or do you want something else?'

The look in Bruno's eyes when he met Jimmy's was measured and deliberately ambiguous, somewhat mocking and challenging, complicit and at the same time intimidating, to which he added the dramatic and sudden suspension of movement: the vodka stopped flowing with the bottle still leaning, suspended, over the glass.

Stay cool, he's testing you, Jimmy thought.

'I don't use.'

Bruno burst out laughing. He placed the bottle on the table and threw his head back, making his laughter sound even more strident.

'That's not necessary,' Bruno said with a certain haughtiness, now reining himself in. 'Look, Jimmy,' he began to explain, calmer now and with an air of sincerity, 'I know Tanaka is your surname, I know you come from a working-class family, people who went through hard times, and you probably think that if you come and tell me that you do drugs once in a while when you're with my daughter, after the way we've welcomed you here, I'm going to want to kill you. But you're wrong. I'm being completely honest with you. I would worry if you didn't do drugs with Virna; because if she doesn't do them with you, she's going to do them with someone else, you know what I mean? And, look, she's already had several boyfriends with sinus problems. The question here is what you are taking, what the hell you were taking that made Virna do what she did.'

'I don't know, Bruno,' Jimmy insisted, not fully convinced by Bruno's speech.

Bruno scrutinized him silently for a few more seconds. Then he poured a little more vodka into each glass, picked his up and, with his eyes glued on Jimmy's, lifted his glass to offer a toast, then drank his down in one gulp.

'Look,' he continued in a deliberate voice, 'I know Virna and her friends, and even most of the families of her friends, their brothers, sisters, cousins; and as you can imagine, there are more than a few stories to tell in a social circle that is so tight and where there are so many opportunities to, well, do things. It's only natural. Now, if you tell me one more time that you don't do anything other than alcohol, and that in addition you have no idea what my daughter is in to, I'm going to throw you out of here on your ass; because I don't know if you're an imbecile or a motherfucking son of a bitch who can lie to my face with that shit-faced grin of yours. OK with you?'

'OK,' Jimmy said, giving up. 'Sometimes we do drugs.'

'Very good. Now we're getting somewhere. And yesterday, what did Virna do? Coke, nothing else?'

'Nothing. Though maybe, in the bathroom, she . . . '

'OK, but generally, what do you do?'

Jimmy hesitated.

'Let's see, cocaine?' Bruno suggested with ironic friendliness.

'Yes.'

'Good stuff?'

'I don't know. For me it is,' he added nervously, looking at the floor.

Bruno stood up, went over to the liquor cabinet, took out a small metal box, came back, placed it on the table, sat down and, after opening it with some effort, took out a small oval mirror, a short, shiny thin metal straw and a small grey cylindrical container he opened carefully.

'Like this?' he asked Jimmy, holding it out. 'Take it,' he insisted when Jimmy didn't move.

The box was made of a heavy metal. Jimmy held it carefully and looked in the narrow opening. Instead of white powder he saw a generous amount of tiny white flecks, which reflected a certain crystalline light as he shifted his angle of observation.

'No,' Jimmy asserted with confidence, and he handed him back the container.

'OK, now we're going to snort a little and you'll see the difference,' Bruno said calmly.

He formed lines of crystals on the mirror with the help of a tiny silver spoon and continued his monologue.

'Do you realize what the problem is? It's the quality of the things you kids consume. It doesn't bother me that Virna uses, what worries me is what she uses. And, look, I'm not talking only about this,' he said, lifting the container he'd shown Jimmy. 'Because this is a luxury, that's true, it's cocaine, and you can want to do it or not. But if you're going to, you've got to do something like this, something good, medicinal; the cocaine they sold in pharmacies in Paris a hundred years ago. If you don't, you're done for. And, look, I don't have any problem getting you this stuff so you'll stop using whatever you're using that made Virna react the way she did yesterday. Do you understand what I'm telling you? I don't know what's with you kids. You grab the first thing that comes your way. The stuff they sell out there is poison, chemicals that crack your head open and fry your neurons. And it's not only a poison, it's also an obsession. You want more and more and more. And you pay more and you obsess more, and each time you go further, you think less and less, and then you don't think at all.'

He paused. He arranged the final flecks at the end of the line and continued his speech as he held the mirror horizontally in the air halfway between them.

'This goes for everything, you know. This system is a fucking circle of doom. Produce more and more cheaply, and make the consumer swallow faster and faster. And the key to keeping the goddamn assembly line moving, you know what it is? That nothing that's consumed is real; what's real is expensive, and gets consumed slowly. That's why the ultimate solution is: nothing can be real. None of the food or the clothes or the music or the books or the drugs that you kids consume are real. It seems like food, like clothes, like music, but it's all just something like those things, made to be devoured immediately. It's a perfect system. A magnificent, gigantic, super-efficient piece of machinery that produces nothing, totally and absolutely nothing.'

Somewhat overwhelmed, he again interrupted himself and, after getting lost in his thoughts briefly, he offered Jimmy what he had been holding in front of him the whole time.

'Here, try this and you'll see. These things are getting lost, and when they finally disappear, that will be it. Then there'll be nothing but dregs, and human beings will kill each other for the carrion.' ∎

SELTZ

Carlos Yushimito

TRANSLATED BY ALFRED MAC ADAM

CARLOS YUSHIMITO
PERU
1977

Yushimito's short stories were first published in a limited edition titled *El mago* (2004). His second collection of short stories, *Las islas* (2006), was warmly received by the critics. His stories, set in *favelas* and *sertões*, are inspired by Brazil, though he has never been there. Fleeing from his native country like his paternal grandfather before him, he moved to the United States in 2008 to study at Villanova University in Pennsylvania. Currently, he lives in Providence, Rhode Island, where he is working on a doctorate at Brown University. There, in libraries and between seminars, he is finishing his first novel. His other books, *Madureira sabe* (2007) and *Equis* (2009), have brought together more stories, some of which have been translated into French and Portuguese. 'Seltz' is a new story.

I was in the back room taking off the costume when I felt his hard cachaca breath next to my ear. It was Bautista, the manager. His face was sweaty. I assumed that, as usual, he must have been partying hard already by the way he twisted his mouth and how his disconnected words rushed towards me. So it wasn't at all odd that I was overcome by a strange feeling of shame. A furtive sense of guilt. For a few seconds I felt as if someone were watching a pair of lobsters copulate in slow motion and that I was standing next to that person in front of twenty television sets all showing the same picture. In slow motion, extremely slow motion.

Zé Antunes says the best advertising strategy for an electronics shop like ours is to keep every television set in the place tuned into the Discovery Channel. 'For example,' he would say, 'let's imagine they're showing a rock concert or a football match: parents associate television with drugs or squandered leisure time. Whenever they show a movie, women in their forties, married and with kids in college, usually remember with nostalgia and subconscious anger that their husbands almost never take them to the movies.' Zé Antunes says the educational channels increase the probability of making sales, and it must be true because to parents education will always seem a good investment and they'll never stint when it comes to that. 'That's the area we should be attacking: the jugular vein of sales,' he declares.

Zé Antunes knows a lot about the animal world, but not as much as he knows about sales and marketing. Which is why I try to listen to him often, so I can pick up all that knowledge of his. But it's different with Bautista. While I stared at his exaggerated gestures, almost certain that his well-pruned nose had poked into a good party that afternoon, I thought about his idea of happiness and about the good deal he'd most certainly have made with the Draco distributor. One thing leads to another; anyone knows that. And Bautista knows the business well because he's the owner's son, and the owner is one of the most important and richest men in Rio de Janeiro.

'Tonight I've got a new disguise for you, Toninho.'

Patting me on the back complicitously, Bautista was still on the alert, not realizing that I had no desire to spend another bad night at his side. That's why, even though he insisted, I didn't raise my head to affirm or deny anything. I went on with my capricious striptease until I recovered my human shape.

He finally gave up, perhaps stymied by my extreme confidence. He made a pistol with his hand, and a trigger squeezed in his eyes fired.

'I'll wait for you in the car.'

He was waiting for me in the hall, not the car.

'Did you make sure to turn the water off all the way?' Zé asked.

I told him I did but the suspicious prick made sure to check for himself. He came back a minute later drying his hands.

'Forewarned is forearmed.'

By then the sliding metal gate had sealed the main entrance. Only the three of us were left inside, bottled up among white tiles and television screens all showing the same screen. A red-maned lion lumbering away with the last piece of a crotch in his mouth, wagging his backside while some hyenas fought over the remains of what had been a zebra. They ate with ardour, with an African appetite. Bautista and Zé Antunes, paying no attention to me, went on chatting animatedly next to the register.

'In the trunk you'll find a jacket and some good hair cream,' said Bautista, interrupting their talk for an instant. He moved his hands, as if his head were a fortune-teller's crystal ball. 'Put on the jacket and get in the car.'

He tossed me the key.

Before we left, Zé handed him a small yellow envelope.

It was the kind used by the accounting department at the end of the month. Zé Antunes has been working in the shop longer than anyone else. It's he who has the job of putting the padlock on the gate, of turning everything off and disconnecting the electricity. He's the last to leave and the first to arrive, except on Tuesdays, when he has the morning off. During the four years I've been working here, I've never seen him miss a day or take a vacation. And I've never heard him complain, curse out or pester anyone who didn't deserve it.

He's a man everyone should imitate.

When I shut the trunk, I felt livelier and more alert than before. I put on the freshly dry-cleaned jacket, finished rubbing the cream into my hair and leapt into the passenger seat. I looked myself over in the rear-view mirror and wasn't terribly disgusted. I turned on the radio. The voice of Daniela Mercury growled from the speakers with the same sensuality as her body: *Vem aí um baile movido a novas fontes de energia. Chacina, política e mídia. Bem perto da casa que eu vivia . . . eletrodoméstico . . . eletro-brasil . . .*

O pen shirt, brown tweed jacket, slick hair. After a few minutes I'd become another Bautista, hardly different from the original, though smaller and less elegant. My chest, a bit exposed, enjoyed the air that kicked its way in, broken into gusts through the window of his Audi. I really liked the role of the carefree man who goes out on a Friday night to get rid of the stress that comes from unpredictable business deals. I had that tense look – as if I were about to explode – that so attracts women. I looked myself over in the side mirror. I looked again and again. Yes, I really did feel elegant, sophisticated. Freed from my usual worn-out, cheap clothes, I was a born seducer: the seducer's instinct was boiling up silently, fighting to burst out of me.

Even so, my new self-image only lasted as long as a flash of light. Bautista is a rich kid who competes in sports, rarely for fun, and wears pricey threads I could never buy, not even with five months' salary. He knows how to handle himself in society and doesn't have to work for things to fit properly in either his body or his life. He's got green eyes like two fireflies in the night and a good bone structure that simply reeks of testosterone accompanied by the smooth aroma of Gucci. I only wish I had his ability to seduce with words, that conductive determination (as Zé would put it), when he wants to get a pretty girl into bed with him.

T ickets?' says one of the two huge bouncers covering the door. He looks me up and down impudently.

'It's OK, Ciro. He's with me.'

Bautista knows how to get around authority by merely using the power of his emphatic smile. After that, they open every door for us. Noting the sweetened faces of the two gorillas, I stand tall in the tweed and walk forward fearlessly. I pass through them. Impatiently, I feel the pulsating energy that pleasure and rank generate. Inside there is a corridor with chrome walls; there you intuit an explosion that finally comes with a surprise that swallows us into that enormous fable with thousands of lives in motion. Instantly, the lights attract us, as if we were two astronauts lost in space.

'The guys at the door are like drug-sniffing dogs,' Bautista says almost shouting as he walks along next to me. 'They can smell poverty from two hundred metres away.'

'They must get lots of practice,' I answer, still holding in my rage. 'I see that black guy who stopped us at the door every day, going up to sell drugs in São Clemente.'

We've barely made our way in when someone swings out to meet us.

'Bautista,' a man says.

I see them hug, kiss each other on the cheek. A thin guy wearing glasses.

'You're not going to tell me we're going to keep on doing business here?'

'As long as the chemistry is right,' he laughs, clutching at his beak.

The man is the Draco distributor.

'Evaristo Rangel.' He holds out a hand.

'Toninho,' I reply.

'My cousin Toni,' Bautista corrects me, secretly shooting me a glance full of hate.

'Aha . . . so you're the famous Toni,' says Rangel.

Curious, he looks me over.

'The famous Toni,' he repeats, turning to look at Bautista.
I feel a bit idiotic, laughing without understanding them.

W e'll spend a good part of the night exchanging empty, pointless anecdotes, tales no one will pay any attention to or remember after. From time to time, they'll make three lines of coke, and I'll snort one so as not to waste the outfit Bautista chose for me. OK, I'll snort more than one. At this rate, it won't be hard to lie. A moment will come when nothing will be true, and they won't notice. Then I'll be the most amusing guy on the face of the earth simply because they've decided I am. I'll say that snake sex is slow, almost like their digestion, and that pigeons screw in a horrible way, almost plucking each other clean, literally that they're the most sadistic and refined of all animals when it comes to pain, especially among themselves. I'll talk to them about things that involve little by way of revelation. I'll laugh at myself, pretending it's someone else who's the idiot who dances for children dressed as a crocodile.

They'll laugh. We'll all laugh. I could tell them, without a trace of sarcasm, that they're a fine pair of idiots and they'll still laugh, wholeheartedly. In the chaos, the moment for changing games will come without a word being spoken. Two black women of a kind I've never seen before will join the party, dresses cut low, calves, thighs, their whole being reeking of sex. When they say hello, the smooth texture of their stockings licks my leg, and I feel I could use another line, but there are no more lines for Toninho. Maybe for Toni there's one more, I say to Bautista. And he laughs. And I dig in. The Draco distributor keeps us supplied with caipirinhas and beer. And the black guy from the door, to prove my point, is the one who will bring us coke.

The women study me with lust. Unleashed, I can almost imagine an orgy right on the table, and when I'm about to touch the thigh of one of them, Bautista takes me to one side and says he's got to take Evaristo Rangel somewhere. 'You're sensational, Toninho. Remind me next month you deserve a raise.' Next month will never come. But at that moment, I give him a hug. And he softly pushes me away because one of the women grabs him from behind, as if he were a teddy bear. She's got a pair of eyes that turn everything to stone. My dick, for starters. My mouth. My self-esteem. I go back to the table alone. Evaristo hugs me and kisses my cheek. 'The famous Toni,' he laughs. And I laugh too, I laugh watching how Bautista and Rangel walk off arm in arm with two colossal beauty queens. A waiter touches my shoulder, sir, he hands me the yellow envelope Bautista left before taking off. I put it in my pocket after taking a cautious look inside. If I were a judicious man, being, as I am, a poor man, I would wait a minute, drink a last beer and go home with extra money in my pocket. If I were wise, I'd drain my glass without looking around. But the first beer multiplies miraculously in my hands, and still sitting at the same table, my glass filled with a renewed and luminous magic, I recognize Julia, ah, the beautiful Julia Oliveira.

S een Bautista?' she asks.
    I shrug.
    'He took off.'
    I see her wounded-cat pupils dilate in the darkness. I sense that her pushed-back hair is an attempted gesture of dignity in the face of abandonment.
    'Son of a bitch,' she whispers, thinking about Bautista.
    Then, with no explanation, she turns her back on me and walks off.
    The second time, I see her aimlessly prowling around the table.
    I'm sorry for her. I stare at her breasts.
    'And who might you be?' she asks, attracted by my curiosity.
    'Toni,' I lie. 'The son of a bitch's cousin.'
    Now she laughs coquettishly.
    'I imagine you've got no idea where he went, right?'
    I won't betray a friend.
    I tell her I have no idea.

'Of course not,' she goes on, as she sits. 'You men always cover each other's ass when you get into trouble. Something about your sex, I guess. An animal instinct, simple self-preservation. We women, on the other hand, take advantage of the first mistake to destroy one another. Why should this be? It must be that we evolved more quickly than you.' Her voice softens, I think she's going to start crying. 'It doesn't matter that he leaves with another woman, as long as he tells me. Understand?'

I don't believe her. It's a trick to get me to talk.

After watching people dance for a while, I feel her eyes getting closer.

'You know how to dance, don't you?'

This time I don't lie when I tell her I do. For five years I danced for the Mangueira samba school, until I got too old to go on living from what I earned in one month of the year and when my parading around in spangles didn't give me enough money to eat. Once, dancing helped me get a legal job, and now it would help me sleep with a pretty girl. Who was it who told me dancing would get me nowhere? What did it matter, somebody said: you are what you live. I felt lucky because of my agility, because of my strong, flexible arms. I had no trouble moulding my body to the strange sensuality Julia radiated; no trouble attacking her strong buttocks with mine. I nailed her with a professional look, making it clear that we were simply a man and a woman doing what they liked on a dance floor. Nothing else committed us. We bounced each other around a good while until our legs begged for mercy, hers before mine, and we went back to the sofas, exhausted. We were two lobsters spied on by a hidden camera, I thought: thousands of televisions watched us close up, the complicity of a good sale, the happiness of a couple of respectable family men. I felt that the red and yellow lights of the next song, the serious voice of Tim Maia, crawling along like a camouflaged commando in the darkness, was heating us up all over again.

'You're a good dancer,' she dropped in my ear.

What she really meant was, 'You're a really good dancer, sensational,' but that feminine reticence restrained her, a reticence I'd taught myself to understand, even to esteem in myself, reading soap-opera magazines in the barbershop.

'Not as good as you,' I lied.

'Now I don't even want your cousin to come, Toninho.'

She remembered my name.

We danced away the rest of the night. We kissed. I made good use of what was left in the envelope. Then, making up some excuse, she took me home. She wanted to know if it was true what people said, that people danced the way they screwed.

When two wolves meet outside a neutral zone, it's inevitable they fight until one of them wins. When they get to that point, the weaker wolf turns over and puts his throat at the mercy of the winner. It's a sign of submission, an instinctive acknowledgement that the other will immediately recognize. It doesn't matter that the loser's blood boils or that his teeth have yet to assimilate the fact that tonight he will enjoy no reprisals. The winner will let him leave, because basic instincts make them respect their collective survival. This phenomenon, the scientists call 'inhibition mechanism'. A genetic key that keeps animals of one species from eliminating one another, when there are so many other species to eliminate – rabbits, deer . . .

I was watching television when Zé Antunes came over.

'You were late this morning,' he informed me.

I suppose Bautista told him everything last night because he didn't chew me out more than was necessary. At a certain moment, he even looked worried.

'You don't look well, Toninho. You must have stayed up until very late.'

The truth is I wasn't complaining. I immediately found my way back from Tijuca, showered in the back room, and was now trying to recoup a bit of energy dozing on the sofa during my few free minutes.

Even when I turned to the good memories I had of last night, the caresses of Julia Oliveira, my head wouldn't stop aching. The pain grew greater, becoming an implacable nail in my head. Standing opposite the television sets, I was watching that ballet of light, the perfect synchronization of the pictures.

I heard Zé Antunes greet the guards, then Roberto, Célia, Clarice and Zacarías.

They all walked along one behind the other and disappeared.

'Imagine we roll the same ping-pong ball again and again in front of some newly hatched ducklings. In that moment, even though we don't realize it, we will perhaps furtively have imprinted the link which will make them associate the revolving motion with the mother's identity. From then on, it will not be strange to see five ducklings follow the ball as they would an adult duck.'

By then, reduced by the whispering voice of the television, Julia was driving her fabulous blue sports car, and I, at her side, was looking through the windshield at the continuous line of the highway, the light posts and the wide fields in the darkness, as if everything conformed to a single, inseparable identity. But, above all, I looked at her. I looked at the reflection of her blue profile. The birthmark on her neck, next to her jugular vein. From time to time, she twisted around, and I saw in her eyes a solid promise, out of my reach.

Maybe for that reason I smiled: because I felt insecure as long as she looked at me.

We open up the shop at ten. I'd only managed to rest for fifteen extra minutes. Far from what I might have thought, the people outside flowed by with a disturbing continuity. It was a long train of infinite heads, hasty marches and unsatisfied needs. It was life in motion. On my corner, opposite the main entrance, I'd managed to get the costume on properly: the big stomach with green spots, the enormous head on top of the small human head; the jaw; the two soft fangs; the pair of well-disguised holes that were my eyes. I was once again the grand crocodile that promoted the electronic devices sold in Mattos Electronics, dancing for children. By using my talent, I quickly attracted and gathered kids and their parents. With the bounce of my long legs, with the strength of my arms, I lured them to the Draco refrigerator department, and there Roberto's skills did the rest. I went back to my corner and kept on dancing. I never stopped for even a moment. Half an hour later, I saw a married couple, followed by Zacarías and an enormous 21-inch television set, along with a complimentary coffee-maker. They were smiling, holding hands tightly.

'Toninhno,' Bautista smiled radiantly.
In his hand he held a catalogue of Draco products, unfolded and splendid. Soon the new collection of washing machines and dryers would come, a genuine advance in technology that was revolutionizing the appliance market all over the continent.

'And we'll have them here before anyone else, in our shop,' he was saying, waving the pamphlet around, sometimes kissing it and tapping it lightly as if it were an ampoule and he was about to give me an injection in my backside.

'Toni,' he patted me on the back.
As always, he had a perfect smile.

One of the advantages of my profession is that I can discreetly keep an eye on everyone who enters or leaves the store. I can make obscene gestures no one sees, look down blouses and be unnoticed. Which is why, when I saw Julia, unique in the crowd, approaching, she did not really take me by surprise. I felt perplexed, frightened, but ultimately protected under the barrier of rubber and cotton. I saw her ride the escalator up, a magnificent vision that cut a path through the masses. Julia, radiant, her face glowing with the vitality that good sex confers on women, passed me by without looking. I knew she'd come all the way from Tijuca just to see me.

'Julia Oliveira,' I heard Bautista saying.
Now I was in a tizzy, because in my own self-involvement I hadn't

foreseen the possibility that the two of them would meet, but that's exactly what was happening.

'What a surprise to find you in my family's humble shop,' he went on.

With a deeply plunging neckline, Julia had turned herself out perfectly to survive the light of day, much more successfully than all the other women I'd ever known combined. I looked at her, subtly made up, spiteful and challenging, but incomparably beautiful and dignified in the face of the Casanova she had before her – who did not deserve her. I felt that, in the heat of the rubber suit, my confidence was beginning to melt, seeing how she faced up to him with a courage I would never have recognized in myself.

'Well, then,' she was saying. 'Know where I can find him?'

'Toni?' laughed Bautista.

I felt a shiver sliding along my long crocodile tail.

'Yes, Toni,' she was saying. 'Toninho. Your cousin. Where is he?'

Bautista located my eyes amid all those people.

'He must be at the yacht club in Ipanema.' I noted a certain level of annoyance this time. 'Like all good citizens of Rio, he likes to bang heads with the waves.'

My soul returned to the crocodile. Now we were side by side.

'I'll go find him in Ipanema in that case. Ciao, Bautista.'

Then she walked past, elegantly sidestepping me, walking quickly. I no longer existed for her.

And I did nothing to change that. I said not a word to her as she left. I allowed the two holes in my disguise to take aim – excessively – at her magnificent backside, while she sank down the escalator, where the ground floor would soon swallow her up.

A little later, Bautista followed her. You could see he was furious with me, though he didn't show it in any obvious way. And I didn't try to interpret it in any other fashion. We were fine just the way we were. It wasn't worthwhile ruining the day. When he passed by, he whispered slowly that I owed him an explanation, and I think he meant more about not having been Toni the whole night than about having screwed his girlfriend five or six times.

I went on dancing, spinning, dancing until Gal Costa gave me a timely break.

Then I stopped the kids who were jumping around me and walked toward the shop, not letting anyone or anything stop me, indifferent to begging or demands. Even so, a boy grabbed hold of my tail. But I violently shook him off, and the little villain ended up by the washing machines. I walked on fearlessly, passing through the threatening words that Zé, Bautista, any customer, any fathers of conservative families, concerned with the proper education of their children, might have for me. On the way, I ran into Célia, who was in charge of cellular technology sales. She cheered me up with the empty smile she used on everybody.

'Whatever. Tell them I had to go to the bathroom.'

'I'll cover for you,' she said. 'But don't expect me to do it for more than five minutes.'

I thought she was going to add 'or I'll come get you', but the door, closed by its own inertia, interrupted my fantasy.

Once inside, I did not go directly to the bathroom as I'd said. First I took off the enormous head and abandoned it next to the tap. With all my strength I wished I could also take off the other, that soft spiral that sank towards nowhere inside my body. I walked towards the mailbox, rummaging through my pockets until I found the little blue envelope I'd bought two hours earlier on the way from Tijuca.

I took out the tablet, dropped it in a glass of water, and sat down to wait, observing how it disintegrated into thousands of milky bubbles. I saw how it sank, how the shipwrecked sailor overcome by gravity grew thinner and thinner until he reached that final convulsion that completely disintegrated him. I thought about the lobsters reproducing in direct proportion to good sales. I thought about Célia smiling at me with something more than sympathy before she disappeared. I thought about Julia looking for me in all the yachts anchored in Ipanema. I thought about Bautista, proud of having the complete Draco catalogue, long before any other downtown shop.

I thought about Daniela Mercury. I thought about the wolves that are pigeons and the pigeons that are wolves. I thought about the animals who let losers live. Perhaps my throat had been exposed long before I knew I'd lose. Or I could toss my own ping-pong balls at life. I could get someone to follow me, at least a couple of metres into what remained of life. Staring at the now peaceful glass, I thought I'd found the answer to many of life's mysteries, but I had no words to share with the world. Nor was any of that necessary. We were only that moment and myself. Vigorous, inspired by a strange dignity, I heard the snivelling of a child and the shout of an indignant father, perhaps my name piercing the walls of the shop. I heard the footsteps that were coming to get me, threatening and, finally calm, even my headache broken into thousands of adrenalin bubbles, I put on the crocodile head and waited for them, standing on my own two feet, ready to fight.

My name was Antonio Carlos Pereira. Toninho.

I was ready. ■

THE <u>ONLY</u> LIST

MARTIN AMIS
PAT BARKER
JULIAN BARNES
URSULA
BENTLEY
WILLIAM BOYD
BUCHI EMECHETA
MAGGIE GEE
KAZUO ISHIGURO
ALAN JUDD
ADAM MARS-
JONES
IAN McEWAN
SHIVA NAIPAUL
PHILIP
NORMAN
CHRISTOPHER PRIEST
SALMAN RUSHDIE
CLIVE SINCLAIR
LISA ST. AUBIN DE TERAN
GRAHAM SWIFT
ROSE TREMAIN
A.N. WILSON

IAIN BANKS
LOUIS DE BERNIÈRES
ANNE
BILLSON
TIBOR FISCHER
ESTHER FREUD
ALAN
HOLLINGHURST
KAZUO ISHIGURO
A.L. KENNEDY
PHILIP KERR
HANIF KUREISHI
ADAM LIVELY
ADAM MARS-JONES
CANDIA McWILLIAM
LAWRENCE NORFOLK
BEN OKRI
CARYL PHILLIPS
WILL SELF
NICHOLAS
SHAKESPEARE
HELEN SIMPSON
JEANETTE WINTERSON

SHERMAN ALEXIE
MADISON
SMARTT BEL
ETHAN CANIN
EDWIDGE DANTICAT
TOM DRURY
TONY EARLEY
JEFFREY EUGENIDES
JONATHAN
FRANZEN
DAVID GUTERSON
DAVID HAYNES
ALLEN
KURZWEIL
ELIZABETH
McCRACKEN
LORRIE MOORE
FAE MYENNE NG
ROBERT O'CONNOR
CHRIS OFFUTT
STEWART O'NAN
MONA SIMPSON
MELANIE RAE THON
KATE WHEELER

U'LL EVER NEED

MONICA ALI
NICOLA BARKER
RACHEL CUSK
PETER HO DAVIES
SUSAN ELDERKIN
STEPHEN GILL
PHILIP HENSHER
A. L. KENNEDY
HARI KUNZRU
TOBY LITT
DAVID MITCHELL
ANDREW O'HAGAN
DAVID PEACE
DAN RHODES
BEN RICE
RACHEL SEIFFERT
ZADIE SMITH
ADAM THIRLWELL
ALAN WARNER
SARAH WATERS
ROBERT McLIAM WILSON

GRANTA 81: BEST OF YOUNG BRITISH NOVELISTS 3

DANIEL ALARCÓN
KEVIN BROCKMEIER
JUDY BUDNITZ
CHRISTOPHER COAKE
ANTHONY DOERR
JONATHAN SAFRAN FOER
NELL FREUDENBERGER
OLGA GRUSHIN
DARA HORN
GABE HUDSON
UZODINMA IWEALA
NICOLE KRAUSS
RATTAWUT LAPCHAROENSAP
YIYUN LI
MAILE MELOY
ZZ PACKER
JESS ROW
KAREN RUSSELL
AKHIL SHARMA
GARY SHTEYNGART
JOHN WRAY

GRANTA 97: BEST OF YOUNG AMERICAN NOVELISTS 2

"Striking . . . Compelling . . . A voice that's immediate, unsentimental, and disarmingly direct."

—MICHIKO KAKUTANI, *THE NEW YORK TIMES*

"Gloriously gifted and alarmingly intelligent, Engel writes with an almost fable-like intensity. Her ability to pierce the hearts of her crazy-ass characters, to fracture a moment into its elementary particles of yearning, cruelty, love, and confusion will leave you breathless." —JUNOT DÍAZ,
Pulitzer Prize–winning author of *The Brief Wondrous Life of Oscar Wao*

"[An] arresting and vibrant new voice . . . Unforgettable."
—ELISSA SCHAPPELL, *Vanity Fair*

"Terrific . . . *Vida* is rich with life. Sabina's story is one of millions of threads of the immigrant experience, but it is universal as well: We all search for our place in the world, for the one who can make us visible."

—COLETTE BANCROFT,
St. Petersburg Times

© ISAK TINER

THE GIRLS RESEMBLED EACH OTHER IN THE UNFATHOMABLE

Carlos Labbé

TRANSLATED BY NATASHA WIMMER

CARLOS LABBÉ
CHILE
1977

Following a family tradition, Labbé likes to recognize the song
of every bird in the countryside. He has published a hypertextual
novel, *Pentagonal: incluidos tú y yo* (2001), the novels *Libro de
plumas* (2004), *Navidad y Matanza* (2007) and *Locuela* (2009), the
collection of short stories *Caracteres blancos* (2010), as well
as the pop music records 'Doce canciones para Eleodora' (2007)
and 'Monicacofonía' (2008). He co-wrote the screenplays for
the films *Malta con huevo* (2007) and *Yo soy Cagliostro*
(in production). In the past he was a member of the bands Ex Fiesta
and Tornasólidos, and is now a literary critic and editor. He lives in
Piscataway, New Jersey. 'The Girls Resembled Each Other in
the Unfathomable' is an excerpt from *Navidad y Matanza*.

To this day, investigators are still adding sightings of Bruno Vivar to the case file of the disappeared Navidad siblings. Every summer since the incident, a dozen witnesses from different parts of central Chile claim to have seen a young man fitting his description: striped T-shirt in various combinations of primary colours; shorts or bathing trunks; leather sandals; extremely thin hairless legs; dishevelled hair in a ragged cut, sometimes brown and other times dyed red. Over and over again, as if his parents' last memory of him had been burned on the retinas of so many who never knew him (the press coverage was as intense as it was brief), they see Bruno Vivar lying in the sand, face down on a towel, staring out to sea, looking disdainfully through some photographs, or swimming in silence. Other testimonies, of course, add specific and equally disturbing details: Bruno drinking at hotel bars, beer in cans or double shots of whiskey that he pays for with a card issued in the United States, while with the other hand he fondles a die that he spins like a top on the lacquered surface of the bar; sitting on a terrace at noon, noisily eating French fries; reading, in the dining hall, a letter delivered to the hotel weeks before; tossing the die and then writing another letter never sent by the local mail.

These bits of information come from different sources: guards; waiters; store clerks; receptionists; cleaning people who at the time also yearned to assemble the missing pieces of the case but who only succeeded in helping the police to declare impossible a verdict of either homicide or kidnapping. It has been tacitly assumed that Bruno Vivar – a legal adult – simply abandoned his family all of a sudden, which isn't a crime in Chile.

The unasked question is why the name of Alicia Vivar, the fourteen-year-old girl, appears only twice in the file. Especially after a detailed review of reports on the reappearances of her brother, Bruno. Because Bruno never once turns up alone. The various accounts agree that he arrives at hotel parking garages in different expensive cars always driven by a man whose smile also appears in police files, though in another section: Boris Real.

Boris Real became known in Chile in 1984 as the young local businessman who, representing a group of Swiss investors who wanted to buy Petrohué Bank, landed in the Capuchinos jail as the result of an anti-monopoly suit brought by the Superintendency of Banks when it was discovered that the Swiss were linked to an Australian investment group acquired by Atacama Bank and, at the same time, to the Norwegian-Spanish group that was acquiring the De Los Lagos Bank and Antonio Varas Bank. Boris Real was tried as the representative of the inscrutable international consortium that attempted to acquire 51 per cent of the Chilean bank, an operation which, it is noted, might have had consequences for the country beyond the strictly financial. The group in question immediately left the country, leaving no trace. At least until the summer of 1999. Of course, Boris Real wasn't the businessman's actual name but rather the alias of Francisco Virditti, forty-one, who acknowledged having headed a group of six shareholders motivated by nothing more than 'legitimate market play', as he states in the only interview he's given.

Seven years later, when the Chilean press could scarcely recall the business conspiracies that served to avoid analysis of the Pinochet recession, there came the regrettable death of Juan Ausencio Martínez Salas. On 5 February, on the seventeenth hole of the Prince of Wales Golf Club, a heart attack ended the days of the Patricio Aylwin administration's undersecretary of education. That afternoon, Martínez Salas was walking the links of the capital's golf club with two friends from his days as an MBA student at the University of Chicago: the board- and video-game executive José Francisco Vivar and Boris Real. A check of the witnesses at the Official Records Office reveals that the given name of the businessman present at the moment of death was Boris Real Yáñez, forty-eight, and there is no request on file for a name change for the individual in question. Perhaps it was a different Boris Real; perhaps Francisco Virditti had been the real pseudonym. Nevertheless, in another newspaper photograph of Real discussing his dear friend, the face is the same as that of the businessman who declared himself innocent before the Superintendency of Banks in 1984. In a press conference on 16 May 1995, the then congressman Nelson Ávila decried the possibility of a secret murder plot after the release of the findings from the autopsy of Martínez Salas, which seemed to suggest traces of poison in the undersecretary's system. The public outcry lasted for two days. As so often, there was vague talk of a political crisis. Then everything was forgotten. Boris Real was subpoenaed at his Vitacura residence before returning to anonymity. According to various accounts, he made a statement to Irma Sepúlveda, the judge in charge of the trial investigating the death of Martínez Salas. Today Boris Real is nearly impossible to find. He has no known address, nor does his name appear in any public record. José Francisco Vivar, approached by the press around the time of his children's disappearance, stated that he was no longer in contact with his friend.

Even more disturbingly, I must report that one July afternoon in 1997, I myself saw all of them: Vivar, Boris Real and the congressman Nelson Ávila strolling along the big beach at Cachagua. They were accompanied by their respective children. Naturally, I urged my companion to edge closer with me. The significance of the situation has only become evident to me since the beginning of the investigation of the incidents of Navidad and Matanza: Boris Real was walking hand in hand with little Alicia Vivar, then a girl of twelve. They were several feet behind the rest of the group. She asked him to come with her to the rocks, to look for shells. She didn't address him formally or call him uncle, but rather Boris. Then they talked about the reddish colour of the clouds at that hour and she asked how long it was until the end of the world.

What they did that summer was to drive around the beaches of central Chile in a Cadillac. Virditti reclined the passenger seat, closed his eyes and, through closed lips, murmured songs that a woman had taped for him five years before. 'Memories are made of these' could be heard. He dragged on a cigarette every so often;

that was the only thing to indicate that he wasn't asleep to anyone looking in from the outside; specifically, from the other end of the beach. There I was on my towel, face down, with a pair of binoculars. Alicia was next to me. Or rather: sometimes she came out of the sea, shivering, and lay down beside me with her arms clutched tight against the yearned-for skin of her body. I set down the binoculars, picked up a fistful of sand and let it fall gently along the path traced by the freckles on her back down to her waist, between the shoulder blades. But she didn't smile. Fist-fuck, she whispered, her eyes closed, and with nothing but that extremely disturbing expression she reminded me that she wasn't happy, that she never would be. Those nights that she spoke to me in English across the hotel corridor from her room in a voice hoarse with tears or laughter, the voice of a woman who has wet herself laughing, she told me horrible children's tales that later turned into the story of her nightmares: a rabbit passing by, her on top of another woman whom I also loved, sucking at her dried-up breast, heedless. Walking over a grave. Boldly she said: the grave I'm staring into now. Do you want to know what I see?

Clearly the Alicia I'm talking to you about isn't the same girl of fourteen, at least not the Alicia Vivar the investigators are still seeking. She got up, she went running into the sea. And she managed to kick sand in my eyes. For peeping! she shouted. Then I had to go running after her, grabbing her where the waves were already over our shoulders and forcing her down under the full weight of my body for the space of half a minute. She came up half drowned and wouldn't speak to me. Then I took her face in my hands to say: my little girl, my lost one, my unreadable book. Right, moron, in your dreams, she answered, before coming closer to bite my lip. That's what I was fated to discover. That we'll never be allowed to experience a desire that we simply can't handle. I'm writing this for her, wherever she is. For me this report can't be neutral: hundreds of associations come between us, just because I was naive enough to believe that love had something to do with words, with the correct use of them. Now I'm afraid to talk; I'll just turn into a professional. But one thing is true. I loved Alicia. Most importantly: I still love her. Whatever the name she's got now.

That's why I'm writing at this time of night. Back from forty hours of work at the laboratory. Drunk. Alone. Lost. Staring into the grave. I know what's right, what awaits me and the splendour. Glimpses. I know, too, that sometimes, in the Cadillac, Francisco Virditti opened his eyes and watched Bruno head for the beach wearing nothing but a bathing suit. Virditti knew perfectly well which girl Bruno had chosen that afternoon, all of them different but resembling each other in the unfathomable. Bruno worked things so as to dive in next to them, make some charming joke, laugh – sidelong glance – and brush against them, as if by chance, in the salt and the spray. So that ten minutes later the girl felt sorry for Bruno Vivar when she noticed his purple lips and offered to share her towel with him. That was the key moment, when they got back to where her things were and she turned pale upon discovering that her towels had been stolen. The shaken look on her face. She reminded me of my sister, or rather my father's daughter, Bruno would tell me much later, between two whiskeys, under the weight of a death threat: my threat. Arrogant twisted idiot, fucking hell, if I had him in front of me this instant he wouldn't get a word out. I'd spit on him; kick the shit out of him. And that's all there is to say. Because at the same time Virditti was laughing his head off in the car. He had crossed the beach, taken the towels, and coolly returned to the passenger seat of the Cadillac as Bruno plied his charms amid the waves. But the game was interrupted when Alicia chose to wait for Francisco Virditti in the back seat of the Cadillac and greet him: idiot, you're the one I wanted to see. I realize that there was nothing I could do to stop her. Then he started the car and sped toward the highway. Where death so often dwells. ■

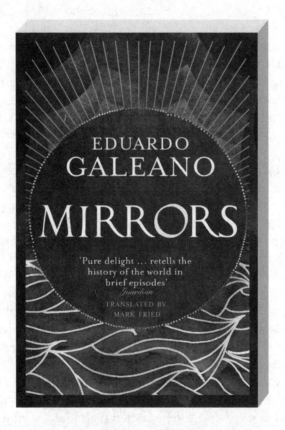

GRANTA

IN UTAH
THERE ARE
MOUNTAINS TOO

Federico Falco

TRANSLATED BY ALFRED MAC ADAM

FEDERICO FALCO
ARGENTINA
1977

Falco was born in General Cabrera, a village in the interior of
Argentina bordering the dry pampas. A writer and video artist, he has
published the short-story collections *222 patitos* (2004),
00 (2004) and *La hora de los monos* (2010), and two books of poetry:
Aeropuertos, aviones (2006) and *Made in China* (2008). A professor in
the departments of Film, Literature and Contemporary Art
at Blas Pascal University in Córdoba, he received a scholarship
from New York University and Banco Santander to study for an
MFA in Creative Writing in Spanish at NYU in 2009.
He now lives between Argentina, Madrid and New York.
'In Utah There Are Mountains Too' is a new story.

All that year Cuqui kept thinking about it, but school work, figure-skating classes, drawing lessons and her friends' sweet-sixteen parties kept her too busy. When vacation rolled around, she again turned the matter over in her mind and came to a conclusion: God doesn't exist. So Cuqui decided she'd become an atheist. The first person she told was her grandmother. The old woman just shrugged: it made no difference to her whether Cuqui was an atheist, a Protestant, a Jew or a Catholic. Later she told her mother over the telephone.

Mom, I don't believe in God any more. I've become an atheist.

Cuqui's mother, at the other end of the line, remained silent.

Mom, did you hear me?

I did, she said.

I've realized that the people who don't believe in God are superior to those who do because they don't depend on anything. I don't want to depend on anyone, Mom.

Cuqui, what's wrong? Why are you telling me these things?

Because that's what I think. She could hear her mother sobbing.

Mom, please don't cry.

Mom, are you still there?

Yes, she said, and then hung up.

Every summer, Cuqui's mother rented out the house they lived in. She left it in the hands of one of the downtown real estate firms and went off to work as a cook in a hotel on top of the mountain. She would give Cuqui a little box with a roll of banknotes and send her to live with her grandmother. The money in the box was supposed to cover her expenses for all three summer months. The real estate people would rent the house to tourists who came to Villa Carlos Paz looking for fun and tranquillity, people who spent their time rock climbing, taking pictures of one another riding burros and chatting with other tourists standing in the lake, the water up to their waists and the sun frying their backs. To pick up some overtime, Cuqui's mother never took a day off, so she never came down to Villa Carlos Paz. But every two or three days she would telephone the grandmother's house and ask what was going on. Cuqui always told her everything was just fine.

Cuqui's grandmother lived in the high part of Carlos Paz, on the slope of the mountain, near the cable car. From her garden it was possible to see the entire lake below, the grey-and-white houses, the downtown hotels, the main street that meandered until it came to an end opposite the church at the Cuckoo Clock Rotunda. The summer Cuqui became an atheist was long, dry and suffocating. Cuqui hated vacation. She didn't like the heat, got along badly with her grandmother, was horrified at the thought of swimming in the muddy lake, and the tourists drove her mad. From lunchtime until sunset it was impossible to go anywhere. The sun shone down on the lake and scorched roofs, pavements and asphalt. Cuqui would fall into bed and stare at her grandfather's library, overflowing with old books, encyclopedias and art magazines. For hours she would think about what to do with her life.

Sometimes Cuqui dreamed about being a model. Not on the catwalk, because Cuqui is short, but a magazine model. She fantasized about someone, some day, discovering her strolling down the avenue and getting her out of Villa Carlos Paz, out of her mother's house, out of summers with Grandma. Cuqui would travel the world, would be photographed by the best photographers and would be on the cover of Italian *Vogue*, the best-designed *Vogue*. Then one day Cuqui had to face facts. She took off her gym shorts, her T-shirt, the sports bra her mother had bought her, pulled off her panties and just stood still opposite the mirror.

The shades were down, barely any light came in. Cuqui looked herself over for a good while.

She was useless, even for magazine photos.

Cuqui had already reached a conclusion about the other problem bothering her: God didn't exist, so she became an atheist. Now she had to get out of Carlos Paz and become famous. But how was she going to stand out? She decided to solve that problem over the course of the summer and spent her time thinking about it. When she got tired of thinking, she silently wandered around the house. Grandma was having a siesta stretched out in bed with her feet raised and the fan on. Cuqui marched around the kitchen, observed the dust and the cobwebs clinging to the windows, the cat hairs on the dining-room chair, the wooden table for four, which could be opened to seat six or eight but which was never used.

The cat yawned in the only patch of shade in the weed-choked, sun-beaten garden. The tall grass curled over, dried out and brown. The blue armchair fading in the hall. Cuqui would sit in it and remain still, not wanting to do anything. She looked at the cars on the street, the tourists walking towards the lake with their beach umbrellas under their arms, a dog scratching its fleas. Cuqui felt the perspiration on her body, her hair sticking to the nape of her neck, the leather on the armchair to which she'd begun to stick, the sweat between her skin and the padding. When she heard her grandmother getting out of bed, she ran to her room again. She lowered the shades, locked the door, and thought some more.

That's how she spent the first month of summer. Then, with no warning, Cuqui fell in love with a Mormon. He was a young, good-looking Mormon with blue eyes and blondish hair. Cuqui met him in the house of the woman who lived just across the street. One afternoon, sitting in the blue chair, Cuqui saw two boys walking under the blistering sun. The boys were wearing white short-sleeved shirts, ties and black trousers. Each had a pack on his back. They rang the bell at the Aguirre house, but no one answered. They knocked at the door of the widower Lamónica's little apartment, but no one answered there either. One of the boys wiped his dripping forehead and took refuge under the big ash tree. The other one knocked at the door of Mrs Pérez's house. Mrs Pérez looked them over for a second through a window, asked what they wanted, hesitated a moment and invited them in.

Mormons in Mrs Pérez's house! Finally something interesting! thought Cuqui as she ran to the bathroom to wash her face and comb her hair a bit. She took off her pyjamas, put on her black dress, made sure her grandmother was snoring opposite the fan, picked up an empty cup and walked out.

She entered Mrs Pérez's house through the laundry-room, pretending to be oblivious.

Mrs Pérez, Mrs Pérez, she called out.

People were talking in the living room. Mrs Pérez came into the kitchen.

I have guests, she said. What do you need?

Cuqui showed her the cup. Could you lend me some sugar?

While Mrs Pérez got the sugar can out of the cupboard, Cuqui peeked into the dining room. The Mormons were sitting in the armchairs facing the window. One was an ordinary boy, his cheeks pocked with old acne scars, his ears a bit big. The other Mormon was handsome. He reminded Cuqui of Joey McIntyre, from New Kids on the Block.

Would you like some coffee? Mrs Pérez shouted to them.

The Mormons looked up and saw Cuqui leaning in the doorway. Cuqui smelled them with her eyes closed. They gave off a sharp aroma of pine forest, soap and cologne.

We don't drink coffee, our religion forbids it, said the Mormons.

Some tea then? Coca-Cola, Sprite? asked Mrs Pérez as she woke Cuqui up and pointed to the laundry room door.

Off with you, she whispered.

I want to listen to them too.

None of that, said Mrs Pérez. Your grandma needs the sugar. Take it to her.

A glass of Sprite would be great, answered one of the Mormons from the living room.

Mrs Pérez opened the refrigerator, closed it, opened it again, and clasped her hands around her head. There was no more Sprite. From the sideboard she took out the little can where she kept her spare change and found a five-peso note.

Take this. She held the money out to Cuqui. Go over to Vicente's and buy me a litre-and-a-half bottle of Sprite. Tell him it's for me so he doesn't charge you the deposit. I'll bring the bottle back tonight. Make sure it's good and cold.

Cuqui ran to the store. When she got back, Mrs Pérez was showing the Mormons some photos of her husband, who'd died the previous winter.

He liked to read, he adored it, said Mrs Pérez pointing to the bookcase behind the armchairs. The Mormons swivelled around and for just an instant looked at the hundreds of *Reader's Digest* selections, perfectly lined up. Years and years of the monthly selections arranged in order of publication.

From the kitchen, Cuqui called Mrs Pérez. She lifted up the bottle and showed it to her.

Ah! The Sprite's finally arrived! said Mrs Pérez. I'll pour some out for you right now.

Mrs Pérez introduced her while she arranged the glasses on a tray: This is Cuqui, the granddaughter of my neighbour.

Cuqui! It sounds just like cookie! said the Mormon who looked like Joey McIntyre.

The other Mormon, the one with the scarred cheeks, explained to Cuqui what a cookie was. Your name sounds just like the English word cookie.

Cuqui wasn't even listening. No one had ever spoken her name in a foreign language.

II

Each Mormon, over his heart, wore a golden pin bearing his name. The ugly Mormon was named Robert and was called Bob. The cute Mormon was named Steve and had no nickname. Bob was older than Steve, had just turned twenty-two and looked very serious. Both spoke perfect Spanish, but the hard pronunciation of English appeared at the ends of words. Steve and Bob told them they believed in God and that Jesus was God's son and that they believed in the Bible. But besides all that, since they were Mormons, they also believed in another book, a sacred book written in America.

Bob's voice was soft and slow. He explained things as if Cuqui and Mrs Pérez were five-year-olds. Steve would nod in agreement and add something from time to time. When Bob finished, Steve opened his backpack, took out two books with blue bindings, and stood them on the table, next to the glasses and tray.

This is the *Book of Mormon*. These copies are for you.

Before Steve could close the backpack, Cuqui saw that inside, along with another pair of books, there was an empty plastic container and a green Axe deodorant missing its cap.

You can read in these books what Bob's told us, Steve went on.

What we would like is that during the week, you two think about what you've heard and that you ask God, in true faith, with a sincere heart, if you should believe us or not, said Bob. He will answer you. If you ask in true faith, He will answer you. OK?

OK, OK, said Mrs Pérez. She had her hands clasped on her lap and was nodding slowly, her eyes half shut with the expression of someone deeply moved.

Bob smiled, turned his head, and looked at Cuqui.

OK?

Yes, of course, said Cuqui.

Before they left, Bob and Steve set a day and hour for their next meeting. Even though Cuqui wrote it down on a scrap of paper, she didn't have to look at it again. Wednesday at three. She would never have forgotten it. She said it over and over. That week, she thought about nothing except Steve smiling at her with his glistening white teeth and his blue eyes flashing light. Steve caressing her hair. Steve holding her close and seeking her mouth. Steve saying to her *Cookie, Cookie, Cookie*. Each time she thought about Steve, Cuqui ran to her room, locked the door and touched herself.

What are you doing in there? asked her grandmother.

Nothing. Leave me in peace, shouted Cuqui. And then she continued.

She went to the supermarket, bought herself a green Axe, and that night, before going to sleep, rubbed some on her pillow and slept hugging it. She dreamed about Steve's white chest. She imagined the beauty marks he might have on his back, the freckles on his shoulders, the golden, thin hair on his chest.

Steve, she murmured in her dreams.

D id you read? asked Mrs Pérez the instant Cuqui knocked at her door the next Wednesday. Her *Book of Mormon* was next to the waiting tray, the glasses upside down on a lacy napkin, and the bottle of Sprite chilling in a wine cooler. Sticking out from between the pages were improvized place-markers – scraps of paper, pamphlets, strands of wool.

Cuqui had no time to answer. Mrs Pérez was already peeking through the window.

Here they come, here they come, and she checked to see that everything was in place. She let them ring and, even though she was standing next to it, waited half a minute before opening the door.

Bob was just as repulsive as before. Steve, on the other hand, was much better-looking than Cuqui remembered. He'd shaved carefully and his cheeks were glistening, smooth and clean. He was not wearing the dark blue tie with light blue polka dots he'd worn the previous week. Now he was wearing one with small checks, a mix of blue-black and gold that looked even better on him. And then there was his shirt, white and short-sleeved like the one he wore the first time, but it seemed smaller, more tightly fitted to his body. It hugged the muscles on his arms. His wide shoulders and straight spine revealed the body of an athlete. Cuqui recalled the men in underwear in the Avon catalogues a neighbour dropped off for her mother every month and felt a wave of heat that devoured her face. She lowered her eyes, pulled her hair forward and looked through her fringe. Bob held out his hand to her. Steve was smiling, a step behind him.

Come in, come in, said Mrs Pérez, gesturing towards the armchairs and pouring Sprite.

Bob and Steve sat down and Mrs Pérez handed them their glasses. They drank silently, all in one swallow, as if they were dying of thirst. Mrs Pérez's living room had filled with the sharp, savage aroma of green Axe. Cuqui realized that Bob and Steve shared the deodorant and that after walking through Villa Carlos Paz at siesta time, they would stop and put some on before entering anyone's house. That's why Steve carried it in his backpack.

When he finished his soda, Bob dried his lips with a handkerchief and asked if they'd read the *Book of Mormon* and if they'd thought about what he and Steve had said.

Mrs Pérez instantly nodded.

Of course, answered Cuqui.

Very well. Today we'll introduce you to Joseph Smith, the founder of the Church of Jesus Christ of Latter-Day Saints, said Bob, and he began to speak. Cuqui was not allowed to hear even half of the story. During the week, Mrs Pérez had mentioned to Cuqui's grandmother that Cuqui was in her house along with the Mormons. That Wednesday, half an hour after 3 p.m., Cuqui's grandmother had told Cuqui's mother by telephone. She let out a howl and ordered her to get her daughter out of there immediately. Cuqui's grandmother crossed the street, rang the bell and said: You're coming with me. Don't say a word.

Cuqui had to go. She couldn't say goodbye to Steve or even find out when he'd be coming back to Mrs Pérez's house.

That night Cuqui's mother telephoned her.

I don't ever want to see you near those people again.

I do what I like, answered Cuqui. I'm an atheist, so what they say doesn't interest me, so just relax. I'm not going to make them atheists, and they're not going to make me a Mormon.

So why go? Your grandmother told me they gave you a book, that you've got it in your room, that you lock yourself away to read.

I like one of the Mormons, Mom, that's what's going on. I'm in love, and I'm going to fight to get him.

You've been brainwashed by them, said Cuqui's mother, bursting into tears.

I've had it with you, said Cuqui, hanging up.

I don't ever want you see you going to the Pérez place again, Cuqui heard her grandmother shout just before she slammed her bedroom door and threw herself on to the bed to cry.

III

From that day on, the heat no longer mattered to Cuqui, the tourists no longer bothered her and she stopped thinking about what she was going to do with her life. Cuqui was in love. There was only room in her head for Steve. She went to the Carlos Paz library and read everything they had about Mormons. She made a list of questions that sounded profound and required long answers and kept it in her pocket. She didn't want to find herself bereft of conversation topics when she ran into Steve and Bob again. She began taking bicycle rides that lasted the whole day. She knew that Steve and Bob were doing their missionary work in her neighbourhood, that they went from house to house, knocking on doors. It shouldn't be hard to find them, but even so it took her a week to pick up their trail. Seven long days of investigation, pursuit and fruitless pedalling.

And then, one day, she saw them sitting in the square, right under the monument to the Volunteer Fireman. Cuqui crouched behind a bush and spied on them. Bob took a plastic container out of his backpack and began stirring up some cold beans. He ate for a good while, while Steve read the *Book of Mormon*. Then they switched. Bob passed the container to Steve, and Steve handed him the book. Cuqui's foot fell asleep. She got up, stretched her legs, pretended to be strolling, and ran to hide behind an evergreen. When Bob and Steve finished eating, they put away the container and went back to their missionary work. For the entire afternoon, Cuqui followed while they preached. She hid in gardens, behind lamp posts, between two parked cars, up in a tree. She never lost them. Late in the afternoon, Bob and Steve went home, and Cuqui discovered where they lived: a tiny apartment on the patio of a hardware store, on the other side of Carlos Paz, near the Cuckoo Clock. The next day she asked the owner of the store if they'd been living there for long.

They keep changing. Every three months, two new ones come, and the old ones disappear. They're nice people.

Cuqui discovered their schedule.

They set out at nine thirty and spend the day on the move. They don't come back here until seven or eight. They turn the light out right away. Cuqui carefully noted their habits, the houses they visited, how much time they spent in each, how often they returned. When she'd learned everything, she began to set up ambushes. She would wait for them on a corner in the shadow of a tree, and would intercept them wearing her best smile: Boys, what a coincidence! she'd greet them before asking the first question.

B ob had more experience. He was older and had done missionary work for a longer time. In the conversations with Mrs Pérez, he'd always been the main speaker. Even so, when it came to Cuqui, he stepped aside and let Steve take over the conversation. Cuqui knew that Bob didn't trust her. Perhaps Mrs Pérez had warned him, perhaps he was jealous. She would take out the list she'd written up in the library and ask the questions with true conviction, but the answers didn't interest her. And she couldn't conceal that. Bob would cross his arms and find somewhere to sit. He didn't even try to answer her, letting Steve take charge. Steve did make an effort to convince Cuqui. He was full of ardour and enthusiasm, as if he needed to make a conversion to get his missionary diploma or as if he wanted to impress Bob, show him how much he knew.

Can you explain to me how the ancient prophets came to the United States from Jerusalem? And what do you think about Darwin's theories with regard to the survivors of the Tower of Babel?

She didn't even give him time to take a breath, and no sooner had Steve finished his answer than Cuqui was wondering if in Utah the Mormons still married several wives, then she'd express her doubts about the possibility of writing out an entire book on sheets of gold, or assert that it was impossible for a man to learn to speak ancient languages in a single day.

Steve would listen carefully. Then, his face full of peace, he would smile.

You need faith, he would say. God is much greater than we are; without faith you'll never understand Him. And then he'd apologize because they had to be on their way, a family was expecting them. But before saying goodbye, Steve promised Cuqui he'd pray for her that night.

Tonight I'll pray for you, Steve would say. I will ask that the Holy Spirit illuminate you and give you the gift of faith and understanding.

Thank you, thank you, Cuqui would answer. She'd get on her bike and leave, happy because that night Steve was going to think about her. Cuqui would then run to her room, hug the pillow redolent of green Axe and imagine Steve sitting next to her on the edge of the bed. He would raise his arm and show her his armpit. Cuqui would press the button. Steve's blond hairs, soft and translucent, would receive the shower of deodorant and be moistened. *Thank you*, Steve would say, and lean over, and before making love to her, he would run his tongue over her eyelids, moistening her closed eyes.

IV

One day, Cuqui had an idea. To talk about something other than religion, she would invite Bob and Steve to dinner. She had the money her mother had left her and could take them to a good restaurant.

We never eat outside the house. At ten we have to go to bed, Bob informed her.

In that case, I'll invite you to lunch.

We always eat with other missionaries or with families that are members of the congregation, said Bob.

No problem. I'll invite you to breakfast, Cuqui insisted.

Bob hesitated for an instant. He looked over at Steve. Steve said nothing.

OK then, breakfast, Bob finally answered.

Cuqui jumped for joy. She got on her bicycle and rode full-speed down Carlos Paz's main street. She was so happy she waved to the newspaper vendors, turning down the pamphlets about rental cottages, excursions on the lake and all-you-can-eat barbecues. She looked over several hotels, visited restaurants that served breakfast, asked about prices, investigated menus and asked what each thing was, how much it cost, if you could have a second helping. She chose the Hotel del Lago. Expensive, but its window over the coast was worth it.

The night before the breakfast Cuqui couldn't sleep. Again and again she reviewed the subjects she'd bring up for conversation, the seating arrangement, the clothes she'd wear. The Hotel del Lago offered an American, buffet-style breakfast. When Cuqui made enquiries, the hostess showed her the breakfast room. It was late and there were only some tourist families at a few tables. Cuqui's feet sank into the soft, bordeaux-coloured rug. The window faced the lake and, beyond it, the dry, brown mountains. There wasn't a cloud in the sky. The centre of each table was occupied by a floral arrangement – roses, daisies and ivy.

Are they real flowers or plastic? asked Cuqui.

The hostess frowned: Real of course.

Cuqui ran her finger over some petals and saw she wasn't lying.

You can eat as much as you want?

As much as you like.

And it's just the way it is in the United States?

Yes, miss; it's an *American* breakfast.

The piped-in music was soft, as fluffy as the rug. A tourist wearing bermudas and a white T-shirt got up to get the newspaper on the counter and went back to his table. A waiter emerged from the kitchen with a huge, round, stainless-steel tray topped with a glass dome. Cuqui imagined Steve and Bob sitting at the window, slowly eating their scrambled eggs and toast. She imagined them laughing their heads off and thanking her profusely for having invited them to have a breakfast just like the ones they had in their own country. Cuqui had them recover the tastes of home. She imagined Bob discreetly getting up, saying he wanted to stroll a bit out on the terrace to get a breath of air, and Steve alone with her, at the light-bathed table. Steve would toss his napkin to one side and rest his hand on Cuqui's. She would feel all its heat.

Thank you, Steve would say, staring into her eyes. Thank you, Cuqui, thanks a lot, she imagined Steve saying before he kissed her. And then, towards dawn, she fell asleep.

She set two alarm clocks, but needed none. She got up before the sun actually rose. She took a quick bath, brushed her teeth and drank a glass of Coca-Cola, so she wouldn't leave the house with an empty stomach. Her long, white dress, strappy sandals and a touch of perfume behind her ears. That was all. Simple, fresh, the ideal outfit for a breakfast overlooking the lake. Cuqui had arranged it all on the chair, so it took her less than a second to get dressed. No necklaces, no earrings. She looked at herself in the mirror. She was perfect. Now it was time to leave.

From her bedroom, her grandmother asked what she was doing, where she was going.

I've got something important, said Cuqui. I'll be back before lunch, she shouted as she shut the door.

Her bicycle awaited her, leaning against the wall. The previous afternoon she'd checked to make sure both tyres were hard and that the chain needed no oil. She wanted no mishaps. Cuqui flew downhill through the empty, still shadow-covered streets, her hem pulled up so it wouldn't get tangled in the spokes or stained by the pedals. Her legs: smooth, shining, freshly shaved. The wind made her hair float and showed her face and Cuqui felt like singing something, a funny song, or, even better, she felt like whistling a melody that would be like background music. She felt she was in a movie. Young and sensual.

She flew along the main street, crossed Carlos Paz in a trice, crossed the new bridge over the narrowest part of the lake and went the wrong way down a one-way street that led down to the Cuckoo Clock. Why not? There was no one coming. The owner of the hardware store was getting out portable barbecues, ladders and armloads of brooms to display on the pavement for potential customers. Cuqui left her bicycle leaning against the lamp post.

Will you keep an eye on it for me? she asked the hardware store owner. He nodded yes: It's safe there.

Cuqui walked along the asphalt alley next to the store. She passed the Goodyear poster, the rolls of chicken wire, the piles of stakes, the posts. Behind, on the small patio, the plants in the vases had died years ago. The window of the Mormons' little apartment was shut. Cuqui knocked at the door. Once, twice. Silence. She checked her watch: it was the time they'd agreed on. She knocked again, and from the other side she seemed to hear a growl, the slight creak of springs.

Who is it? asked a voice that seemed like Bob's.

Cuqui.

Just a minute, said Bob.

Cuqui heard whispering and stumbling steps. The muffled sound of tossed sheets. More whispering and, finally, the key that turned in the lock.

Bob was wearing basketball shorts, a T-shirt two or three sizes too big and his hair was like tangled straw.

Ready for breakfast? asked Cuqui as she looked through the half-open door. She saw a plastic table covered with dirty dishes, piles of the *Book of Mormon*, open bags of crackers and a sugar bowl with no lid. She saw two plastic chairs with the Cervecería Córdoba logo on their backs. She saw a poster of Jesus' face tacked to the wall and under the poster a bed whose sheets were on the floor with one pillow against the headrest.

What time is it? asked Bob as he scratched his head.

Seven thirty, the time we agreed on, answered Cuqui.

Behind Bob, sitting on the bed in his underpants and wearing another huge T-shirt, Cuqui could see Steve yawning and rubbing his eyes. Steve put on a baseball cap – backwards – smiled and waved to Cuqui.

We'll need fifteen minutes, said Bob.

Fine, no problem, I'll wait for you here, said Cuqui, taking two steps back.

Yes, OK, wait for us, said Bob.

It was only when he closed the door and she turned a bit and looked toward the blue sky and the lot behind the hardware shop that Cuqui noticed the wave of foul air loaded with moisture and odours that wafted from the Mormons' apartment and enveloped her. A smell similar to the sweat she'd noticed from time to time on the boys in her school, but mixed with remnants of sleep, dirty sheets, dry saliva on lips and with something sweeter, like apples, or flavoured cereal, or a slice of cake forgotten in the refrigerator.

Cuqui shut her eyes and took a deep breath to inhale it completely. The smell by then had diminished, and she could barely find a few confused traces that she engraved on her memory. She understood that it was the smell of Steve when he slept and that the deodorant was only a disguise to fool others. Only she knew his intimate life.

Nevertheless, it annoyed her that in this intimacy there was also a bit of Bob's smell.

V

Even though Cuqui insisted they eat all they wanted, Bob and Steve barely finished a cup of milk and a slice of bread each.

There were few people in the dining room. A family at the other end and a couple of retired folks at the tables closest to the buffet.

And Bob and Steve there, opposite Cuqui, with their ties and white shirts and the blond hair plastered down with gel, the part on the side, perfect, the backpacks filled with the *Book of Mormon*, their trays in their hands. Outside, the sail of a windsurfer cut the surface of the lake, moving along so slowly it seemed stationary.

You can have more, said Cuqui. As much as you like.

This will be fine, said Bob, sitting down.

No, not in that chair, said Cuqui. Yours is the other chair, that's Steve's.

Bob and Steve exchanged glances but said nothing. Steve sat where Cuqui wanted him to sit. She tried to initiate a conversation. She talked about the heat, the drought, the danger of forest fires, exchange rates, an accident on the funicular. Bob and Steve listened in silence.

Steve is leaving today, said Bob, when Cuqui finally stopped talking. We've decided it's better he go to another mission, far from here.

Cuqui didn't understand, and for an instant went on talking about something else. Bob had to repeat what he'd said:

Steve is leaving today. He leaves this evening.

Cuqui thought they were joking with her. It couldn't be true.

Is that true? she asked Steve. Tell me, look me in the eye. Is it true?

Steve lowered his eyes and took a long drink of milk.

Why would he lie? said Bob.

I'm not asking you, I'm asking him, Cuqui blurted out. Steve, is it true?

Yes, said Steve, his eyes fixed on the tablecloth.

Steve had indeed said yes. Cuqui felt that the lake was disappearing, that the sun was shining so brightly it turned everything white, that a black hand was pulling her guts down. Her eyelids trembled. That was the void.

Could you leave us for a moment? she asked Bob, making an effort to pull herself together. I'd like to speak to Steve alone.

That's impossible, answered Bob. We missionaries have to do

everything together. It's one of our ways to resist the attacks of the demon.

Enough, Bob, said Steve.

But –

It's OK, Bob, I know what I'm doing.

Bob got up and walked away without saying another word.

The previous night Cuqui had fallen asleep reviewing the list of subjects for conversation. Now none was of any use; but each item was still there, curled up in her head, piled one on top of the other, keeping her from thinking. Cuqui closed her eyes.

I love you, she said.

Steve blushed.

Cuqui went over to him. Tried to kiss him. The smell of green Axe, so near, and yet as if on the other side of a wall.

No, said Steve, pushing her away. No, he said again.

Cuqui's eyes filled with tears.

Is it because I'm an atheist? Is that it?

Steve didn't answer.

It's because I'm ugly.

Steve signalled to Bob to come back.

Cuqui got up and without saying goodbye walked to the cashier. She didn't want Bob to see her cry. In her bodice she had a banknote, one her mother had given her in the little box. She flattened it out on the counter, paid the bill and left.

She saw them again that afternoon at siesta time. Cuqui knocked at their door and Steve appeared. He was just finishing up his packing. Cuqui invited him to take a walk.

Bob has to come too. Cuqui accepted. They walked towards the lake. In front of the Cuckoo Clock a crowd was gathering. It was five minutes before the hour and the tourists were waiting with their cameras raised, focused on the door from which the little wooden bird would appear.

I brought you this, so you'll remember me forever, Cuqui said to Steve.

It was a tin heart, the kind they sell at the kiosks. The heart cut through the middle so there were two identical halves. Each half had a hole in it so it could be put on a chain and worn as a necklace. Cuqui had separated the two halves and then cut the half she was giving to Steve in half. She gave the half with the hole to Steve and the other to Bob.

So the two of you will remember me, she said. Take it wherever you go. Keep it with you on your missions and when you go back to the United States. Keep it with you forever.

The clock's bell began to ring, the double door opened and the wooden cuckoo with the open beak appeared.

Cuckoo! Cuckoo! Cuckoo! screeched the bird.

I'll pray for you every night, said Steve.

Great, said Cuqui.

The bird went back in, and the doors shut for a second. Then they opened again just as quickly.

Cuckoo! Cuckoo! Cuckoo! screeched the bird once more, and the mass of tourists again took pictures.

I have to ask you one last question, Cuqui said.

Yes, of course, said Steve.

Cuckoo! Cuckoo! Cuckoo! screeched the wooden bird for the third time.

What is Utah like? asked Cuqui.

I don't know. I've never been there. My family is from Arkansas, said Steve.

In Utah there are mountains too, just like here, said Bob.

Cuqui smiled. She shaded her eyes with the palm of her hand so the sun wouldn't dazzle her and she looked out at the lake, the hotels along the shore, the main street and its shops, the dry peaks around Villa Carlos Paz.

Thanks, that's what I wanted to know, she said, turning aside. Then she left.

Bob and Steve stood there, silent, among the tourists taking flash photos. Each one held in his hand a piece of the tin heart.

Then the wooden bird disappeared behind the door and did not come out again. The tourists put away their cameras and little by little began to disperse. Cuqui pedalled at top speed, climbing the hill towards the cable car. She wanted to get to her grandmother's house quickly, throw the green Axe into the garbage and lock herself in her room to think. She had to recoup the lost time. Only one month of summer was left. ■

PHOENIX POETS

FROM CHICAGO

Ziggurat
Peter Balakian

"Peter Balakian's *Ziggurat* ingests calamity and dissolves it into almost exhilarating rhythm and image, pushing the language until it feels like it's breaking into something new. The work aims to reveal the human capacity to integrate and, after hard passage, transcend."—Sven Birkerts

CLOTH $25.00

Tourist in Hell
Eleanor Wilner

"Wilner is a poet of incomparable erudition and gifts of insight. There is no other contemporary poet who has addressed, as she has throughout her distinguished career, the world legacy of history and myth with such a keen sense of wonder, curiosity, and, in the end, literal re-vision."—Susan Stewart

PAPER $18.00

The University of Chicago Press • www.press.uchicago.edu

GRANTA

SMALL MOUTH, THIN LIPS

Antonio Ortuño

TRANSLATED BY TANYA HUNTINGTON HYDE

ANTONIO ORTUÑO
MEXICO
1976

Ortuño, born in Guadalajara to Spanish immigrant parents, has
been, in this order: an outstanding student; a dropout; a worker in a
special-effects company and a private tutor. *El buscador de cabezas*
(2006) was selected by the Mexican press as the best first novel of
the year. His second book, *Recursos humanos* (2007), was a finalist for
the Herralde Prize. In addition, he has published a collection of short
stories, *El jardín japonés* (2007). His new collection, *La señora rojo*,
will be available at the end of 2010 . His writing has been translated
into English, French, Italian, German, Romanian and Hungarian.
'Small Mouth, Thin Lips' is a new story.

6 May

I receive this letter:

You do not ask me, Doctor, to write a text that explains myself to you and my other jailers. No, you demand that I carry on for another, taking up lines stolen from someone who shared my misfortune. Let me tell you right now: it can't be done. Nothing I have written up until now has served to explain myself. I have no choice but to assume – given that I find myself imprisoned and my death imminent – that there is no hope my prose will ever come close to what I am. How, then, am I to write something that isn't *mine*?

Relentless nausea, as well as indifference, prevented me from delivering these pages to you on your last visit. It's no easy matter, fantasizing behind bars. And it is even more arduous to resign oneself to doing so beneath the light of this lamp, and over the smooth surface of this table, which illuminated and supported Gustavo López in vain. I cannot help but consider it an unwholesome presage, Doctor, your furnishing me with these implements, while revealing to me at the same time their former owner's identity: a friend murdered in some adjoining cell.

My father taught me that using another man's personal items, or occupying his recently vacated seat, can prove to be inconvenient. A shameful sensation overwhelms me every time I see that circle of light over the table, Doctor: that of a toilet seat still warm. I said I felt nauseous, but actually what I feel is hatred. Because even once you've discovered that my being here is all wrong, an aberration, you will still deliver me up to the firing squad or, at any rate, you won't lift a finger to keep them from dragging me before it.

Did you attend Gustavo's execution? Did you look on impassively, serenely, and were you able to smoke a cigar? Did you feel any pain when the volley was fired, even if only that of losing a patient? I force myself to write, still horrified by the heat of the lamp and the sense of the table weighing down my body like a shroud on a cadaver.

I knew Gustavo and, although perhaps he wouldn't have called himself my friend, I can say I esteemed him. When other writers crossed the street to avoid bumping into me, Gustavo alone kept allowing me to buy him beers and hold conversations about Sunday football.

During our first interview, Doctor, you seemed puzzled as to why the man who wrote the national anthem had been arrested. You can gauge, then, the dimension of the surprise and terror that corrode me. I have not been imprisoned, like so many others have, for not believing, but rather for *believing too much*. My conviction and fanaticism are so smooth and so seamless that they have been mistaken for irony.

I can write no more. I hope these lines will serve, at least in part, as a kernel of what you hope to receive.

With the warm greetings of
Ricardo Bach

17 May

The first sign of Bach's hypocrisy was his pathetic reference to Gustavo López. A real man would not have acted grateful as a puppy upon receiving the enemy's attentions or friendship. Thus, from the start, I had the advantage of knowing the utmost depths of the prisoner's mind: he is a lamb in search of affection. His intention has been to portray himself as docile and confused, while at the same time vindicating his militancy, as if such partisanship did not require the kind of virility he seems incapable of showing.

Bach is fair-skinned. His mouth is small and his lips thin. He composes certain gestures of helplessness, shielded by the two deep rings under his eyes, which have moved more than one warder to pity. I suspect they are eager to sodomize him, but the security camera and the guards I have standing watch have thwarted this. Dressed in a prisoner's uniform and without any hair gel available, Bach has had to come up with ways to maintain that genteel veneer he seems so proud of. The tailored suits, the tortoiseshell comb and the polished shoes have been replaced by overalls and work boots, and the characteristic short mane from his portraits has given way to a crew cut.

He welcomes me with gleeful gesticulations and shadows me like a lapdog, offering me a seat with a lordly and effeminate gesture that I find humiliating: as if I were an old lady being waited on. He sits down on the cell's straw mattress and smokes the cigarettes I have provided with childlike zest.

His answers are precise. He has turned out to be so thorough that I find myself reining him in. Gustavo López, back when I treated him, would let the cinder of his tobacco fall to the ground, and his greatest show of hygiene consisted of reuniting it by stomping out the butt with his shoe. Bach makes an effort, in contrast, to keep the floor of his cell spotless and has procured (perhaps via some warder who has grown fond of his winking grey eyes) a broom, a dustpan and a basket he uses to rid himself of every last molecule of ash.

I have visited him three times. His courtesy is so intensely elaborate, I have begun to entertain the theory that he is mocking us. How else to explain the atrocious 'Ode to My Jailer's Phallus' that he handed in together with his first report and that I have resisted including in this notebook?

On the other hand, Bach seems to possess an endless supply of items that are difficult for others to come by. His cot is covered by a wool blanket, instead of a urine-soaked sheet. Every time I hand him pen and paper, he stores them with joyous gestures next to other provisions he keeps in a lacquered wooden box. He has even offered me coffee and, to my surprise, revealed a metallic pot, filter and all, that he then proceeded to heat. I haven't gone so far as to denounce his privileges to my superiors, but if I have truly eliminated (or at least obstructed) any possibility of his obtaining such items through clandestine embraces, only mesmerism can explain the prison staff's apparently blind obedience to him.

Bach seems animated, despite the puerile despair with which he writes. A single glance at his works (*Virilities* being his most demented title: a cantata to an astronaut who has been reproduced through cloning in order to conquer the universe, and who celebrates his career every step of the way with orgies during which he copiously mates with copies of himself) has awakened in me the kind of antipathy I hadn't felt for years. I comprehend why, according to his confession, other writers in the city would cross the street when they saw him. I comprehend why his co-religionists hastened to put him in jail. A man like Ricardo Bach ought to be hanged.

19 May

Cherished Doctor,

Woe and fear have not subsided, despite our enlightened and pacifying talks. I have dreamed of a band of fierce priests, their garments spotted like jaguar skins, leading me to a mountain of fire and tossing me, naked, into its steaming maw. And yet I have also dreamed that an old man of amazing agility throws himself in after me at the last moment and manages to bring me safely ashore. What meaning might this dream have, Doctor? Perhaps there is someone kind enough to circumvent my destruction, before the final hour tolls in the bell tower of my life? I wish you were here with me now, Doctor. I would feel more at ease in your presence, the most consoling by far that has populated these, my final days.

Awaiting you impatiently,
Ricardo Bach

20 May

Bach's insinuations trouble me. Not because I see myself being compelled, like a small bird under a serpent's spell, to rush over to his cell and possess him. No: I am certain that this imbecile is mocking us, and I need to determine how we shall crush him. Gustavo López delivered the required texts with sincerity and thus his perdition was consummated. But subduing a shifty character like Bach will require more subtle stratagems.

Perhaps my initial judgement was mistaken and this is no lamb we are holding captive, but rather a jackal. Thus, our first step should be to withdraw all dispensations and substitute them with other, less convenient ones. He shall have no wool blanket, but rather a pink down quilt. He shall not sport a prison uniform, but be compelled to dress in a T-shirt and short pants, like a boy. He shall have no pen and paper, but rather a machine that allows us to view his rough drafts. We shall maintain the toilet in his cell in a state of indefinite repair, permitting but one daily visit to the restroom used by the general prison population. For the time being, all lights will be turned off at Federal Penitentiary Number One at night, except for those illuminating Ricardo Bach's cell.

29 May

Doctor,

The most wretched of your patients now writes to you. I know I mustn't blame you for the humiliations that have been inflicted on me, since your mission is to facilitate my healing. That is why I turn to you, to beg that I be provided with only the basic implements that are enjoyed by other inmates of this prison. I do not want these children's clothes that they compel me to use, nor this effeminate quilt they have placed on my bed. I understand that my coffee-maker must have seemed like an extravagance, but substituting it with a hand-lotion dispenser defies all comprehension. The cold light burns my eyes, Doctor, and the lack of a toilet, given that mine is still out of order after nine days of repairs, has caused me to suffer unspeakable torments. If I haven't written on the machine provided for me, it isn't out of suspicion, my dear friend, but rather because my deteriorated health and mood have prevented me from doing so. Help me so that my creature comforts may be reinstated, or at least let me be treated like everyone else, and ask the guards to remove the posters of small animals and scented soaps from my cell. If someone were to come to my aid, I guarantee that precious, or at least curious, information will be placed at his disposal regarding the men held captive in this prison: news of the kind I tend to learn in the yard, which for the time being I am reluctant to visit, dressed like a child, or like a victim facilitating aggression (I remain in my cell unless they bully me into leaving by kicking me in the stomach, something that has already occurred). I know, for example, that the prisoners have a special nickname for you, the pronunciation of which demeans you while elevating their own corroded wit. Come to my cell, ensure that my toilet and coffee-maker

are reinstalled and my prison uniform returned to me, and
I promise I will be your faithful ally in this prison, your eyes
and ears in the yard and your tireless examiner of hallways.

Tremulously yours,
Ricardo Bach

4 June

I found Bach emaciated, but my arrival revived him considerably.
He has informed me that through my intervention – he seems to
believe that I am indeed capable of what I am capable of, a feature
none too common among the inmates – his clothing has been returned
to him and his toilet now functions, at least during most of the day.
I have given orders that three hours pass between his evacuations
and any possibility of flushing, so that his dungeon might acquire the
distinctive smell of human shit that greeted me upon arrival.

I provide him with cigarettes and personally bestow a new
coffee-maker on him. Before he can ask, I offer an explanation for
my absence: convalescence from the flu. Before I can continue, he
scrabbles around among the personal items he keeps in his lacquered
box and hands me some petrified cough lozenges. Seeing me
contemplate his gift mistrustfully, he snatches it away and smashes
the package against the table three or four times, until the pieces have
come apart and are rendered edible.

Submissively, he remains silent until, direct and to the point, I
interrogate him regarding my nickname. He blushes and begins to
relate the details of every conversation between prisoners over the
past week: the whispering about guard brutality, the murmuring
against the bad food, the meaningless disquisitions regarding what
does or does not take place on the outside. One madman swears that
the explosions heard at night are caused by bombs with which his
comrades intend to break him out of prison. I take note and then

complain that he has not revealed the nickname to me as promised. He smiles. 'Don't force me to show my hand, Doctor. Allow me to retain that innocuous fact for the time being, until I am able to make some confirmations.'

Ricardo Bach is fairly attractive, for a queer.

10 June

Doctor,

I have reread the pages written by Gustavo López that you have so kindly provided me with. I fear that my rhetoric will prove useless for the mission you have asked of me. Resuming a draft of alien prose, especially when the underlying motivation is an intimate confession, lies beyond my interest and, I suspect, my capacity. I still tremble whenever I recall Gustavo's execution. I imagine the sensations overtaking him: the chest inflated with blood, phlegm and gunpowder; the extinguished breath. Continuing to write someone else's confession is tantamount to a violation, like the rape of another's experience. It is a confiscation and a betrayal. Unless, of course, I were to convert Gustavo López's sentimental manuscript into that of Ricardo Bach's, an even trickier text, given that confidence has never been a theme that interests me and naturally, therefore, repels my style. You are insistent, Doctor, and threaten to return my apron and slippers to me – garments, by the way, that you formerly denied having anything to do with. You indulge in watching me from the other end of the security camera that records my imprisonment and ask me, as incessantly as a mosquito, for the nickname ascribed to you. Given that you represent my last hope, which is, in the end, the only one allowed within the narrow scope of a condemned man, I will endeavour to satisfy you. Run, upon reading this message, to the monitor where you are accustomed to analysing me, turn on the machine that reports my words to you and, sooner rather than later, you shall find the required lines. Do not ask for more: I don't find myself capable of giving you the satisfaction more than once.

Exhausted,
Bach

12 June

He suffers. Or at least so it seems, contemplating him through the camera. But Bach is an actor. Tomorrow we shall see if the results are as desired. Each text he snatches from his delirium will modify, disavow and permanently erase Gustavo López's; each one will become either his equal or his caricature. He will be stripped of all dignity and idiosyncrasy, and Gustavo López will have died, delectably, for a second time.

13 June

On the machine, in lieu of the requested information, I find a text filled with insults addressed to my own dear mother, which Bach attributes to me. Fucking queer.

18 June

I have been told that, before his arrest, Bach was highly regarded among the scribblers of the faculty: they were the principal and virtually the sole consumers of his writing. Perhaps it is in light of this minimal success that his attitude has become so extremely arrogant and brusque. Following the prank he played on me, I had him beaten, after which he refused to see me on two separate occasions: they must have convinced him blow by blow.

I perceive, upon returning to his cell, that he is in full decline. He can't be more than thirty, but the physical deterioration inflicted by prison is notorious. His clothing hangs from his skinny arms and bunches up over his sunken chest. His mop of hair falls out by the handful, and his girlish face continually displays the grimace of acid reflux. One of his eyes has been swollen shut by a bruise and his gums bleed, perhaps from poor hygiene, perhaps from the beating that has left him prostrate on the straw mattress. I offer him a cigarette and this small tribute softens any haughtiness that remains. He leaps at it, then puffs with satisfaction.

The first thing he says is that he has had a lot of experience as the patient of psychologists, so at this final juncture he is nonplussed at having to deal with one more. He answers the new questionnaire in a slow, firm hand, poorly writ, but comprehensible. I attempt to interrogate him about his works, but he resists. Now, he states, nothing matters. He confesses that he has yearningly dedicated himself to the task of winning over his fellow prisoners as an audience for future readings. I, who have come prepared with a few disquisitions demonstrating the unbearable morbidity of his case, decide to believe in this sham redemption and take a different tack.

After another cigarette and a pledge to bring him books, I secure his promise to get back to work. Before I can take my leave, he approaches me and corrects me once again: 'Politics is something that has always been alien to me, that I have limited myself to contemplating. Destiny is what landed me in jail, Doctor. And I wish to write about that, because it will explain me better than a thousand manifestos.'

I comprehend that Bach has decided to forgo his defensive posturing in the hope that his death penalty will be rescinded. In order to encourage him to start immediately, I give him the rest of the cigarettes and instruct that he be provided with paper and a set of ballpoint pens instead of a computer. He smiles, exposing his reddened gums. I feel certain that he will take advantage of these sheets to write against me.

If for no other offence, his kind ought to be imprisoned for ingratitude.

21 June

Following the gift of cigarettes, Bach has ceded a few sheets to me written in a delinquent, reflective style that has little to do with his youthful works. In desperation he insists that, given enough time and paper (he takes the cigarettes for granted, something I continue to find revealing), the rewrite may be accomplished.

'I'm a disgrace, Doctor. I'll bet you haven't diagnosed this in your reports, but I'm a butcher, a vulgar man. I don't ask to be freed. I want only to be treated. Forget my circumstantial (out of ignorance) opposition (or at least that's what I've been ordered to think) to the government and remember that I am a man who has suffered.'

I fail to understand how he can deliver such solemn speeches without losing that little grin, the blood streaming from his gums, cleaned every now and then by that thin pair of lips as if they were windscreen wipers on a car.

I stress that his death sentence cannot be altered under any circumstances by my intervention, that the power to rescind the sentences of inmates has been denied me, even if I declare them to be insane. He receives this information without bowing his head or losing his composure.

'I'm not asking you for my life, Doctor, but for enough time to put down on paper what I've learned, what I hold in my head right now. Not words that escape meaning: pure meaning, pure reflection. Don't deny me this.'

I give him more cigarettes and tell him that I would be interested, of course, in reading one or two chapters in his hand. Once he feels sure of himself, once his style starts to improve and the smile on that horrendous mouth becomes more sincere, I will deliver him, hands bound, to his executioners, and I will keep his unfinished work, beautiful as an armless statue.

Perhaps he senses my machinations, because as I am preparing to leave, he remarks, 'Do you know what they call you in the prison yard, Doctor?'

I show my lack of interest in the affair by departing immediately. His laughter chases me down the hall.

What they call you? What they call you?

23 June

I congratulate Bach on his work so far and promise he will have enough time to complete the rest. He looks satisfied as he lights a cigarette and adjusts his glasses. (How did the wretch get his hands on glasses?) He claims the low light we've provided has given him headaches and a severe eye irritation that camomile has failed to alleviate. I ignore how he was able to get tea in this prison, impervious to all human needs, but I suspect the warders. I ask him if one of the guards has ever assaulted him. He responds with a guffaw that displaces for an instant the mask of affability that he assumes before me, revealing the dark depths of his contempt.

'No, Doctor. My flesh, as you can see, is weak and can no longer be found appetizing. If my ability to obtain camomile concerns you, I can tell you that, in exchange, I had to give up some of the cigarettes that you have so attentively provided. The partner in this trade was another inmate, a professor with whom I converse sometimes. We sunbathe together. It is innocuous traffic and I trust that you won't denounce him. I have friends among the prisoners.'

I ask him how many. He laughs.

'I have friends, Doctor.'

I assume he has improvised this story, since there are no such friends or strolls or professors with camomile bursting out of their pockets. Bach's intention is that I order an electric light to be installed in his dungeon, or perhaps even a chair where he might compose in comfort – he now writes lying on his cot, which makes his handwriting excessively shaky.

I am anxious to leaf through his pages. I order that he be given an extra ration of tea. He must have perceived the irony, because he smiles. Now that I think of it, he hasn't stopped smiling.

24 June

I must confess: Bach's pages interest me. Even more so after confirming, thanks to the travails of a pair of agents who were commissioned for the task, that they do contain some truth about his life.

But enough. I cannot allow myself the luxury of ceding such privileges and concessions to a prisoner. Hundreds or thousands more await me. I lament never reaching the end of his adventures, but if we want to break him – and we do – now is the time.

The first thing he notices is that I haven't brought him cigarettes. His smile becomes, perhaps, more forced. But it doesn't wane. Behind me, two guards enter the cell, carrying the table and the lamp. Bach is, one might say, euphoric. When I confiscate his sheets of paper, he starts laughing with pleasure.

'I see, Doctor, that our agreement has come to an end. Some nights I thought you might actually allow me to finish, or even be capable of sending my texts abroad. There, someone could publish me, and my name wouldn't be lost forever, like waste in a sewer. I can only laugh. I suppose you aren't coming back, and I will remain here, forever silenced. But you blink. So, I will be taken before the firing squad. I see. You might think, my friend, that I shouldn't have wasted my time. My answer is that I was merely taking stock of my resources. This circumstance, death, will not detain my evolution. Even now, I'm thinking of phrases and chapters that exist only because I conceive of them. Posterity is a realm that doesn't belong to me.'

Annoyed by this diatribe, I bid him farewell. Bach nods and extends his hand, which I shake vehemently.

Upon hearing the bars close and the lock biting into its tail, I gloat. I return to my office and my dinner, my waltzes and tonight's file. To the certainty that we have silenced a man before his words could save him.

What a pity: I'm in no mood to read files.

While dining on my oatmeal I review, joylessly, the brief pages by Ricardo Bach that I shall keep forever incomplete and concealed.

At dawn, there's a knock at my door.

I have to admit it. I didn't expect to see him there, wearing that smile. ■

GRANTA

GERARDO'S LETTERS

Elvira Navarro

TRANSLATED BY NATASHA WIMMER

ELVIRA NAVARRO
SPAIN
1978

Navarro, born in Huelva, published her first book, *La ciudad en invierno* (2007). In 2009 she published *La ciudad feliz*, which won the Jaén Prize for best novel and the Tormenta Prize for best new author. She has collaborated with magazines including *El Cultural*, *Ínsula*, *Turia* and *El Perro* as well as the newspapers *Público* and *El País*. She teaches writing workshops and has her own blog (www.elviranavarro. wordpress.com), as well as Periferia (www.madridesperiferia. blogspot.com), a work in progress about the neighbourhoods of Madrid that explores peripheral and undefined spaces through writing. 'Gerardo's Letters' is an excerpt from her novel in progress.

Two roads, separated by half a mile of wasteland, flank the hostel, and I suggest that we cross over to see whether we can find some patch of countryside, but Gerardo says it's late, we'd better explore the fields. We walk straight ahead until it's completely dark, and we return guided by the lights of the hostel and the cars. We can't even see our sneakers, and looking down produces a kind of dread, as if we were about to plunge into the void or step on a nest of scorpions. When we reach the basketball courts I instruct Gerardo to hold my ankles while I do sit-ups. The ground is cold and it's hard to bend; having Gerardo crouching in front of me, with his head brushing against my knees, begins to seem unpleasant, and I stop at what seems a reasonable limit for a beginner. I feel absurd and it occurs to me that this is the nature of couplehood: the abjection of observing and participating in the other person's obsessions. Like my sit-ups at ten at night on the dark basketball court of a hostel a mile from Talavera. Maybe there's something positive about this that I've lost sight of, or maybe this foolishness applies only to defunct couples, like me and Gerardo, who claim that everybody else in the world takes such things for granted. 'You're crazy,' he tells me when I try to explain what I mean, and then I feel this craziness of mine as a searing loneliness, even real madness. When I'm with him I lose my sense of judgement, and since Gerardo is the keeper of reason, I suddenly fear that without him I won't be able to function in the world.

We get to the dining room just as they're about to put the trays away. It's not even eleven; we ask an old woman in a net cap why they're closing so early. The old woman says that if we wanted to eat late we should've stayed at a hotel. The menu: shrivelled peas with something that looks like York ham but turns out to be chopped cold cuts, and breaded cutlets in perfect ovals whose greasy coating hides some kind of processed chicken. All I eat are the peas. The chopped meat and the processed chicken are the same pale pink colour. 'The cutlets are raw,' says Gerardo. At a big table the girl from last night is talking to three boys of about the same age, who must be the other high-school students. They've finished eating, and they're smoking, flicking their ash on the tray; then they put out their cigarettes in what's left of the peas. The girl doesn't look at us.

'I'm going to shower,' I tell Gerardo as we enter the room. I take my robe, toiletry bag and flip-flops out of my duffel bag, and when I'm about to open the door Gerardo says:

'You can get undressed here. I won't touch you.'

I undress with my back to him. I'm conscious of his efforts to communicate his lust; it registers as a disagreeable weight on the back of my neck that makes me get tangled up in my trousers and fall down. I stand up and leave wearing my robe over my bra and T-shirt. Fortunately the hot water works and I stand under the shower head, which spits out water in fits and starts, until my fingers are wrinkled and the bathroom mirror is steamy. I don't want to go back to the room; I pace back and forth, opening the doors of the shower stalls, where those little black bugs that seem to inhabit every dank place collect. I make a racket with the doors and stir up the bugs; a whole swarm ends up flying around the mirror, which is dripping with water. My feet are cold and I decide to get in the shower again, but the sides of the stalls are covered with insects now and I don't have the strength to shoo them away. I go back to the room. Gerardo is lying in bed masturbating, with his pants around his ankles. He doesn't look at me. I gather up my clothes as fast as I can and, trailing the cord of the hairdryer, I leave the room before he comes.

I return to the bathroom; the insects have retreated to the nooks and crannies of the showers and are now undetectable. I'm afraid there won't be any outlets; if there aren't, I can go to the TV room and dry my hair there. I imagine the four high-school students sprawled on the vinyl sofas, watching a celebrity survival show.

Asking the high-school students for permission to make a noise with my hairdryer while they watch their show doesn't seem very appealing; and yet I'm determined not to go back to the room, even if Gerardo thinks the creepy gnome of a hostel manager has chopped me into bits and stuffed me in the pool-bar freezer. This is a good moment for us to break up once and for all: at six in the morning, while he's asleep, I'll go up for my duffel bag and call a taxi. A break-up plan like this might be out of the question for another couple without involving the police and having the hostel searched for the vanished loved one; but Gerardo and I have become accustomed to bad behaviour and extravagant gestures. If I decide to spend the day hanging upside down from a tree, he'll leave me there, though he might tell me twenty times that I'm a nut. This is another one of the things that, until a year ago, made leaving him unthinkable, because I hate normal life, and in some sense and despite the awfulness, with Gerardo I seem to be safe from a certain kind of normality. With him, through the process of taking everything to the limit – rage, contemplation, disgust – I attain a kind of exasperated life and I'm convinced that this exasperation must violently propel me somewhere.

Luckily there are outlets in the bathroom. I've forgotten my comb and try to untangle my hair with my fingers. Finally I settle for smoothing the top layer and the fringe; the climate in Talavera isn't dry enough to make my hair straight, though maybe that has nothing to do with Talavera but with the dampness of the hostel, and, specifically, the microclimate of the showers, the strange miasma that rises from the tiles and smells like a mixture of plumbing and swamp. The incipient dreadlocks make my hair stand straight out and then fall, like a crinoline, though what bothers me most is not having my eyelash curler or my green eye-pencil to revive at least some feature, a revival that might incline me towards a kinder appraisal of myself. I come out of the bathroom with the hairdryer; I have to pass the door of the room to get to the stairs and I walk on tiptoe. Gerardo must have been listening for me because when I reach the first landing he opens the door. I start to run; at the reception desk, I stop. I'm euphoric.

'Natalia?' says Gerardo from two floors above. I don't answer.

'Natalia, is that you?' he repeats, and my euphoria turns to pity. Not being able to console him with a 'Yes, it's me; I've gone downstairs for coffee from the machine,' makes me want to cry. And it makes me want to cry that I can't find a middle ground between my joy on the stairs and my sympathy for his loneliness, for his confusion and trust in me despite everything. No, I say to myself, I shouldn't take pleasure in having run away instead of saying 'It's over', in having treated him without the least bit of respect, the kind of respect that involves being able to get along on the most basic level, that involves talking things out rather than gleefully fleeing as if he were a leper and I were made powerful by revealing his abjectness to him. We've spent nine years losing respect for each other but pretending to understand the most important things. Nevertheless, I walk on, not caring whether I make a noise or not, or if he's coming down the stairs and will see me walk away for the second time.

I go into the TV room. It's empty. It's Saturday; how could I not have realized that the high-school kids would almost certainly be out in Talavera tonight. At one end of the room is the PC the girl talked about, and when I see it I feel the faint urge to check my mail, the sense that simply by virtue of not having visited my in-box all day, an urgent message is waiting for me. I sit down and push the power button; I hope no password is needed, since the last thing I feel like doing now is going in search of the gnome. The PC takes a while to start, and it's so cold that I plug in the hairdryer and rest it on the edge of the keyboard as once again I curse Gerardo and at the same time feel sad because everything is full of his opinions, which have become my own. Now I'm censuring myself for the eagerness with which I wait for access to cyberspace, and this censure is him telling me he can't stand people who don't know how to live without the Internet.

Four irrelevant emails await me. I write to a couple of friends, and then I log on to Messenger, but on a Saturday at 12.30 everybody has better things to do than to chat. I need to do something; huddled here in this crappy hostel with the hairdryer resting on my left instep, I don't know whether I'll be able to stand the strain of the wait. And yet leaving my hideout means facing Gerardo, since he's the one roaming around the hostel, he's the one who's gone outside to sit in the grass and smoke a joint.

A bright fluorescent light shines from the pool bar, and I know Gerardo sits there with the gnome. The light wipes out any semblance of the intimacy of night, and when I cross the threshold I feel as if I'm about to be subjected to an interrogation. I'm dressed, but at this hour and in the presence of the gnome and Gerardo, it's as if I were naked; I feel as if all my thoughts are revealed, and I don't have the strength to turn away. At one end of the bar, sitting at a table, two high-school students are drinking beer. Gerardo and the gnome are drinking too, and Gerardo is smoking a joint. He looks distraught, and I know he's completely absorbed in the conversation. Even so, he can't help saying to me:

'The TV room doesn't belong to you. Those kids probably wanted to watch a movie.'

The high-school students show no sign of having heard him. They're adolescents, and they don't give two shits about anything. Their eyes are red; I suppose Gerardo has already passed them a few joints. The noise of the hairdryer has kept me utterly ignorant of the night-time goings-on at the hostel, which is the kind of spot that Gerardo and I like to frequent: a strange place, with no music, where the possibility exists of acquiring some kind of unusual knowledge or experience (usually sordid), the kind of place that's part of the life on the edge that I mentioned before. Here is where I think I discover – in a different way to Gerardo, since he keeps his feet more firmly planted on the ground – something very valuable that I can't get anywhere else, and for which I need Gerardo. Without a loving hand to guide me to these haunts, which I'm unable to give up, I feel lost. I ask the gnome for a Mahou; he points at the refrigerator, which annoys me. I can't find the opener, but I don't want to ask for it; I search on the bar, where there are piles of glasses, cups and spoons. Gerardo reaches over and hands it to me; he's probably been holding it all this time as he watched me.

'Thanks,' I say. He doesn't answer. He's nodding at something that the gnome is telling him about how to fix a cistern, something that requires the engagement of every single one of his brain cells. I stand behind the bar until I finish the beer and get another one; then I come out and I don't know what to do next. There are two doors to the bar, one that leads to the reception area and one that leads outside. I don't know whether the second door is open, but luckily the key is in the lock. I go over and push the door softly in order not to attract attention. My push is so gentle that nothing happens, and I turn the key hard both ways, which leaves a mark on my skin. I have no choice but to press my body against the cold metal of the door to see if the lock will give. In the stillness of the bar, where the high-school students are talking in whispers or not talking at all, and where Gerardo and the gnome look like two actors on a stage, my movements remind me of the woman who works at a cheap restaurant where we're regulars. This woman swears as she waits on tables, cursing as if she were praying, her voice rising and falling. Her mad litany and the tap of her heels interrupt the murmur of the diners, who sometimes laugh but usually ignore the poor lady's verbal incontinence; she, meanwhile, carries on normal conversations between obscenities, managing things so that no one is offended, or maybe not needing to manage things, since the voice that shits on everyone's mother is different from the one in which she holds normal conversations, as if she had a demon lodged in her throat.

At last I manage to open the door, and I hurry out without looking back; I have the feeling that I won't dare to return, though my beer is already half finished. I'm drinking at a dizzying speed; I want to settle as soon as possible into that pleasant state of alcoholic equanimity that will allow me to stroll blithely in front of Gerardo and the gnome, as well as the high-school students, since now I can't avoid my inclination to humiliate myself in order to be taken back again. It's also possible that my compulsive drinking, and my belief that when I'm drunk I'm going to saunter around boldly, actually conceals my desire to submit to Gerardo and, through him, to be welcomed into the world. Gerardo has already won everyone over, and I noticed what a dirty look the gnome gave me for not sticking with my boyfriend, for showing that I'm not worthy of the nice guy who's sucking up to him on a Saturday night at his hostel.

Under the effect of the first two beers, I'm off to get my third. I float towards the bar; the opener is in my power, though that doesn't matter any more because Gerardo, the gnome and the students have moved on to G&Ts. The students are carrying on an animated conversation now and the buzz has cleared the air, so I venture to sit on the billiards table. I've left the door open and the cold night air filters into the bar and stirs up the smoke from the joints and the cigarettes, carrying it upward before it's dispersed. For a moment, I have the impression that small clumps of fog are brimming from the ceiling.

The gnome looks at me and the disapproval has vanished from his face, giving way to a repulsive desire. I fix him with a look of disgust. Gerardo notices his buddy's behaviour and hesitates; turning his back on him means being left defenceless, but remaining by his side makes him uncomfortable. The gnome has drunk enough not to detect the change in Gerardo; I suppose he thinks that since we're fighting and Gerardo has grown strong in his company, he can treat me any way he likes. Impossible to hint subtly to him that he's making a mistake, that Gerardo is already getting ready to give him the boot, even if what awaits him is a confrontation with me in the room. I get up and grab four beers to get me through the fight. I tell the gnome:

'Put it on our bill.'

Meanwhile, Gerardo swallows what's left of his gin and tonic and gets up, shaking the gnome's hand distastefully. The gnome whispers an obscenity and points at me, and then he laughs. Gerardo doesn't reply. The little man is confused and mutters a curse.

We return to the room and the first thing I do is grab my brush and jerk it through the knots at the nape of my neck. Meanwhile, Gerardo opens a Mahou, smokes a joint, goes to the bathroom to brush his teeth. I've plugged in the hairdryer again; I don't care if I wake up the couple next door. When Gerardo comes back I'm curling my eyelashes and putting on eyeliner. He doesn't say anything; he even seems to understand my belated primping in preparation for what awaits us, and once he understands that I'm preparing to leave, and once I understand it too – since at first I don't know why I have this compulsion to fix myself up, to brush out the snarl of knots at last and look pretty in the mirror with my made-up eyes – we feel sad. It's four in the morning; I tell him that I'm going to take a beer for the road, and will he please come downstairs with me, because I'm scared of the gnome. I put sixty euros on his bed, which is quite a bit more than we owe at the hostel; he takes it because he's short of money. I call a taxi on my cellphone. There's no one at the bar any more and it smells of the hash that Gerardo has been sharing with the high-school students. The taxi takes half an hour to come; it's terrible torture, and we cry. A white van appears, similar to the gnome's, though with a regulation light. The taxi driver looks at us as if someone had stabbed a family member and we were on our way to identify him; when he sees that Gerardo is staying and that we're wishing each other luck, he starts to look less concerned, and I begin to adore his easy manner; suddenly he strikes me as incredibly healthy and alive, and I'm so happy that this is the mood in which I'll be conveyed from the hostel to the train station, on this night that's almost as dark as the night before, and in which all that's visible are the highway stripes. ■

GRANTA

THE BONFIRE AND THE CHESSBOARD

Matías Néspolo

TRANSLATED BY FRANK WYNNE

MATÍAS NÉSPOLO
ARGENTINA
1975

Néspolo, born in Buenos Aires, currently works as a journalist and
lives in Barcelona, on the shores of the Mediterranean, with his
three daughters, his wonderful wife and a dog called Jonás. In 2005,
he published his first collection of poems, *Antología seca de Green
Hills*, and in the following years several short stories in various
anthologies. The latest anthology, *Schiffe aus Feuer: 36 Geschichten
aus Lateinamerika* (2010), was published in Germany. In 2009, he
edited an anthology with his sister, Jimena Néspolo, *La erótica de
relato: Escritores de la nueva literatura argentina*, and published his first
novel, *Siete maneras de matar a un gato*. which will also be published
in English as *Seven Ways to Kill a Cat* (2011). 'The Bonfire and the
Chessboard' is an excerpt from his novel in progress.

I
THE BONFIRE

The first thing 'El Tano' Castiglione did when he landed was to burn the papers. He had arrived on the island at dusk, and by the time the ferryboat had disappeared around the bend of the river, he had clambered down from the jetty and dumped the contents of his backpack on to the muddy riverbank. He made a few quick swipes, rescuing the food, what few clothes he'd brought, a couple of books and a blank notepad. The rest he torched with the match he used to light his cigarette.

The night was drawing in quickly now and the impromptu bonfire might give him away. El Tano kicked the charred papers with the toe of his boot, poked the fire to let it breathe. Flecks of ash rose through the smoke like black butterflies. He let his mind wander, following the larger pieces of char as they fluttered out over the water. The sky was veering now from purple to black. As he tossed his cigarette butt on to the remains of the fire, he remembered that his own papers were among the burning documents and, against his will, he let out a wild laugh. A dog barked at something, somewhere out between the islands. El Tano's laugh died with the last tongue of blue flame. He stamped out the embers, not angrily or resentfully. Methodically. Ashen butterflies exploded into tiny moths, taking wing.

He slung the backpack over his shoulder and plunged between the willows, following the bare grass track that led from the jetty. He moved swiftly and easily. In the distance, he could make out the cabin raised on stilts about a metre and a half off the ground. A boat hung from the eaves. This was a detail he hadn't expected, and it made him wonder if this was 'El Negro' Brizuela's place. The island had no name. But he knew the name of the tributary that branched off just past *el remanso del Irlandés*. El Tano had disembarked at the second jetty upriver. The first jetty was nothing more than a couple of tree stumps. Washed away by the river, the ferryman had said. Besides, from Brizuela's directions, which El Tano had been conscientiously repeating to himself, this had to be the right island. But seeing the boat hanging from the eaves, he began to wonder. El Negro hadn't said anything about a boat. It was logical: without a boat, anyone coming up river would be completely cut off. But it was the kind of logic you expected from a practical man. And El Negro was not practical. Quite the opposite.

El Tano climbed the ladder to the shack cautiously, as though at any moment he might be run off with a shotgun. He reached up and ran his hand along the lintel, a rough-hewn beam that jutted out an inch or two above the door. The key was there. Just like Brizuela had said. But something was wrong. There was no chain, no padlock. The door was open. He nudged it gently with his foot and slipped the key back where he had found it.

The sound of footsteps made his skin prickle. The place was in darkness.

'Roberto! Hey! What are you doing here?'

El Tano hesitated. The rasp of a match broke the silence, its flame outlining the slim figure of a girl lighting a kerosene lamp. She turned the wick down so it wouldn't smoke, slipped the tulip-glass shade into place and hung it on a nail.

'Don't just stand there, come in . . .' she said, pushing a lock of hair behind her ear.

'I'm not Roberto. You've got me mixed up with someone else.'

The girl stared at him, puzzled. She opened her mouth but no words came out. El Tano stepped inside and set down his backpack. He would be spending the night here anyway. He had no choice.

'What are you being like that for? It's Vero. Don't you recognize me?'

She curled her lip in an expression of reproach. She had full, well-defined lips and a long, thin, freckled face. El Tano looked her up and down, racking his brain – nothing. He'd never seen this girl before; if he had he would remember. She obviously had him confused with someone else. He considered playing along but something in her eyes stopped him. Her pupils were like shards of graphite sunken in the honey of a pair of magnificent eyes which, despite their colour, had not a hint of sweetness about them.

'We know each other?' El Tano gently tested the water.

'You're freaking me out, Roberto,' she said softly. 'What's the matter with you?'

If this was all an act, the girl had talent. El Tano tried to twist his mouth into something he hoped was a smile but it froze halfway in an expression of irritation. Or disgust. Half-heartedly, he started checking out the shack.

'Nothing's the matter,' he said. 'Just tired, is all.'

The reply had been instinctive, unthinking, but as he heard himself say the words, he felt goosebumps, as though he were taking on this other man's identity without resisting. He hadn't planned to play along but he was doing it anyway. It didn't matter. Right now it suited him to be someone else. Anyway, if this girl wanted to think he was Roberto, or Juan de los Palotes, he couldn't stop her.

The cabin was clean and had everything he might need to hole up for a while. There was a wooden dining table and three rickety chairs. A counter ran along one wall with a small gas stove on it and shelves above with pots, pans, canned food and some candles. Next to the counter, under the small window, was a sink with an old-fashioned hand-cranked pump. He worked the handle vigorously and fresh water spilled out. He bent down, drank from the spigot and splashed his face. The girl handed him the towel hanging on a nail by the window. She smiled. El Tano took the towel without a word. Her eyes still bothered him.

At the far end of the cabin were a couple of cushions – burlap sacks – scattered around a wooden crate that served as a coffee table. On the table was a block of cheese, three sticks of bread, an open bottle of wine and a rolled-up piece of sheet music. He kicked one of the sacks. It was soft, clearly stuffed with wool or rags because the kick made no sound.

Ignoring the girl's stare, he pulled back the curtain to the bedroom: a worm-eaten wardrobe; a wooden pallet with a double mattress; a rumpled blanket. Night was beginning to leach though the open window. He could hear bugs bouncing off the window-screen. He was about to wander back out of the bedroom when he noticed a dark rectangular shape against the peeling planks.

'What are you looking for?' the girl asked, pulling back the curtain.

'Nothing special. Why? You hiding something?'

The girl just laughed. By the glow from the living room El Tano examined the dark rectangle. It was a photograph. Five or six people partying, a celebration of some kind. He recognized only two: the girl and Brizuela, though it took him a minute to recognize El Negro. In the photo he had long hair. It made him look very young.

When he came out of the bedroom, he threw open the door to the bathroom. It was the only place left to check. It wasn't so much a bathroom as an upscale latrine. There was a toilet but no cistern – just a bucket that had to be filled from the hand-cranked pump. A five-gallon can hung from the ceiling with a rubber shower head attached. The drain was a hole in the floorboards. At least there was a shower.

Now that he had given the place the once-over, El Tano decided there was just one problem. A problem that was about five foot ten with a fine pair of legs. Looked at the right way, she wasn't so much a problem as a godsend. A gift. But El Tano wasn't one for such subtleties. He was running out of patience.

'So, who do you take your orders from?' he said abruptly.

'I don't take orders from anyone, *nene*. What's got into you?' The girl shot him a look, putting a pan of water on the stove. 'No one tells me what to do, not since I left home when I was sixteen.'

She talked with a posh, nasal accent. The whole thing was an act.

'So what the fuck are you doing here?'

'Same as you. It's like every question . . . It's like you don't know . . .' Her act was bulletproof. She took a bag of rice and a can of tuna from the shelf. She looked heartbroken; the honey in her eyes seemed about to trickle down her cheeks.

El Tano gave a snort, pushed his backpack against the wall, lit a cigarette and stepped out under the eaves to smoke. He needed to calm down, to think things through. He gripped the railing hard until his arms stopped shaking. His cigarette ash hung, suspended, a coiled grey worm reluctant to drop. It didn't fall until he ripped the cigarette butt from his lips and flicked it into the darkness. He pounded his fist on the belly of the boat. It sounded sturdy. Solid. He stopped for a moment and listened to the concert of the night. A host of noises he could not identify, hushed, overlapping, lulled by the murmur of the river. When the mosquitoes began to feed on him, he went back inside.

'So, how long you been here?' he asked, settling himself on a burlap sack and taking a swig from the bottle of wine.

'We've got glasses,' the girl said. 'Don't be so crude.' She brought a couple over to the coffee table, filled El Tano's and poured a small glass for herself. 'About a week. What day is today?'

'Thursday.'

'I got here exactly ten days ago,' she said, taking a sip and then licking her upper lip.

'So, what do you think?'

'It's really peaceful out here. Like stepping into another dimension. But I guess I've been a bit bored, to be honest.'

El Tano gestured vaguely. Raised his eyebrows, shook his head as though he knew exactly what she meant.

'There's no electricity, which is a bit of a bitch,' she went on. 'I didn't realize. I even brought my laptop, can you believe that?'

'You've got a laptop?'

'Of course. Why?'

'So I'm guessing you're loaded?'

'Jesus, Roberto, please! Don't start with the class struggle shit, I hate it when you do that.' She tugged viciously at the lock of hair she had pushed behind her ear earlier, so it looked like a vertical groove between her eyebrows.

'I'm not starting anything, *nena*. Calm down. Just thinking out loud, is all.'

'You are starting, like you always do. You're just spoiling for a fight.'

El Tano drained his glass and refilled it. She was clearly some rich *hija de papá* and this Roberto guy was probably fucking her. At least they bickered like they were a couple. That much was clear.

He changed the subject, said the first thing that came into his head.

'How often do the ferries run?'

'Four times a day,' the girl said, throwing four handfuls of rice into the saucepan. 'There's one first thing in the morning which is always empty. Then there's the one at noon and another in the afternoon that run the islanders' kids to and from school. Little brats. Always screaming and fighting . . . they're like animals. Then the last ferry is at sunset, the one you came on.'

'You seem to know them all.'

'No, not really, I hardly leave the island,' she said, standing on tiptoe to lean all her weight on the can-opener. 'It's not like I need to. There's a floating shop that comes. It's a bit expensive, but they've got most things.'

She was struggling to open the can of tuna. El Tano sat back, enjoying the sight as she leaned over the table, cursing under her breath. With every thrust of the can-opener, she swayed her ass. It was tight, round, perfect. It defied gravity. Every now and then, she glanced round to see if he was watching her. He started to think maybe she wasn't having trouble opening the can, maybe this was a private show. He lit another cigarette and smoked it down to the end.

El Tano poured himself a little more wine but choked on the first sip.

'What the fuck are you doing with that thing, you crazy bitch?' he spluttered.

The girl was coming towards him with a big kitchen knife. She screwed up her face and stared at him.

'You don't want cheese?' she asked, brandishing the knife, a smile frozen on her lips.

By the time El Tano had stopped coughing, she had cut the cheese with quick, precise movements into a dozen evenly-sized pieces. With a flick of her wrist, she scooped a couple on to the blade and brought it up to his chin, like it was a spoon, the blade turned towards him.

'Have some,' she said.

El Tano cleared his throat, careful not to move his head, and accepted the cheese, fingers trembling. She took the knife away and sliced the bread with the same quick, skilled movements.

'You handle that thing like a pro,' El Tano said. 'I'm not too sure I like that.' His hand hovered, holding the cheese.

'Oh, don't be silly, Roberto,' she said, still holding the knife and squeezing his knee with her free hand before suddenly jumping to her feet. 'Shit, the rice is going to burn.'

El Tano let out his breath, then ate the cheese. The girl took the pan off the burner, turned off the gas and piled the overcooked rice into two bowls. She divided the tuna between the two white mounds of rice and carried the bowls to the table, scooping the bread into a third bowl as she passed.

'Shall we eat?'

El Tano brought over the wine and the glasses. The girl fetched a couple of spoons. El Tano's chair creaked as he went to sit down.

'Here, take that one.' The girl pushed the third chair towards him. 'It's a bit more sturdy.' The rush seat looked frayed and about to give way but the frame and the legs felt more solid.

They ate in silence. As he swallowed the last mouthful, El Tano stretched out his legs with satisfaction.

'You want a little more wine?'

Before he could answer, the girl poured herself a small splash and filled his glass, just as she had done earlier. This was his fourth. If he hadn't had so much wine, all this attention from a stranger would have got on his nerves. Made him suspicious. But by now El

Tano was seeing things very differently. He was no longer edgy. It was as if this was some bizarre drama and he had no choice but to play it out to the end.

'You mind telling me what's so funny?' the girl asked in a neutral tone as though she got the joke but was also reproaching him for something.

'Don't mind me. The wine's gone to my head.' El Tano proffered a cigarette, which she waved away with a look of disgust. He brought one to his own lips and let it dangle there, unlit.

'Now you're a bit more chilled, do you mind if I ask you something?'

'Ask away.'

'Just promise you won't get mad, Roberto . . .' She twisted the unruly lock of hair around her index finger again.

'It all depends, *nena*. I don't know till you ask.'

The girl collected the plates, put them in the sink, pumped some water and left them to soak. Seeing El Tano light his cigarette, she handed him the empty tuna can to use as an ashtray. She sat down again, took a sip of wine and brushed the crumbs off the table with the back of her hand. She was playing for time.

'What were you burning down on the riverbank?' she asked suddenly.

'Nothing. Just garbage.'

'Then why were you laughing like that?' He felt the girl's eyes drill into him again. Cold.

El Tano looked away, took a long drag on his cigarette.

'I wasn't laughing. Maybe it looked like I was.'

'You were laughing, I heard you . . . You see, *you are* acting weird.' She shook her head as though dismissing something obvious, sighed and gave him an exaggerated smile.

El Tano tried to force a laugh but only managed to cough. He reached over to stub out his cigarette in the can. She caught his hand as it hovered in the air.

'Come on, let's go to bed. Or were you planning to sit up and watch TV?'

'Who do you take me for, *nena*?' El Tano replied, jumping to his feet and slipping an arm around her waist, without quite knowing what he was referring to.

II

THE CHESSBOARD

He offers me white and counters with the Scandinavian Defence. It's like he knows. It's my Achilles heel. I can't handle the Scandinavian Defence. Been trying to get my head round it for years and I just can't do it. It's a risky gambit on his part but I can't think of a way to turn it to my advantage. I can never think of a way to develop it, I always get bogged down. Unless the other player makes a serious fuck-up – like El Tano always did – the best I can hope for is a draw. The sort of tedious mind-numbing game where you want to forfeit or resign just to get it over with. And that pisses me off.

Everyone at El Torre Blanca knows I hate it, they know me. Every now and then one of them will open with the Scandinavian Defence just to wind me up. Even though they know they're in for a dirty drawn-out game. They know that there's no way I'm going to let them get away with it. But they do it anyway. Just to piss me off. Ruin my day.

And now this son of a bitch I don't know from Adam is trying to fuck with my head. Worse, the guy doesn't even look up from the board. He makes like he's concentrating, like he needs to think about his every move when he's playing straight out of a textbook. What does he take me for, a moron?

I look over the guy's head at Bruno who's shitting himself laughing. I make a face like I'm asking who the fuck is this guy but Bruno shrugs, sticks out his bottom lip, eyes wide, and shakes his head. He obviously hasn't got a clue. Neither do I. First time I've seen him in here, that much I do know. Just one look at him and you know he's as out of place as a lollipop up someone's ass. Smart suit and tie, hair slicked back, white shirt, cufflinks. Neatly folded handkerchief sticking out of his jacket pocket. All he needs is a carnation in his buttonhole. The guy's actually wearing a Rolex, and it doesn't look like a knock-off. Just look at the way he picks up his bishop . . . And his fingernails. Jesus Christ, Mr fucking Manicure. This is all I need, some asshole who wants to play the dandy.

And there I was thinking he was just one of those office jerks who parachute in sometimes. Rank amateurs who come after a hard day pencil-pushing. They usually hang round for a couple of months, make fools of themselves then go home with their tails between their legs and never come back. Good riddance. They want to play chess, let them play the senile old codgers down at Parque Rivadavia or Parque del Centenario. I'm not a snob, it's just that down here we take chess seriously. Here at El Torre Blanca we've got standards. That's why Juanjo comes down to train with us, and he's got international ranking points. And some of the kids who play here are shit hot. They all play professionally. I gave up years ago. Like Bruno. But we still play. Still fight to the death.

But this is not just some guy in a suit. He knows exactly what he's doing. He knows not to develop his queen too early, not to get trapped behind his pawns, not to use up his time. But that doesn't prove anything. You can get all that from books. What's he up to now? The Lasker Variation? Bring it on. Give it your best shot. Let's see how far that shit you've learned by heart gets you, because a couple of minutes from now whatever you learned from your chess books will do you fuck-all good. There's no such thing as a foolproof mid-game. Especially what I'm about to throw at you, you'll see . . .

Strange thing is he didn't even talk to anyone. How did he know? One of the kids could have told him: You want to wind up El Negro, open with the Scandinavian Defence. But no, this guy strolled in, came straight over and challenged me. He waited while me and Soriano finished our game, then sat down opposite without a word. Oh, he was all show, I'll give him that, made sure not to crease his designer suit.

'Look, Brizuela, I'm going to be straight with you.'

Wow, Mr Manicure can actually talk. And I don't waste my time. Fine by me, but I'd check your game clock if I were you, because for someone playing the Lasker Variation you're running way behind.

'And you are?'

'Emanuel Lasker. Pleased to meet you.'

Yeah, and I'm Garry fucking Kasparov! You're trying to put me off my game. And what's with the hand? You want to shake hands? Who the fuck do you think you are?

Fine. No one can say I'm rude. It's not my style. That's it, Mr Manicure, shake. That's right.

'I thought you might be, I mean from the opening gambit . . . So, what can I do for you, *maestro*?' You can come the chess master all you like, Mr Manicure, but you won't find this move in your books. Let's see who you try to pretend to be next. And don't try to distract me because I'm planning to take that fucking knight of yours, and that'll be the end of you.

'Where can I find El Tano Castiglione?'

Fuck. Now the guy really is putting me off my game. That's the last thing I was expecting. El Tano must be in deep if this guy is looking for him. He told me he needed to disappear for a while, asked if I could help him out, let him hole up in my cabin in the Delta for a couple of weeks, but I thought he just needed to skip town, do a bunk from the place he was staying. He owed, like, five months' rent. Or I thought maybe he was trying to get away from that crazy bitch he'd been seeing on and off. That's why I didn't ask any questions. Looks like he had other reasons for getting out of Buenos Aires. El Tano is clearly in serious shit. And that worries me. Worries me a damn sight more than the fluke move this guy's just pulled. Without even thinking. Because now it seems Mr Manicure doesn't even need to look at the board, doesn't need to think before he moves. It's like he knows my next move before I do. Hang fire, Brizuela, give yourself thirty seconds to study the board. Take a minute, you're all right for time. Chill. What's this guy playing at? Is this a serious move or a bluff?

'I've got no idea, *maestro*.' The clown raises one eyebrow. Who does he think he is, Humphrey Bogart? 'What do you want El Tano for?'

'And precisely what business is that of yours, Brizuela? Don't stick your nose in. Just tell me where to find him and I'll give you a one-piece advantage. Might make the game a bit more interesting.'

'No need, *jefe*. Don't worry about me, I'm taking you down one way or another.' I'm calling the shots here. The guy is bluffing. If I've got my calculations right, we can trade pieces and I'll still be a pawn up. And whatever mid-game strategy he thinks he's got going, I don't see it.

'Why don't you leave me your details, *maestro*? If El Tano drops by, I'll get him to call you. What do you say?'

'Don't play the innocent, Brizuela. Tell me where El Tano is or the game is about to get a whole lot more complicated. And I'm not just talking about your queenside.'

Shit . . . should have seen that coming. I'm a pawn up all right, but I don't like the look of that open diagonal. And in a couple more moves he'll have lined up his rooks. But what the hell is he trying to pull? I don't get it . . .

'Don't play the hard man, Lasker. And don't make threats, it doesn't go with the designer suit. Or things are about to get a little twisted. And I'm not just talking about your tie.'

I'm talking about those rooks and that open diagonal, because I'm figuring you're not packing a gun under that fancy jacket. So you can quit playing the dime-store hood because any which way you look at it, you're going down. Right now, I'm trying to signal to Bruno to round up the boys just in case I do need to work you over but I can't even get the dumb fuck to look this way. He's with Medina watching a game of speed chess between Juanjo and old man Soriano. I'm guessing Juanjo's wiping the floor with him.

'I'm not making threats, don't get me wrong. Look, Brizuela, here's the deal . . . Is it OK to smoke in here? You want a cigar? I've got a couple of fine Cubans I just know you're going to love . . .'

Holy shit. He is packing. That whole little routine, taking the cigar case out of his inside jacket pocket just so he can flash the butt of his gun. And it's an automatic. Mr Manicure is playing hardball.

OK. That means we're dancing a very different tango. Time to play a tight defence. Reinforce the kingside, hang on to my pawn advantage. I don't run scared, I don't back down, it's not how I play. But I'm not planning on eating ground glass either. To let Mr Manicure know I'm prepared to play nice, I offer him a light, grab an ashtray from the next table and set it next to the chessboard. Beside the game clock. Time is ticking away – but it's his time. There's no panic. The way things are going, unless I fuck up, with a pawn advantage I'm guaranteed a draw.

But give the guy his due, he was right – the Cuban is sweet. I'm enjoying it. Christ, it's hot in here. There's sweat dripping down my forehead. What is it with old man Soriano always closing the window at the back? He's always does that. I've told him a thousand times to leave it open, get a through breeze so the air doesn't get stale, but the old guy's pig-headed.

'So, like I was saying, here's the deal: El Tano's got something of mine and I want it back. I find him, he gives it to me, everyone's happy. End of story. You getting this, Brizuela? We know he headed up to the Tigre Delta last night. Took the train. What we don't know is where exactly he's headed. And the Delta is a maze, all those little islands . . . but I don't need to tell you that, you know the place. So, anyway, I'm not about to start playing the Boy Scout. I haven't got the time or the inclination. Am I making myself clear?' Mr Manicure lines up his rooks on the same file and winks at me like I didn't see this coming at least three or four moves back.

Either the guy is underestimating me, or he's playing me for a fool.

'So, what do you want from me, Lasker? I'd love to help you out, but I've got no idea where he is . . .' A drop of sweat trickles between my eyebrows and dribbles down my nose.

I wipe my forehead on my sleeve and look for Bruno through the smoke. Now he's sitting with the rest of them. They've all got their backs to me. The only person standing is Juanjo, who's moving between the tables, playing a simultaneous exhibition. Looks like Bruno didn't even see me signalling. Probably better that way. Wouldn't want anyone to catch a bullet on my account. Things are getting heavy here. On and off the board.

'Oh, I think you do know . . . don't play dumb, Brizuela, it doesn't suit you. And, trust me, it'll only be worse for you if you do . . . Elvira told me you've got a cabin out in the Tigre Delta. Why don't you just cut the shit and just tell me how to get there? Simple.'

That drunken old hag, that fucking lush . . .

She set me up. What a bitch. She was always bleating about loyalty and solidarity during the dictatorship but at the first sign of trouble she's happy to grass me up. To put El Tano in a box. Because I'm guessing Mr Manicure here isn't heading up there to give him a pat on the back. With a face like butter wouldn't melt. The guy's probably a professional hit man. So I'll tell him what he wants to know, lie a little, string him along. He doesn't care, he's been ordered to do a hit, he gets paid, it's a job. Simple as that. He doesn't give a shit who's who or what's what. Mr Manicure's hands aren't shaking. You can see that.

What's your next move, Brizuela? Better make your mind up, the clock's ticking and this time it's my game clock that's running down. I don't want to move but I've got to. You've always got to move, even when there's nowhere to go. It's the rule. Chess is like life . . . You can move the most insignificant piece on the board, the one that least alters the situation, but it's a move just the same. You're just playing for time, just putting things off, sooner or later you find yourself right back in the same mess. Or something worse. You can't back out.

Advance pawn. Nothing. It's just a shack, a bolt-hole so I wouldn't be homeless. Mr Manicure narrows his eyes but he doesn't look at the board. He holds my gaze. And smokes. He's still waiting for me to play, even though my clock is stopped now.

'It's just an old shack, it fell down ages ago. Probably got washed away last time the river flooded. I haven't been there for years. It's in the ass-end of nowhere, out there in the islands . . . What makes you think El Tano's headed out there?'

'You tell me . . .' Mr Manicure flicks his ash, a gentle tap of his thumb on the underside of the cigar, takes a deep drag and advances his knight queenside.

He moves it delicately, like the piece is made of glass, but there's nothing delicate about that knight, it's as armour-plated as Alekhine's gun. And it's about to blow a hole in me. In a couple of moves, he'll have it supporting his doubled rooks. I've been expecting this but I've got nothing to counter it with. If I break up my defence, he'll bring his queen down that open diagonal and it's mate in four. Think, Brizuela, think. Change the game, force his hand. The fewer pieces you've got, the better the defence. You know that, you're no rookie . . .

'I don't think El Tano's out in the Delta. He'd have said something.'

Mr Manicure raises one eyebrow again. He's not buying it. If they trailed him here to Retiro, it means they must have been following him since Wednesday, which is when he came here crying into his beer.

'I'm serious, Lasker. If you don't believe me, fine . . . I'll give you directions to the cabin. No skin off my ass. But you're wasting your time going out there, all you're going to get is eaten alive by mosquitoes. I'll tell you, this time of year, they're like fucking planes. Besides which, you'll probably get lost, the place is a nightmare.'

'Then you'll just have to come with me . . .'

'No. No need for that . . . I'm not saying you won't find the place. I'd draw you a map, give you directions, you'll find it. Don't sweat it. '

Careful, Brizuela, you're in this up to your neck. Watch what you say, get yourself in any deeper and there's no way out.

I can turn this thing around. I can get out of this by the skin of my teeth. I can force him to trade for the bishop. It's a sacrifice, I'm not denying it, because there's no way I can take it back. With a bit of luck I'll be another pawn up, that's it. But it's a brilliant move because the guy's got no choice but to take it, and it's a game changer: queen, knight, rook.

'So, what's it to be, Brizuela?'

Mr Manicure reluctantly takes the piece, raps the button on his game clock with the base of my bishop. He's running out of patience. That's a good sign.

I take my time explaining the route for him, down to the last detail, giving him reference points even where there aren't any. And while I'm doing that, I'm trying to work out where I'm going to send him off course. How close I'm going to let him get to the cabin. It's like when you give someone a fake phone number. The best thing to do is recite your number slowly and just change one digit. If you only change one, it's easy to remember. If you make something up, you'll just screw yourself. Because you're going to have to repeat it, once, twice, three times . . . as many times as you have to. And you'll wind up giving yourself away.

Mr Manicure is playing fast now. He's just noticed that I've shifted up a gear. If I don't get him on time, I'm screwed. He's got seven minutes on the clock, I've got twelve. I advance my remaining pawns, supporting them with my rook, talking all the while. The more complicated my directions the better. I'm going to send him up shit creek, I'm going to send him up the *brazo de Bragado* just before you come to *el remanso del Irlandés*, send him off to get lost in the river weeds. The ferryboats don't go up Bragado. He'll have to hire a boat. Pay some *mencho* to take him. I don't think I'm going to be able to queen but he's got no chance. If he's hoping to checkmate me with just a rook and a knight, he's got his work cut out. And I'm not going to make it easy for him.

I'm still reeling off directions. Mr Manicure is sitting, staring at me. He doesn't ask any questions, doesn't ask for any explanations. Must have a photographic memory. From the next table, I grab one of the score sheets we use during tournaments and ask for a pen so I can draw a map on the back. Mr Manicure takes a ballpoint from his inside pocket, holding his jacket open just a little too long. Son of a bitch wants to make sure I get another good look at that gun he's packing.

I draw the map, move my pieces, talking all the time. I'm like a machine. He's got three minutes left. Come on, Brizuela, you've got him nailed. Don't think, keep going. You've got him.

I offer him a pawn to see if he'll take the bait and Mr Manicure looks me straight in the eyes. I should keep talking, play dumb, distract him, but I can't. Panic is setting in. This is my last chance. He's the one who needs to take his time now. If he takes the pawn, we trade rooks and it's a stalemate. He's still got a minute and a half. If he plays fast, plays well, he can still checkmate me. But Mr Manicure takes the pawn and winks at me. The bastard saw it coming . . . Then he pretends like he's all surprised, raises his eyebrows, lets his jaw drop, deliberately overacting.

'Congratulations, Brizuela. Good game.' He gets to his feet and offers me his hand.

I shake his hand again, but unwillingly. I don't even get up. I don't like this. It's not funny. If he was trying to humiliate me, then handing me a draw like this is much worse than wiping the floor with me with a checkmate. The son of a bitch knew exactly what he was doing . . .

'When I get back from the Delta, I'll let you know how my trip went. And we'll have a little rematch.' ∎

Portobello

Winner of the Spanish Critics' Award 2009

Translated from the Spanish by Mara Faye Lethem

'What a novel ... lush, intricate
and rewarding' *Herald*

PORTOBELLOBOOKS.COM

GRANTA

THE CUERVO BROTHERS

Andrés Felipe Solano

TRANSLATED BY NICK CAISTOR

ANDRÉS FELIPE SOLANO
COLOMBIA
1977

Solano, born in Bogotá, has published the novel *Sálvame, Joe Louis* (2007) and has worked as features editor for *SoHo* magazine. In 2007, he lived in Medellín, Colombia, where he rented a room in a notoriously violent neighbourhood and worked in a factory for six months. Based on this experience, he wrote the article 'Seis meses con el salario mínimo', finalist for the prize awarded by the Fundación Nuevo Periodismo Iberoamericano, chaired by Gabriel García Márquez. In 2008, the government of South Korea invited him to serve a six-month literary residence in Seoul, where he met his wife. He has served as writer-in-residence at the University of Alcalá de Henares. 'The Cuervo Brothers' is part of his novel in progress.

The City

The Cuervo brothers claimed to have been transferred from a school whose name we had never heard of. The older one started in the second year, a class below me. The younger one joined in the last year of primary school. From the very first week there were all kinds of stories about them. As the months went by, these grew like the number of bullfrogs in the rainy season. During these holidays, I've classified them all in a notebook. Going over them carefully, I've established four categories:

1. Sex
2. Sinister
3. Diabolical
4. Martian

As was to be expected, the first rumour spread about them was that they were queer. Gay as butterflies, but not very brightly coloured. Brown or perhaps black, those with just a flash of yellow or aquamarine blue. When we started having girlfriends, my best friend Diego told me that one night, after seeing *Alien 3* with María Adelaida in the Embajador, he caught sight of the older brother selling himself on the corner of the Terraza Pasteur shopping mall. He got into a green jeep in a parking lot and began sucking off an old guy who looked like a military man. While he was face down, the guy was playing with his false teeth, or so Diego said, without the trace of a smile. The wildest story in this category was about their bodies. According to the person telling it (I can't remember now who that was), the brothers were born hermaphrodites, and someone saw them binding up their breasts in a toilet before a PE class. After that we got on to their families. As soon as we learned they lived on their own with their grandmother, crime was added to the sex stories we swapped during break time. The worst of these concerned the double life their mother had lived. She had been a high-class whore, but their father found out when they were only little and slit her throat.

He was in Gorgona prison, and had five years left to serve of his sentence. When he got out, he was going to reclaim them, and would kill everyone who had made fun of them. I remembered, though, that in a history class once, we had been told the island prison of Gorgona had been closed in 1977, when the only inmates left were poisonous snakes.

The sinister stories all started with a melodramatic incident. At first there was a rumour they had escaped from an orphanage south of the city. The wealthy spinster they were now living with helped them run away one night through a drainage pipe, and took them to live in one of the 1940s mansions that still survived in the neighbourhood around the school. Most of them had been pulled down or converted into car workshops, but the house where the Cuervos lived was just as it had always been, with its lofty English appearance. Others said they were her legitimate grandsons, flesh of her flesh, but that every weekend she chained their hands and feet, locked them in the basement, and only gave them wheat broth and stale bread to eat. That's why they smelled so badly when they came to school on Mondays, it was said. The most dreadful aspect of the whole thing was imagining them having to eat that thick soup, that slimy gruel we all hated when it was served up in the school canteen. Some boys even said the dungeon they were kept in communicated directly with the basements in Avenida Jiménez, the ones near the spot where Gaitán was killed, and that his real killer had escaped through them. I myself invented the rumour that the younger one suffered from a strange illness which meant he could only see in black and white, and that was why his eyes were wrinkled like prunes. Nobody liked that one. So I invented a syndrome which gave him convulsions and made him clasp his balls if he spent too long in the open air. That explains why he never plays football, I said, to clinch the argument.

Zorrilla was the one who started the diabolical rumours when the sex ones faded out after the older brother was seen on a date in a cafe after school, whispering in the ear of one of the female dental assistants who visited the school. Something we could not deny, and which filled us with rage, was that, despite being very skinny, the Cuervo brothers were by no means ugly. It would have been much easier for all of us if they had been. Zorrilla, who had one leg withered from polio, would slap it as he told us time and again in the alleyway behind the library, next to the church, that he hadn't been able to resist the temptation, and one Friday evening had slipped into the brothers' house. He only managed to get as far as the interior courtyard, where he saw a slaughtered calf covered in a cloud of flies that were buzzing horribly. Sometimes when he told the story it was a calf, at others a sheep. In the end he settled on a billy goat, after Gómez told him that was the animal the Devil took shape in whenever he wanted to come down from the world beyond. We all enthusiastically agreed they were in league with the Devil and that their grandmother had been a witch. None of us questioned how Zorrilla, with his gammy leg, had climbed over the two-metre wall surrounding the Cuervos' old house.

Navarro was ultra-Catholic, and almost as scary as the brothers. He was the source of one of the least popular stories, which I've classified under the heading: The Sect. I put it in the 'Diabolical' category just to prove I was including everything. Navarro claimed they were the sons of a pastor in the Unification Church, founded by a mysterious Korean. The Church had called on their father and mother to abandon them and travel the countryside spreading the holy word of the founder, who saw himself as the true Messiah.

But it's the Martian stories that are still my favourites. I called them that because they portrayed the brothers as real aliens. Some boys claimed the Cuervos had never worn jeans, drank their own urine mixed with Coca-Cola, that at Hallowe'en they went out wearing their school uniforms, saying that was their disguise, that they made knives at home and bartered them for marijuana with the street sellers on Avenida Caracas, that they were fencing and Graeco-Roman wrestling champions, but had been thrown out of the Bogotá league for being queer.

The boys from lower forms added many more details to the brothers' weird habits. They claimed the two of them didn't eat tomato sauce, spoke Latin to each other, shaved their armpits, collected clothes hangers, only read encyclopedias and had never watched TV. Perhaps these last two were stories with some vestige of the truth to them. I'm saying that because I can prove it. My mother was their grandmother's accountant for seven years and went to see her at least every six months. She sometimes told me snippets about the brothers, such as, for example, that she had never seen a television set in the house. If I tried to find out more about them, she would tell me not to be such a gossip. Let them be, don't you see they haven't got any parents? she would say.

What nobody expected, and me least of all, was that late in '93 it was the Cuervo brothers themselves who opened the doors of their house to me and revealed almost all their secrets. When it comes to the truth or falsehood of the stories about them, I have to admit I never bothered to correct any of the rumours, despite the first-hand information I had. To some extent we needed those stories, and it was not for me to give the Cuervo legend its *coup de grâce*. When we first began to talk about the brothers we all led humdrum existences. Without meaning to, they enlivened them for a while at least, thanks to their secret lives that were as tangled and mysterious as a jungle . . . so different to our predictable hormonal chaos, our first nights out getting drunk, and games of football that from one day to the next ruthlessly wiped the exploits of Mazinger Z or Dr Hell from our hearts. We never talked about it, still less constructed theories on the subject, it just happened, but when everything seemed to indicate that the time had come to get seriously involved with girls, one by one the boys forgot them; I remained irretrievably caught up with the two brothers, their grandmother, their house. The Cuervos offered me a life at a moment when I was acutely aware of my own mediocrity, which was threatening to overwhelm me. I was neither rich nor poor, good-looking nor ugly; I wasn't talented but I wasn't stupid either. I was Mister Average, right on the borderline. Besides, I didn't have a name that could match theirs. I was called Nelson and lived in a flat with my parents, who were both civil servants whose insipid lives consisted mostly in breaking their backs to be able to keep me at that school and to have holidays at the coast. My parents were so decent they didn't even offer me the possibility of hating them as an excuse. That's why I don't feel the slightest remorse about not having corrected the myths created around the Cuervos. The brothers themselves silently encouraged me not to feel bad about it, and occasionally concocted some brilliant eccentricity that I could describe at school and so gain a modicum of popularity that tipped the balance to the right side. Before the older brother left home they confessed that far from humiliating them, they were flattered by all the stories. Of course, none of this means they weren't extremely strange. Goodness, it's the Cuervo brothers we're talking about!

One of the more sinister rumours had it that when the drug traffickers began exploding car bombs, the brothers used to go to the scene of the explosion and take photos of the burned-out wrecks, the buildings with shattered windows, the mutilated, wounded, and even of the dead bodies. Although no one at school ever saw these photos, I discovered them one evening when they left me alone in their second-floor library. They had classified them in different folders. There were some of the bomb at the *El Espectador* newspaper office, and the DAS security headquarters, others of the one in the Quirigua neighbourhood, or at the Carulla supermarket on 127th Street in 1990, close to my auntie's house. I remember that last one very well. It was a Sunday, Mother's Day. The bomb went off an hour after we bought a cake with confectionery roses on it in the shopping mall where the bombed supermarket was. They also had photos of the bomb at the 93 Centre. It was dreadful to imagine them catching a bus to the scene of the explosion, then standing there in the midst of the tragedy, calmly taking photos. I calculate that when the DAS bomb went off they must have been thirteen and fifteen, if that. And now I come to think of it, when the school put into practice an evacuation plan in case of an attack – the son of an army officer who was at loggerheads with a drug baron was studying with us – the Cuervo brothers started carrying gas masks in their satchels. Diego and I saw them and asked where they had got them. They said their grandmother had bought the masks in the flea market. As extravagant as ever, Zorrilla assured everyone they must have belonged to their grandfather.

The first time I went to their house, the grandmother received me in a small reception room that was obviously for brief, informal visits. The proper living room was a few metres further on. It was about half as big as the whole of the flat where I lived, with heavy furniture, a bar with bottles that did not seem to have been opened in years and crystal glasses, a radio and different-sized rugs covering a shiny parquet floor. There were no ornaments or paintings – the grandmother hated them. One wall that was almost three metres high had mirrors stretching right up to the ceiling. I had seen her once before, when she went to school for our first reports. On that occasion she had spoken behind closed doors to the head of studies and the headmaster. It was agreed that her grandsons would be the ones to pick up their reports and take them home to sign. If there was any serious problem, she would come to the school, but she was sure there would be no need. Later on, we learned that the brothers had not had to take an entrance exam, or even to fill in any forms to come and study with us. One of their grandmother's relatives was a priest. He held an important position in the religious order which ran the school, so the brothers were accepted without a problem. We also learned they had never been to school before. They had invented the name they mentioned on their first day, which was why none of us had recognized it. The grandmother, who had been one of the first women lecturers at the National University, had given them lessons at home. From early on, the older brother had shown remarkable ability in maths, to such an extent that apart from the allowance he received from his grandmother, he earned more money by giving demonstrations in state schools. Once or twice a month our headmaster would give him permission to do this, provided he mentioned the name of our school, and of course wore school uniform. His younger brother always accompanied him. He was solemnly introduced in community halls, neighbourhood centres, football grounds and even rural schools outside the city as 'The Astonishing Human Calculating Machine'. The event, or rather the performance, consisted of doing mathematical calculations with five-figure numbers in a matter of seconds. The younger brother asked a volunteer for the first part of the operation, and he provided the second, or the other way round. Then the star of the show closed his eyes, went into a brief, electrifying trance, and gave the result without the slightest hesitation. A teacher would copy it down on a flip chart. The teacher would then use a normal calculator to perform the same operation and compare the results. He was nearly always the first to applaud enthusiastically. Every year the older brother added two numbers. In the months before his departure, he could do ten-figure multiplications, and solve square roots of up to five digits. The brothers spent part of their earnings from this on fireworks at Christmas: as was only to be expected, their grandmother did not give them money to burn. Every 16th of December the Cuervo brothers offered a firework display from their balcony. The owner of the house wanted nothing to do with it. Only their elderly maid, Pastora, took part. The display lasted the time it took for five Roman candles to burn down. Pastora lit them one by one, and held them up towards the sky. As there were hardly any other families living in the neighbourhood, the garage mechanics, drunks and a few street sellers were the only people who saw the Cuervos acting as pyrotechnic masters – because there was much more to it than merely lighting volcanoes or sparklers. The brothers designed a plan that would set off whole series of explosions, mixing bangs and blinding lights. Pinned to a corkboard in their study they had a diagram of the previous year, full of different coloured notes and amendments. It looked like one of the complicated exercises at the back of my dreaded physics textbook.

But I was talking about the grandmother. I arrived at their house expecting to be greeted by a mouldy, eccentric old woman who would terrify me. I was sure she would be such a dreadful sight that I would refuse the job even though she had offered me three times as much as I had dared ask for. In fact, after my mother had told me they were looking for a guitar teacher, I had agreed to go to the house simply to be able to set foot in their world and to meet their grandmother face-to-face, to see her hairy, drooling chin and then tell the tale at school, with a few choice additions of my own. When I saw her walking straight-backed down the stairs without even touching the wood and metal banister, dressed impeccably and with a clear face, I was terribly disappointed. She was one of those people who would never be anything other than formal unless it was absolutely necessary. She would never offer me a glass of water. Bemused by her presence, my confused hormones led me to wonder how old she was. In her face I discovered a beauty worthy of a magazine cover. That evening, the only unusual thing about her was a ring in the shape of a giant beetle that she was wearing on her first finger. That and her hands. They had so few wrinkles or marks on them they were like my mother's, and she had only just turned forty. And so I had no option but to agree to give guitar lessons to the Cuervo brothers twice a week after school. That was a few months before the official power cuts, which meant we had no electricity in our homes every evening and night. During the long year that power rationing lasted we bought candles or storm lamps to see each other's faces, and the gasoline smell from the generators saturated the streets at nightfall. ■

OLINGIRIS

Samanta Schweblin

TRANSLATED BY DANIEL ALARCÓN

SAMANTA SCHWEBLIN
ARGENTINA
1978

Schweblin graduated in Film at the University of Buenos Aires and runs her own design agency. In 2001, she was awarded first prize by both the National Fund for the Arts and the Haroldo Conti National Competition for her first book, *El núcleo del disturbio* (2002). In 2008, she won the Casa de la Américas Prize for her second book, *Pájaros en la boca*, as well as Mexico's FONCA grant for the promotion of culture and art. Her stories have been translated into German, English, Italian, French, Portuguese, Swedish and Serbian, for publication in numerous anthologies, magazines and cultural publications. 'Olingiris' is a new story.

There was space for six. One was left outside, in the waiting room. She walked in circles about the space. It took her a moment to realize she'd have to stifle her eagerness until the next day, or the next, or until they called her again. It wasn't the first time this had happened to her. The ones who entered climbed the white stairs to the first floor. None of them knew the others particularly well. They stepped into the changing room in silence. They hung up their purses, they took off their coats. They took turns washing their hands, and took turns as well fixing their hair before the mirror, tying it back in a ponytail, or with a headband. All friendliness and silence; grateful smiles and gestures. They've thought of this all week. While they worked, while they looked after their children, while they ate, and now they are there. Almost inside, almost about to begin.

One of the Institute's assistants opens the door and invites them in. Inside, everything is white. The walls, the shelves, the towels rolled into tubes lying one on top of the other. The gurney, in the centre. The six chairs surrounding it. There's also a fan above, whirling smoothly, six silver tweezers lined up on a towel atop a wooden stool, and a woman lying on the gurney, face down. The six women settle into the chairs, three on each side, arranging themselves around the woman's legs. They wait, observing the body, impatient, not quite knowing what to do with their hands, as if before a table, with dinner set, but unable to begin. The assistant hovers about, helping them push their seats even closer. Then she gives out the hand towels and, one by one, the six tweezers from the stool. The woman on the gurney remains still, with her face down. She is nude. A white towel covers her from the waist to the middle of the legs. She has her head buried in her crossed arms, because it is appropriate that no one should see her face. She has blonde hair, a thin body. The assistant turns on the fluorescent light, a few metres above the bed, which brightens the room and the woman even more. When the light flickers a bit, the woman on the gurney shifts her arms almost imperceptibly, readjusting herself, and two of the women observe this slight movement with reproach. When the assistant gives the signal to begin, the women fold their hand towels in four and place the small cloth square before them, on the gurney. Then some of them push their chairs even further forward, or rest their elbows, or fix their hair one last time. And they get to work. They raise the tweezers above the woman's body, quickly choosing a strand of hair, and then bring them down open, with purpose. They tweeze, they close, they toss. Each dark follicle emerges perfect and clean. They study it for a second before leaving it on the towel, and they go for the next one. Six seagull beaks pulling fish from the sea. The hair on the tweezers fills them with pleasure. Some do the work to perfection. The full hair hangs from the tweezers, orphaned and useless. Others struggle a bit with the task, making more than one attempt before they manage it. But nothing deprives them of the pleasure. The assistant circles the table. She takes care that they're all comfortable, that all have what they need. Every now and then, a pull, a pinch, provokes a slight trembling of the legs. And so the assistant halts and turns her gaze to the woman on the gurney. She curses the fact that the rules of the Institute require that they be face down; with their faces hidden, it's impossible to scold them with a glare. But she has her notebook, which she removes from her apron pocket, jotting down all excesses. The woman on the gurney hears the screech of the rubber sandals when they stop abruptly. She knows what that means. A point deducted, a demerit. Sooner or later they'll add up and be docked from her pay. Her legs are filling with little pink dots. By now they barely tremble, because the tweezers have numbed her irritated skin, now only vaguely aware of a light burning.

II

When the woman on the gurney was ten years old, she lived with her mother near the river. It was an area which sometimes flooded, forcing them to move to her aunt's, who lived a few metres higher, in a house on stilts. Once, when the woman on the gurney was doing her homework in her aunt's dining room, she saw through the window a fisherman skulking around her house, her mother's house. He had come on a boat, which he tied to some trees. A pair of high boots protected him from the water, which rose almost to his knees. She saw him disappear along one side of the house and reappear on the other. He peeked through the windows. But at no point did he knock on the door or the glass. When the mother saw him, she gestured for him to come in. The woman on the gurney could see them as long as they stayed near the window. Her mother offered him hot tea and they sat at the table. Then they moved away. When the woman on the gurney returned from her aunt's house, they spoke of the trips he took, of his work as a fisherman, of the river. He offered to take her out fishing the next day. Because it was the season of floods and there was no school, her mother said it was all right. He took the woman on the gurney to where the river opened into the lake. At that point the boat hardly moved, advancing smoothly along the mirrored water, and she was less and less afraid. It was then she realized she was a little cold, and a little hungry. Day was just beginning to dawn. The fisherman prepared his rod, hooked his bait and began to work. She asked if her mother had prepared them something for breakfast, but the fisherman hushed her and gestured for quiet. Then she asked if he had an extra jacket in the boat. The fisherman hushed her again.

'Are you my father?' she asked finally.

The fisherman stared at her for a moment and it occurred to her to smile. But he said: 'No.'

And they did not speak again.

The mother of the woman on the gurney always wanted her daughter to study and move to the city. She demanded her daughter get good grades and was sure to warn her that if she didn't work hard now, then she'd pay for it when she was older – and dearly. The woman on the gurney studied. She did everything her mother told her. The school was two kilometres from the house, and she went by bicycle. When it flooded, they read her the homework by telephone. In high school she learned typing, English, a little computing. One afternoon as she was returning home, her bicycle chain broke. The woman on the gurney fell to the mud, ruining the notebooks she carried in her basket. A young man driving a pickup truck along the road saw her fall, drew level with her and got out to help. He was very kind. He gathered her notebooks, which he cleaned with the sleeves of his coat, and offered to take her home. They carried the bicycle in the back of the pickup. They talked a little along the way. She told him what she was studying, that she was preparing to move to the city. He seemed interested in everything she said. He wore a very thin gold chain with a small cross hanging from his neck. She thought it was lovely. She did not believe in God, nor did her mother, but something about the young man made her think her mother would like him. When they arrived, she asked him to come round later, to eat with them. He seemed delighted by the idea, but said: 'I leave for work soon. I'm a fisherman.' He smiled. 'Can I come tomorrow?'

'No,' she said. 'I don't think tomorrow is a good idea. I'm sorry.'

The woman on the gurney was twenty years old when she came to the city. She was pleased to see that the houses were not built on stilts, which ruled out floods and fishermen. The city seemed warm, and it made her woozy during those first days. On Sundays she called her mother and told her a few things about her week. Sometimes she lied. She didn't do it maliciously; she did it to pass the time. She told her mother that she'd gone out with new friends. Or that she'd gone to the movies. Or that she'd had something very tasty in a neighbourhood restaurant. Her mother loved to hear these stories, and sometimes she could hardly wait to hang up and call her sister, so that she might hear the stories too.

The woman on the gurney had some savings and had signed up for a technical degree. But the cost of food, rent and tuition was very high, and soon she had to interrupt her studies and look for a job. One afternoon when she was buying bread, a woman at the store, with whom she sometimes shared her problems, said she had a job for her. She said she'd earn more money, and have time to study. The woman on the gurney wasn't dumb. She knew the work might be something unpleasant that no one else wanted to do, or something dangerous. But she said that, as long as there was no obligation, she'd be interested to see what it was all about.

The woman from the store took her by car to a nearby avenue, and stopped in front of a two-storey building with a sign on it that read 'Institute'. Inside there was a confused gathering of women. One of them, wearing a peach-coloured uniform which also read 'Institute', asked the women to reorganize themselves into a line and threatened that anyone out of line would lose her turn. The women quickly queued up. Another woman in a suit recognized the woman from the store and immediately came up to them. She ushered them into an adjoining room and asked the woman on the gurney to fold up the cuffs of her trousers so she could see the downy hair on her legs. The woman on the gurney thought for a moment she'd misunderstood the request. But the woman repeated it. And then she thought it was ridiculous, and that this surely was not a job for her. However, she did not see any danger in showing her hair, so she rolled up her trouser legs and showed them. The woman in the suit put on her glasses and studied the tiny hairs, illuminating them with a small flashlight she kept in her pocket. She scrutinized the ankle where the hairs were not yet strong, and also the calf. Only when she appeared to be convinced it would work did she explain what the job consisted of, the general terms and the pay. The woman on the gurney didn't know what to say. Because the work was very simple, the schedule acceptable and the pay excellent. Her mother had told her so much about the scams in the city that she forced herself to concentrate on where the danger or the lie might be hidden. But everything still seemed perfect to her. And she accepted.

III

When there's no more hair left on the legs, they look red and alive. The woman on the gurney is still. The six women seem tired, but satisfied. Finally, they lean back in their chairs, sighing, resting their hands in their laps. The assistant gathers the hand towels, where the women have left the hair. Before taking them, she folds them in half twice, to make certain the hairs don't get lost, and just like that puts them carefully in a plastic trash bag, which, once full, she ties with a double knot. Only then does she turn to help the women sit up, pulling out their chairs, straightening out the collars or the shoulder pads of their jackets that might have been moved. Then she takes the trash bag, delicately, careful not to tilt it, opens the door and leads the women to the dressing room. When they are all inside, the assistant returns to the hallway, closing the door behind her. Sometimes the women comment on their turn, they laugh, or ask questions about previous times. The assistant hears them talking as she descends the white stairs. She knows she must deliver the bag before going back to the woman on the gurney.

IV

The assistant was born in the countryside, within a family that lived on the harvest and the vineyards. They had a country house surrounded by gardens, and were comfortable without being rich. The assistant liked fish, and the father, who was almost never home, sent her enormous books with full-colour illustrations of fish from all over the world. She learned their names and drew them in her notebook. Of all the fish, the one she liked best was called Olingiris. It had a thin, flat body, with a large tube-shaped snout. Turquoise and yellow. The book said it was a delicate fish, because it only ate coral polyps, and those couldn't be found in many places. She asked for one, but they explained to her that she couldn't have fish in the countryside. The assistant showed her mother a book that explained how to install and maintain a fish tank, but the mother said, though they might get the fish tank and the appropriate food, the fish would die of sadness. The assistant thought that perhaps her father might not feel the same way, that she could show him the photos and he would understand. But when he finally came home, she couldn't find the book about fish tanks anywhere.

The assistant had many brothers, but they were older and worked with her father, so she was alone most of the day. When she turned seven she began to attend the rural school. One of the men who worked for her father came by to get her at seven thirty, left her at school at eight and came back for her at noon. The assistant had a hard time adapting to this new rhythm. Things did not go well at first. Her mother hired a private tutor, and so the assistant studied at school in the mornings and at home in the afternoons. Because the tutor knew of the assistant's interest in fish, she built her exercises around that topic. Sometimes she read her some poetry, and once, when they were studying punctuation, the tutor proposed writing some verses. The assistant accepted the challenge, and the tutor seemed charmed by the results. She gave her an assignment to write a poem using the names of her favourite fish. The assistant approached the homework with much interest. She cleared her desk, leaving only a few blank sheets of paper, a pencil and an eraser. She wrote a poem about fish, but they were make-believe fish; about what she sometimes felt in the morning, when she'd just woken and didn't know quite who or where she was. About the things that made her happy, those that did not, and about her father.

One afternoon the tutor told the assistant that she had a surprise for her and took from her bag a large package, about the size of a binder, gift-wrapped. Before she'd let her open it, the tutor made her promise it would be a secret, that she'd never tell anyone about the present. The assistant agreed. She tore the wrapping paper, and when she saw what it was, she thought an entire lifetime wouldn't be enough to give the tutor something as valuable as what she'd just received. It was the book about fish tanks. It wasn't the exact same copy, but it was the same book, a new one, identical.

By the age of twelve the assistant's grades were much improved, and her mother decided a private tutor was no longer necessary. For a time the assistant would include the tutor in her fish drawings. She made a few of her tutor kissing an Olingiris, and another of her tutor pregnant by an Olingiris. She wrote a few poems for her mother to send to the tutor, but received no reply.

When the assistant finished high school, she began to look after her father's finances and helped take care of things on the farm. She no longer painted or wrote, but she kept a framed photo of the Olingiris on her desk; and sometimes, when she was resting, she'd pick it up, look it over carefully and wonder what her tutor might be doing, and what it would be like to live as an Olingiris.

She didn't marry or have children. She left the countryside when her mother's first symptoms of illness appeared, the same year the drought ruined the vineyards and the harvest. They decided that the assistant would move to the capital with her mother, and they'd live in an apartment her father had bought some years before. The assistant brought along the book about fish tanks that her tutor had given her. The apartment wasn't very big, but it was enough for two. It had a window looking out on the street and a lot of light. They bought a table and two pine beds, and the assistant tore a few pages from the book and pasted them to the walls as if they were framed pictures. She learned to cook, make the beds and wash clothes. She found a job in a dry-cleaner's. Once the clothes were clean, one had to place each piece in the steamer, taking care that no wrinkle was left. Press down the top, wait a few seconds, repeat it all again with the rest of the garment. One also had to fold it and perfume it. Sometimes there were difficult stains; one had to take them to the back, to the sink, give them a special treatment. When this happened, the assistant always chose the first tap, and while she waited those ten seconds which the product required, she would look in the mirror, into her eyes.

When the assistant's mother died, the assistant quit her job. She found, among her mother's clothes, the book about fish tanks, the original one, the lost one. She cleared the pine table and opened both books to the first page. She reread them side by side, many times. She thought perhaps she could find some difference; because, though at first glance they appeared to be the same, she remembered the first one somehow altered. It was difficult to explain. She was simply certain there had to be some difference. But she couldn't find it. She closed the books and felt very sad. She felt they were no longer necessary to her, and she put them both away beneath the bed. She waited at home for many days. When she ran out of food and money, she went out to walk around the neighbourhood and found a 'help wanted' ad on a building that read 'Institute'. The job was simple, and it paid well. She was accepted immediately. The money from the first months was enough to paint the apartment and buy new furniture. She threw away the pages she had hanging from the walls. Mornings, she went out in her uniform from the Institute. She opened doors, filled out forms, led women to the dressing room, opened the main room, prepared the materials, watched each successive woman on the gurney, collected the hair, closed the bag, turned in the bag, said goodbye to the women, paid the woman on the gurney, turned out the lights, locked the door. At home, she put away the groceries, made dinner, ate in front of the television, washed her things, showered, brushed her teeth, straightened the bed and went to sleep. Sometimes she ran out of forms and had to go to the stationer's for more. Or the women on the gurney moved and she had to deduct points from their pay. Or she didn't find what she wanted to eat, so she had to go to bed early.

v

The assistant went to the reception and saw through the window that it was already dark. She put the bag on a shelf, next to three identical bags, beneath the receptionist's desk. Just then, the door to the street swung open and the woman entered along with the cold. She was small, but stout. She wore a heavy coat and the same high black boots as usual, which to the assistant had always seemed like those a man would wear, a fisherman, though by now she was accustomed to them. The woman mumbled a greeting, and the assistant responded with a timid nod. The woman put both hands on the tabletop. The assistant saw that the usual car was waiting in the street, its engine running. She handed the woman the four bags, one by one. The woman took them firmly, two in each hand, and left without saying goodbye. Her only words were: 'Don't forget to turn out the lights before you lock up.'

The assistant said she wouldn't forget and stayed there a few moments to watch the woman get into the car. The women came down, changed into their clothes, and said their goodbyes before stepping out into the street. Only the woman on the gurney remained, who was likely waiting for her, ready, upstairs. The assistant went up, opened the door to the room and was surprised to see the woman on the gurney was still nude. She was still sitting on the gurney, hugging her knees, her head bent down between her arms. Her back trembled. She was crying. This was the first time something like this had happened, and the assistant didn't quite know what to do. She thought about leaving the room and coming back a few minutes later, but she took out the notebook instead, reviewing her numbers aloud, and then offered the woman on the gurney a receipt along with her pay. The woman on the gurney looked at her, for the first time. And the assistant felt her stomach tighten just slightly, mechanically; her lungs filled with air, her lips parted, her tongue was suspended in the air, as if waiting, as if she were about to ask something of the woman of the gurney. Something like what? That was what kept her quiet. If she was well? Well in regards to what? It's not as if she were really going to ask, though the distance between their bodies was appropriate and they were alone in the building; it was only something floating through her head. But it was the woman on the gurney who slowed her breathing and said, 'Are you all right?'

The assistant waited. She wanted to know what was happening, understand what was happening. She felt something seize her, something strong in her throat, a sharp pain that took her back to the image of those books on the pine table, the pictures of the two Olingiris, one next to the other, and, as if this were a new opportunity, she looked desperately for some difference, in the eyes, in the scales, in the fins, in the colours. ■

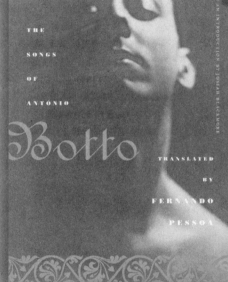

GRANTA

WAYS OF GOING HOME

Alejandro Zambra

TRANSLATED BY MEGAN MCDOWELL

ALEJANDRO ZAMBRA
CHILE
1975

Zambra is the author of the poetry collections *Bahía inútil* (1998) and *Mudanza* (2003), the novels *Bonsái* (2006), *La vida privada de los árboles* (2007) – published in English as *The Private Lives of Trees* – and the book of essays *No leer* (2010). His novels have been translated into various languages. In Chile, *Bonsái* won the Critics' Prize and the National Council Prize for Books for the best novel of the year in 2006. He is currently working on a book of short stories called *Berta Bovary*. He lives in Santiago and is a literature professor at the University of Diego Portales. 'Ways of Going Home' is from the opening of his third novel, which will be published in 2011.

Once, I got lost. I was six or seven. I got distracted, and all of a sudden I couldn't see my parents any more. I was scared, but I immediately found the way home and got there before they did. They kept looking for me, desperate, but that afternoon I thought they were lost. I believed I knew how to get home and they didn't.

'You went a different way,' my mother said later, angry, her eyes still swollen.

You were the one who went a different way, I thought, but I didn't say it.

Papa watched placidly from the armchair. Sometimes I think he spent all his time just sitting there, thinking. But maybe he didn't really think about anything. Maybe he just closed his eyes and received the present with calm and resignation. That night he spoke, though: 'This is a good thing,' he told me. 'You overcame adversity.' Mama looked at him suspiciously, but he kept on stringing together a confused speech about adversity. Back then, I had no idea what adversity could possibly mean.

I lay back on the chair across from him and pretended to be asleep. I heard them argue, always the same pattern. Mama would say five sentences and Papa would answer with a single word. Sometimes he would answer sharply: 'No.' Sometimes he would say, practically shouting: 'Liar,' or 'False.' Sometimes he would even say, like the police: 'Negative.'

That night Mama carried me to bed and, perhaps knowing I was only pretending to sleep and was listening attentively, curiously, she told me: 'Your father is right. Now we know you won't get lost. That you know how to walk alone in the street. But you should concentrate more on the way. You should walk faster.'

I listened to her. From then on, I walked faster. In fact, a couple of years later, the first time I talked to Claudia, she asked me why I walked so fast. She had been following me for days, spying on me. We had met a short time before, on 3 March 1985 – the night of the earthquake – but we didn't talk then.

She was twelve and I was nine, so our friendship was impossible.

But we were friends, or something like it. We talked a lot. Sometimes I think I'm writing this book just to remember those conversations.

The night of the earthquake I was scared but also, in a certain way, I enjoyed what was happening.

In the front yard of one of the houses, the adults put up two tents so the children could sleep, and at first it was chaos because we all wanted to sleep in the one that looked like an igloo – those were still a novelty back then – but they gave that one to the girls. We shut ourselves in to fight in silence, which was what we did when we were alone: hit each other furiously, happily. But then the redhead's nose started bleeding, so we had to find another game. Someone thought of making wills, and at first it seemed like a good idea; after a while, though, we found it didn't make sense, since a stronger earthquake might come and end the world, and then there wouldn't be anyone to leave our things to. Then we imagined that the earth was like a dog shaking itself so people fell off like fleas into space, and we thought about that image so much we found ourselves laughing, and sleepy.

But I didn't want to sleep. I was tired like never before, but it was a new tiredness that burned my eyes. I decided to stay up all night and I tried to sneak into the igloo to keep talking to the girls, but the policeman's daughter threw me out, saying I wanted to rape them. I hardly knew back then what a rapist was, but nevertheless I promised I didn't want to rape them, I only wanted to look at them. She laughed mockingly and answered that that was what rapists always said. I had to stay outside, listening to them pretend that their dolls were the only survivors; they mourned their owners, crying spectacularly when they realized they were dead, although one of them thought it was for the best, since the human race had always seemed repellent to her. Finally, they argued over who would be in charge. The discussion seemed long to me, but it was easily resolved: there was only one original Barbie among the dolls. She won.

After a while, I found a beach chair among the rubble and shyly approached the adults' bonfire. It was strange to see the neighbours gathered together, perhaps for the first time. They drowned their fear in cups of wine and long looks of complicity. Someone brought an old wooden table and threw it on the fire as if it were the most normal thing in the world. 'If you want, I'll throw the guitar on too,' said Papa, and everyone laughed, even me, though I was a little disconcerted, since Papa didn't usually tell jokes. That's when Raul, our neighbour, came back with Magali and Claudia. 'This is my sister and my niece,' he said. After the earthquake he had gone to look for them, and now he was coming back, visibly relieved.

Raul was the only one in the neighbourhood who lived alone. It was hard for me to understand how someone could live alone. I thought that being alone was a kind of punishment, or a disease.

The morning he arrived with a mattress strapped to the roof of his old Fiat 500, I asked Mama when the rest of his family would come; she answered, sweetly, that not everyone had family. Then I thought we should help him, but after a while I understood, surprised, that my parents weren't interested in helping Raul, that they didn't think it was necessary, that they even felt a certain reluctance towards that young, thin man.

It was said around the neighbourhood that Raul was a Christian Democrat, and that struck me as interesting. It's hard to explain now why a nine-year-old child would be interested that someone was a Christian Democrat. Maybe I thought there was some connection between being a Christian Democrat and the sad circumstance of living alone. I had never seen Papa speak to Raul, so I was surprised to see them sharing a few cigarettes that night. I thought they must be talking about solitude, that Papa was giving our neighbour advice about how to overcome solitude, though Papa must have known very little about the subject.

Magali, meanwhile, was holding Claudia tight in a corner, away from the group. The two of them seemed uncomfortable. I remember thinking that they were uncomfortable because they were different from the rest of the people gathered there. Politely, or maybe maliciously, one neighbour asked Magali what she did for a living; she answered immediately, as if she'd been expecting the question, that she was an English teacher.

It was very late and I was sent to bed. I had to make space for myself, reluctantly, in the tent. I was afraid I might fall asleep, but I distracted myself listening to the stray voices in the night. I understood that Raul had taken the women home, because people started to talk about them. Someone said the girl was strange. She hadn't seemed strange to me. She had seemed beautiful. 'And the woman,' said my mother, 'didn't have the face of an English teacher.'

'She had the face of a housewife, nothing more,' added another neighbour, and they drew out the joke for a while.

I thought about the face of an English teacher, about what an English teacher's face should be like. I thought about my mother, my father. I thought: what kinds of faces do my parents have? But our parents never really have faces. We never learn to look at them the right way.

I thought we would spend weeks or even months outside, waiting for some far-off truck carrying supplies and blankets. I even imagined myself talking on TV, thanking all my fellow Chileans for their help, like people did during the storms. I thought about the terrible floods of other years, when we couldn't go out and we were practically obliged to sit in front of the screen, watching people who had lost everything.

But it wasn't like that. Calm returned almost immediately. The worst always happened to other people. In that lost corner west of Santiago the earthquake had been nothing more than an enormous scare. A few shanties fell down, but there was no great damage and no one died. The TV showed the San Antonio port destroyed, as well as some streets I had seen or thought I had seen on rare trips to downtown Santiago. That was where the true suffering was.

If there was anything to learn, we didn't learn it. I think it's a good thing, now, to lose confidence in the solidity of the ground, that it's necessary to know that from one moment to the next everything can come tumbling down. But at the time we went back, just like that, to life as usual.

When we were back in the house, Papa ascertained that the damage was slight: nothing more than some fallen plaster in the walls and a cracked window. Mama mourned only the loss of the zodiac glasses. Eight of them broke, including hers (Pisces), Papa's (Leo) and the one Grandma used when she came to see us (Scorpio). 'No problem, we have other glasses, we don't need any more,' said Papa, and she answered without looking at him, looking at me: 'Only yours made it.' Then she went to get the glass with the Libra sign and gave it to me with a solemn gesture. She spent the following days a little depressed, thinking of giving the rest of the glasses to a Gemini friend, a Virgo friend, an Aquarius friend.

The good news was that we wouldn't go back to school right away. The old building had been significantly damaged, and those who had seen it said it was a pile of rubble. It was hard for me to imagine the school destroyed, although I didn't feel sad, only curious. I remembered, especially, the bare spot at the edge of the lot where we played in our free time, and the wall the middle-school kids would write on. I thought about all those messages flying in pieces, spread out in the ash on the ground – bawdy sayings, phrases in favour of or against Colo-Colo, or in favour of or against Pinochet. One phrase I found especially funny: Pinochet sucks dick.

Back then, I was and I always have been and I always will be in favour of Colo-Colo. As for Pinochet, to me he was a television personality who hosted a show with no fixed schedule, and I hated him for that, for the stuffy national channels that interrupted programming during the best parts. Some time later I hated him for being a son of a bitch, for being a murderer, but back then I hated him only for those inconvenient shows that Papa watched without saying a word, motionless, without acceding any movement other than a more forceful drag on the cigarette he always kept glued to his mouth.

The redhead's father took a trip, around then, to Miami, and he returned with a bat and a baseball glove for his son. The gift produced an unexpected change in our routine. For many days we switched from soccer to that slow and slightly stupid game which nevertheless hypnotized my friends. It was absurd: ours must have been the only place in the country where the children played baseball instead of soccer. It was hard for me to hit the ball or to throw it right, so I was quickly sent to the bench. The redhead, who had been one of my best friends, suddenly became popular. He now preferred the company of the older kids who, attracted by the foreign game, had joined our group. And that's how, because of baseball, I was left practically friendless.

During those weeks of leisure we didn't need to know if it was Wednesday or Thursday or Sunday. In the afternoons, resigned to solitude, I left the house, as they say, to wear myself out: I walked in wider and wider circuits, though I almost always respected a certain geometry of circles. I exhausted all possible routes, saw all the blocks, noticed new landscapes. The world didn't vary much: the same new houses, built quickly, as if obeying some urgency, but nevertheless solid, resilient. In a few weeks the majority of the walls had been restored and reinforced. It was hard to tell there had just been an earthquake.

I don't understand that freedom now. We lived in a dictatorship; people talked about crimes and attacks, martial law and curfew, and all the same nothing kept me from spending the day wandering far from home. Weren't the streets of Maipú dangerous then? At night they were, and during the day as well, but the adults played, arrogantly or innocently, or with a mixture of arrogance and innocence, at ignoring the danger. They played at thinking that discontent was a thing of the poor and power the domain of the rich, but no one was poor or rich, at least not yet, in those streets, back then.

One of those afternoons I saw Raul's niece again. I didn't know if I should say hello. And then I saw her again several times in the following days. I didn't realize that she was actually following me. 'It's just that I like to walk fast,' I answered when she spoke to me, and then came a long silence that she broke by asking me if I was lost. I answered that no, I knew perfectly well how to get home. 'It was a joke, I want to talk to you, let's meet next Monday in the supermarket bakery, at five.' She said it like that, in one sentence, and left.

The next day my parents woke me up early because we were going to spend the weekend at the Ovalle reservoir. Mama didn't want to go and she dragged out the preparations, confident that lunchtime would come and the plan would have to change. Papa decided, however, that we would have lunch at a restaurant, and we left right away. Back then, it was a real luxury to eat outside the house. I sat in the back seat of the Peugeot thinking about what I would order, and in the end I asked for a steak *a lo pobre*. Papa warned me that it was a big dish, that I wouldn't be able to eat it, but on those rare excursions I was given free rein to order what I wanted.

Soon, there prevailed that heavy atmosphere in which the only possible topic of conversation is the lateness of the food. Our order was so late that in the end Papa decided we would leave as soon as the food came. I protested, or I wanted to protest, or now I think I should have protested. 'If we're going to leave, let's go now,' said Mama resignedly, but Papa explained that this way the restaurant owners would lose the food, that it was an act of justice, of revenge.

We continued our journey ill-humoured and hungry. I didn't really like going to the reservoir. They didn't let me wander very far by myself and I got bored, though I tried to have fun swimming for a while, fleeing from the rats that lived among the rocks, looking at the worms eating the dust and the fish dying on land. Papa settled in to fish all day, and Mama spent the day watching him, and I watched Papa fish and Mama watch him and it was hard for me to understand how that was, for them, fun.

I faked a cold on Sunday so they would let me sleep a little longer. They went off to the rocks after giving me endless superfluous instructions. A little while later, I got up and turned on the tape player so I could listen to Raphael while I made breakfast. We had a tape of all his best songs, which Mama had recorded from the radio. Unfortunately, my finger slipped from the 'Play' key, and I pressed 'Record' for a few seconds. I ruined the tape right in the chorus of the song 'Qué sabe nadie'.

I was desperate. After thinking a bit, I decided the only solution was to sing over the chorus, and I started practising the words, putting on a voice until it seemed convincing to me. Finally, I decided to record; I listened to the tape several times, thinking, somewhat self-indulgently, that the results were good enough, though I was a little worried about the lack of music during those seconds.

Papa would yell at me, but he didn't hit. He never hit me, it wasn't his style; he preferred the grandiloquence of phrases that were impressive at first, since he said them seriously, like an actor in the final episode of a soap opera: 'You've disappointed me as a son, I can never forgive you for what you've done, your behaviour is unacceptable,' etc. I nevertheless nurtured a fantasy that some day he would beat me almost to death.

The return trip was excruciating. As soon as we set off for Santiago, I declared I was tired of Raphael, that we should listen to Adamo or José Luis Rodríguez. 'I thought you liked Raphael,' said Mama. 'Adamo's lyrics are better,' I said, but this only led to a discussion about whether Adamo was better than Raphael, during which even Julio Iglesias was mentioned, which was in any case absurd, since no one in our family liked Julio Iglesias.

To demonstrate Raphael's vocal quality, my father decided to put in the tape, and when 'Qué sabe nadie' came on I had to improvise a desperate plan B, which consisted of singing very loudly from the beginning of the song, figuring that when the chorus came my voice would just sound louder. They yelled at me for singing so loudly, but they didn't notice the adulteration in the tape. Once we were home, however, as I was digging a small hole next to the rose garden to bury the tape, they found me. There was nothing I could do but tell them the whole story. They laughed a lot and listened to the tape several times.

That night, however, they appeared in my room to tell me I was grounded for a week, and couldn't leave the house. 'Why are you grounding me after you laughed so much?' I asked, angry. 'Because you lied,' said my father.

I couldn't, then, keep my date with Claudia, but in the end it was better, since when I told her that story she laughed so much that I could look at her without anxiety, forgetting, to some extent, the strange bond that was beginning to join us.

It's hard for me to remember the circumstances in which we saw each other again. According to Claudia, she was the one who sought me out, but I also remember wandering long hours hoping to see her. However it happened, suddenly we were walking next to each other again, and she asked me to go with her to her house. We turned several times and she even, in the middle of a passageway, told me we had to turn round, as if she didn't know where she lived.

We arrived, finally, at a neighbourhood with only two streets, Neftalí Reyes Basoalto and Lucila Godoy Alcayaga. It sounds like a joke, but it's true. A lot of the streets in Maipú had those absurd names: my cousins, for example, lived in First Symphony Way, near the Second and Third Symphony, next to Concert Street, and close to the passages Opus One, Opus Two, Opus Three, etc. The street where I lived was called Aladdin, between Odin and Ramayana and parallel to Lemuria. Obviously, towards the end of the seventies architects had a lot of fun choosing names for the streets where the new families would later live, the families without history, willing or perhaps resigned to living in that fantasy world.

'I live in the neighbourhood of real names,' said Claudia that afternoon of our re-encounter. She stared at me, looking slightly nervous. 'I live in the neighbourhood of real names,' she said again, as if she needed to start the sentence over in order to go on: 'Lucila

Godoy Alcayaga is Gabriela Mistral's real name,' she explained, 'and Neftalí Reyes Basoalto is Pablo Neruda's real name.' A long silence came over us, which I broke by saying the first thing that came into my head: 'Living here must be much better than living on Aladdin Street.'

As I slowly pronounced that stupid sentence, I could see her pimples, her pink-and-white face, her pointed shoulders, the place where her breasts should be but where for now there was nothing, and her hair, unstylish because it wasn't short, wavy and brown, but rather long, straight and black.

We spent a while talking next to the fence, and then she invited me in. I wasn't expecting that, because back then, no one expected that. Each house was a kind of miniature fortress, an impregnable bastion. I myself wasn't allowed to invite friends over, since Mama always said everything was dirty. It wasn't true, the house sparkled, but I thought that maybe there was some kind of dirt that I simply couldn't see, that when I grew up maybe I would see layers of dust where now I saw only the waxed floor and shining wood.

Claudia's house seemed fairly similar to my own: the same horrible raffia swans, two or three little Mexican hats, several minuscule clay pots and crochet dishcloths. The first thing I did was to ask to use the bathroom and I discovered, to my astonishment, that the house had two bathrooms. My idea of wealth was exactly that: I imagined that millionaires must have houses with three bathrooms, or even five.

Claudia told me she wasn't sure her mother would be happy to see me there, and I asked if it was because of the dust. She didn't understand at first but listened to my explanation, and chose to answer that yes, her mother didn't like her to invite friends over because she thought the house was too dirty. I asked her then, without thinking about it too much, about her father. 'My father doesn't live with us,' she said. 'My parents are separated, he lives in another city.' I asked her if she missed him. 'Of course I do. He's my father.'

In my class there was only one boy with separated parents, which back then was a stigma, the saddest situation imaginable. 'Maybe they'll live together again some day,' I said, to make her feel better. 'Maybe,' she said. 'But I don't want to talk about that. I want to talk about something else.'

She took off her sandals, went to the kitchen and came back with a bowl filled with black, green and purple grapes; this struck me as odd, since in my house they never bought such a variety of grapes. I took advantage of the chance to try them all, and while I compared the flavours, Claudia filled the silence with general, polite questions. 'I need to ask you something,' she said finally, 'but not till after lunch.'

'If you want, I'll help you fix the food,' I said, even though I had no idea how to cook. 'We're already having lunch,' said Claudia, very seriously. 'These grapes are lunch.'

It was hard for her to get to the point. She seemed to speak freely, but there was also a stutter to her voice that made it difficult to understand her. Now I think she was cursing the fact that she had to talk in order for me to understand what she wanted to ask me.

'I need you to take care of him,' she said suddenly, forgetting all her strategy.

'Who?'

'My uncle. I need you to take care of him.'

'OK,' I answered immediately, so dependable, and in a split second I imagined that Raul was suffering from some horrible disease, a disease maybe even worse than solitude, and that I would have to be some kind of nurse. I saw myself walking around the neighbourhood, helping him with his wheelchair, blessed for my generous solidarity. But evidently that wasn't what Claudia was asking me to do. She spilled out the story all at once, staring at me the whole time. I had agreed to what she wanted too soon, confident that later on I would figure out what she had really asked me to do.

What I eventually understood was that Claudia and her mother couldn't or shouldn't visit Raul very often. That's where I came in: I had to watch over him; not take care of him but rather keep an eye on his activities and make notes about anything that seemed suspicious. I was to be her informer. We would meet every Thursday, at the random meeting point she had chosen, the supermarket bakery, where I would give her my report.

Afterwards, we would talk for a while about other things, 'Because,' she said, 'I'm really interested in how you're doing.' I smiled with a satisfaction in which fear and desire also breathed. ∎

A FEW WORDS ON THE LIFE CYCLE OF FROGS

Patricio Pron

TRANSLATED BY JANET HENDRICKSON

PATRICIO PRON
ARGENTINA
1975

At the age of twenty-eight, Pron learned how to ride a bicycle through the snow in Germany, the country where the majority of his favourite childhood authors were born. He is the author of three volumes of short stories – *Hombres infames* (1999), *El vuelo magnífico de la noche* (2001) and *El mundo sin las personas que lo afean y lo arruinan* (2010) – and four novels – *Formas de morir* (1998), *Nadadores muertos* (2001), *Una puta mierda* (2007) and *El comienzo de la primavera* (2008). Pron holds a doctorate in Romance Philology from the Georg-August University in Göttingen, Germany, and currently lives in Madrid, where he works as a translator and critic. 'A Few Words on the Life Cycle of Frogs' is a new story.

I

A few years ago, when I was young and hadn't yet read Siegfried Lenz or Arno Schmidt – and neither, as it happens, Kurt Tucholsky, Karl Valentin or Georg C. Lichtenberg; moreover, I hadn't read Jakob van Hoddis, Kurt Schwitters or Georg Heym, the sad, unfortunate Georg Heym – and when in spite of everything I wanted to become a writer, I lived beneath the living Argentine writer. Fortunately, this statement isn't metaphorical. I didn't live under the living Argentine writer in the same way that some Argentine writers live under the influence of others and all under the influence of Jorge Luis Borges; rather, I really lived under the living Argentine writer and was his neighbour and the depositary of a puerile mystery that would interest only me but would change everything.

II

Naturally, I didn't know that I would be the neighbour of the living Argentine writer; I was simply looking for an apartment, and a friend who spent long periods of time away from the capital had agreed to lend me his, in a city where I wouldn't live very long, anyway. I'd grown tired of the city in the provinces where I was born and decided to go to the capital; there, I thought, I could be near the things that interested me and far from the things that didn't, or simply in another place, with other faces and streets with different names laid out in another fashion, and where perhaps there might exist a person with my name who thought differently and did things in another, perhaps more satisfactory way.

I wasn't at all original in this, given that the literary life in that country consisted primarily of youth from the provinces who aspired to become writers and travelled all the way from the sad provinces to the capital, and there they lived badly and never sent letters to their families, and sometimes they returned to the provinces and sometimes they stayed and became writers of the capital with full rights, that is, writers who only wrote about the capital and its problems, who tried to pass off its problems as those of a poor city in southern Europe and not those of a Latin American capital, which is what that city really was. One of those problems – though of course one of the least important – was those very writers from the provinces, who typically visited the literary workshops of other writers from the provinces who'd arrived in the capital some time ago and who were no longer writers from the provinces, or they pretended not to be, or the writers wrote in squalid pensions or in houses they shared with friends, usually from the same provinces, and later they worked in shops or drugstores or – if they were lucky – in bookstores, almost always with ridiculous schedules that ended up impairing their ability to dedicate themselves seriously to writing and, as a result, sooner or later, the writers from the provinces ended up hating literature, which they practised dog-tired, writing in crowded buses or on the metro, since writing otherwise robbed the hours of sleep necessary to put up with their bosses and customers and the weather and the long rides on the bus or the metro, and because this always seemed to be one step further than the place where they had arrived; the writers from the provinces always gave the impression that they would achieve literature with their next story or poem, that they were at the gates of a discovery that they weren't in a condition to realize, though, because unfortunately to write one needs to have slept at least six hours and have a full stomach and, when it's possible, not to work at a drugstore. Further: one can write having slept badly and while feeling atrociously hungry, but never while working at a drugstore; it's sad but true.

III

One day, the day that I moved, I was carrying two boxes of books in one hand while with the other I tried to fit the key in the lock of the building's main door, and I saw the door give way and on the other side, opening it just for me, was the living Argentine writer. The living Argentine writer let me pass and called the elevator for me and asked if I was going to be living in the building, and I said yes and he said his first name and I said mine and he said that he lived on the fifth floor. Then the elevator arrived and he opened the door and I thanked him and threw myself inside with my boxes, as if I had some urgent reason to get away from the ground floor, and still, before the elevator started to rise, I shivered at the thought that the elevator wouldn't work, that it wouldn't unglue from the floor, as if it had gum stuck to its shoes, and that the doors would open and once again I'd find myself face-to-face with the living Argentine writer without knowing what the hell to say or instead telling him everything: my name, my age, my fucking blood type, and my unconditional admiration for him.

IV

My situation was relatively different from that of the other writers from the provinces who regularly arrived in the capital, like insects that assault a cadaver and eat it and lay their larvae inside and so obtain some life from death. I hadn't left any cadaver behind; I had some money and a few assignments – I was a journalist, a relatively bad one but for some reason in demand – and besides, I had a place to sleep. An apartment, I supposed, where I would write my first truly cosmopolitan works, insufflated with an air that I believed only blew in the capital, which for its part bragged about the quality of that air. Naturally, I was an imbecile or a saint.

At that time I wrote stories that were more like farces, stories that were dumb and sadly ridiculous. In one, a boat caught fire along the coast of a city, and its residents gathered to contemplate the spectacle and did nothing to help the crew because the spectacle was so beautiful, and so the boat sank and the crew members died, and when the only survivor of this disaster made it to the coast and asked for help, the city's inhabitants beat him for ruining the spectacle. In another story, a horse appeared which had been dressed like a man so that he'd be allowed to travel on a train; part of its education took place on this long train trip, and when the train finally reached its destination, the horse – which had somehow learned to talk – demanded to be called 'Gombrowicz' from this point forward, and he wouldn't let himself be saddled; I still don't understand what I wanted to say by that. I'd also written a story about this guy who invited a girl he liked on an outing to the countryside, but then the girl constantly changed the radio station in the car and ate with her mouth open and did things that made this guy think he could never declare his love to her and maybe it was better that way, and I think everyone died at the end in an accident or something like that. In that story I'd tested my talents for comparison and simile; I'd written things like, 'He and she had never seen each other before. They were like two little doves that had never seen each other, either'; and 'The boat peacefully steered itself towards the still pool, just like a car driven by a madman heading towards a group of children.' Those were the things I was writing: occasionally, certain people have inferred an unambiguous relationship between a person's imaginative capacity and the quality of his or her fiction, but they leave out the fact that imaginative excess can have catastrophic results for the quality of what one writes, and still, that imaginative capacity is indispensable to every writer's beginnings; it gives him breath and sustains him and makes him believe that his errors are correct and that he is or can be a writer. Well, I had too much imagination during that time.

V

After living in my friend's apartment for a few days I'd discovered a few things, one of which was that perhaps I wouldn't write my first important works in this place. Although the problem wasn't really the place, but rather, my friend's library: I would open a book at random and read a page or two and remain completely demoralized for the rest of the day. I tried to alternate writing with an old typewriter I'd found in a corner, whose typeface I liked a lot, and writing by hand, but sometimes I sat down to sharpen my pencils until an idea emerged and I thought and thought and when I looked again I discovered that the pencil I'd just taken out of its box had been reduced to the size of a fingernail and pencil shavings floated all around me, wood turned on itself, over and over, like the stories I'd wanted to write and hadn't written. Just a few days after arriving at that house, I no longer wanted to write; in fact, I didn't even try. It was like I knew I'd wasted time at the station and the train had passed, and now I had to walk to the fucking end of the world, to arrive there with my feet destroyed and discover that everyone else had left a while back and they'd left the bill on the table without paying and a few dirty plates that I'd have to wash in the kitchen to cancel the bill.

VI

One day, when I tried to open the elevator door without letting go of my shopping bags, a boy in the lobby came up to me whom I'd never seen before, and he was with the living Argentine writer. I started to think about the writer again and his books and I stood frozen in a corner of the elevator: there was the best writer in the country, someone whose books I'd read over and over, who had offered me inspiration and comfort in times I didn't want to remember. He was the writer whose books I ran out to buy as soon as they were published or stole from bookstores without a bad conscience, convinced that good literature had no price, but if it did, it would be better if it didn't have a price for me, who had no real money and walked several hours a day to save on bus fare. To begin with, the living Argentine writer had published a book of stories, which I'd read the moment they appeared and were very important for me, since before that book I didn't know anyone could write like that; I had the impression that at the time no one knew it was possible to write like that except the living Argentine writer, who also spent time on the best-seller lists, had beautiful girlfriends, and rock stars for friends. After this book came another, then another; each one of these was dictated by an efficiency that was almost obscene for all those who couldn't attain it, and I suppose this didn't make things very easy for him. The living Argentine writer wore strange hairstyles and was good, he was very good, and the rest of us could only insult him in silence and think of absurd ways to limit that talent and prodigality and, secretly, learn from it; these things aren't contradictory in literature, whose aficionados are sometimes like a wizard's students who would like to learn all of the wisest man's tricks, but at the same time fervently wish for the tricks to explode between his fingers. That's the great game of literature, and this is the game that the living Argentine writer played and all of us played, each one in his own way, and yet this took nothing from the fact that the living Argentine writer's books had now been translated into other languages and he enjoyed this modest kind of fame that writers have, and now I know he was like those trees one sees on the steppe or in the highlands or the deserts, and that take root there in their existence of few numbers; they do it by burying themselves strongly in the earth. So had that writer buried himself in me, and here he was opening the elevator door for me and asking how I liked my new apartment; just as I was going to reply with a formality the boy said: 'My papa is going to buy me a truck when I'm big, and I'm going to run everyone over.' I smiled and the doors of the elevator opened, and I slipped out of the elevator, and the writer closed the door behind me and made a sign at me with his hand, but I didn't understand if this sign was a gesture of goodbye or an indication that I should stop. A jar of strawberry jam fell to the floor while I struggled with the lock of my friend's apartment door, and the jam left a red mark on the floor, like the testimony of a virgin who has just stopped being one.

VII

One night, maybe the third or fourth that I spent in that apartment, as I asked myself whether one day I would write something in that apartment, I heard sounds coming from the floor above me. They were the sounds of footsteps that went from room to room in an apartment that was clearly much bigger than mine. I stayed still, absorbed, listening to those footsteps as if they were the most interesting, mysterious footsteps that I had ever heard. As the minutes passed, the footsteps followed an irregular rhythm, very different from the noise new houses make to adapt themselves to us, with their almost physical effort: the steps stopped for a few moments, and when I thought I wouldn't hear them any more, they went back to travelling the whole surface of my ceiling, stopping at a point, and then continuing immediately or stopping for a long time. As I listened to them, I thought I was gaining access to the private life of a person about whom I knew nothing, while at the same time, in a certain way, I knew everything, and I felt ashamed of this involuntary meddling in his life, and in order not to listen to his steps any more, I turned on the TV at the foot of the bed and sat down to watch a movie that my friend had left in the VCR.

VIII

In the movie, a young man suffered a minor accident and had to spend a few days in the hospital; on returning to his house, for some reason he believed that his father was to blame for his suffering that accident, and he began to follow his father, observing him, always maintaining his distance. The father's behaviour showed no sign of being dangerous, but the son, observing from his distance, interpreted the father's behaviour in the following way: if the father entered a store and tried on a jacket, the son thought it had to do with the jacket with which – since his father had never worn this type of clothing before – he planned to disguise himself to perpetrate his crime. If the father looked through a travel catalogue in the barbershop, the son supposed that he was looking for a place to escape after committing the murder. In the son's imagination, everything the father did was linked to a murder, only one, which the son thought his father would commit, and given that the son loved his father and didn't want him to go to jail – and as he further believed that the victim of his father's crime would be him – he began to lay traps to deter him from committing the murder he supposedly predicted or to impede its execution. He hid the jacket, burned his father's passport in the sink, and destroyed his suitcases with knives. As for the father, these domestic mishaps couldn't be explained – his new jacket had disappeared; his passport, too; the suitcases he had at home were broken – these things surprised but also irritated him. His habitually jovial nature soured, day by day, and something he couldn't explain, something hard to justify, but at the same time as real as an unexpected downpour, made him feel as if he were being followed by someone. On his way to work, he obsessively watched the faces of his fellow passengers on the metro; if he walked, he looked behind him at every corner. He never saw his son, but his son saw him and attributed the father's nerves and irritability to the anxiety provoked by his imminent crime.

One day the father told the son about his qualms, and the son tried to assuage him. Don't worry, it's all in your imagination, he said, but the father remained nervous and highly strung. That same afternoon, during one of his regular pursuits, the son caught the father by surprise buying a pistol. When the father got home that night, he showed the weapon to his wife and son, but then an argument took place. The wife, who had doubted her husband's faculties for some time, wanted to seize the weapon from him; there was a struggle that the son watched, not knowing what to say, until he let out a scream and got between them, trying to seize the weapon too. Then the pistol went off and the mother fell dead. When the son looked down, he understood that his intuition had been right but at the same time wrong, that he'd predicted the crime but was incapable of imagining that he wouldn't be the victim, and moreover, that the author of the crime would be him and not his father, and that the father would be little more than the instrument of an imagination run wild that wasn't his own, and everything would be an accumulation of real facts, profoundly real, but poorly interpreted. Since my friend had recorded the movie off the TV, when it ended, there were commercials for yogurt and cars, and that night the lights from those commercials stuck to my face until the tape ran out.

IX

The next night I heard the living Argentine writer's footsteps over my head again, and little by little I began to attribute these steps to what I thought was every writer's routine: get up to take a book off the shelf, sit down, page through it, put it back, write, go get a cup of coffee, drink it standing in the kitchen, go back, keep writing. Now I know how the living Argentine writer does it, I told myself: the living Argentine writer doesn't sleep and he spends the whole night writing, I thought, and little by little, my observation of that routine made me wonder what meaning it could have. The living Argentine writer was already prestigious and had a relatively large and, above all, loyal readership, and he was Proustian in the sense that he was principally a stylist, and his style was already totally formed, and he could dedicate his life to going out drinking or watching French films in which nothing happens or making lace or doing whatever else writers do when they're not writing. I asked myself whether the living Argentine writer didn't write primarily for himself, since that's what would make him a writer and not any other thing, for example, someone who fixes cars or takes children to school, and I also asked myself how the living Argentine writer did it, how the existence of great books written by others before, books so fucking good that I could never write them since they presupposed things like a good education and not suffering cold or hunger and not having grown up filled with dread, how the very existence of these books didn't prevent him from writing his own. Then I thought that perhaps the writer saw those books and their authors as examples to follow and tangible proof that the incessant practice of literature could save it from its own errors and defects and so save its author as well, and this certainty, more imagined than real, stayed with me and incited me and made me think that I was wasting my time, tossing and turning in bed instead of writing, and so I started to write again, too: I simply took one of those worn-down pencils that were all over the apartment and began to write. I didn't write anything particularly good, nothing that I could carry down the mountain and show to a people who wandered the desert so that they would preserve it for generations, but it was enough to get the wheels turning again. This time, however, there was a difference, small but substantial: I'd decided to write without revision and in the way I'd been told not to and quickly, against all objections, against popular opinion and against common sense and to write also for the sake of writing, like the writer did at night, without thinking about my sad condition as a writer from the provinces or thinking about what someone else would want to read and without any intention of satisfying a reader's appetite.

X

While I was living in the apartment my friend had lent me, the living Argentine writer's footsteps echoed over my head night after night, and I, who couldn't sleep – not so much because of the noise of the footsteps themselves, which was negligible, but rather because of the conviction that I would be wasting my time doing anything but writing – I started to use these nights to write, running an absurd race against the living Argentine writer, about which he knew absolutely nothing, filling pages and pages with words that would some day be my answer to what the living Argentine writer had written, taking what he had written as a point of departure and then going somewhere else, which was how he and others had written before and how I should have written, too, and others would after me. Sometimes I fell asleep, but as soon as I heard the footsteps, I went back to writing right where I left off, as if pushed by a command both superior to and preceding myself, who had acquired a sort of literary instruction destined only for me, apparently, a kind of literature class given only for my benefit and that could be summarized in just one word, repeated to the point of nausea: work, work, work. I worked. Little of what I wrote mattered; I myself have forgotten it. I knew that what I was writing wouldn't be accepted even in the underground magazines – those that represented the saddest, most underground spectrum of the underground itself – where I'd published before, benefiting, I suppose, from the condescension with which certain prodigal souls praised the works of youth and imprudence – but I kept writing, and at some point, I had five or six stories, one of which was relatively good. No one died in it – a total novelty for me, of course – and it seemed no one came out scalded by some violent and terrible situation. Really, the story was like a dream, one of those placid dreams you have when you fall asleep under the sun and from which it is so unpleasant to wake up. The writers from the provinces are usually rescued from their dream of becoming writers, a terrible dream, difficult to abandon, when their parents die in the provinces and leave them an apartment or a small factory or, in the worst case, a widow and a few mouths to feed, and the writer from the provinces must return to his province, where invariably he ends up establishing a literary workshop; there, he preaches the goodness of the capital and convinces his students that there, in the capital, something really happens, and sooner rather than later, the students end up leaving for the capital, and so the whole cycle repeats itself, like the life cycle of frogs. I already knew that my parents wouldn't die for some time, and however things went, I wasn't going to abandon the dream of literature, I was going to keep dreaming, and this dream was personal and non-transferable and couldn't be shared without the risk of being completely misunderstood, but I also knew that I'd accepted this misunderstanding and decided to resist it no longer and was willing to be dragged along by it, as if by a bad wind, wherever it wanted to carry me.

XI

One day, the story that was a little less bad was accepted by an important magazine. Not by one of those magazines that projected themselves just above the underground, but an important magazine, one of those magazines where you supposedly only published if you knew one of the editors and had fucked them. Well, I didn't know any of the editors, and as such, I hadn't fucked anyone, but there I was, in that magazine, publishing one of the stories I'd written while listening to the living Argentine writer's footsteps come and go all night from an imaginary shelf full of books to an imaginary desk, and these footsteps were a commandment and a lesson that only a mastery of technique, developed through incessant practice, made one a good interpreter of himself and others; that is, a writer.

A few days later, when enough time had passed to be some while, and my story had been published in the magazine where you could publish only if you knew one of the editors and had fucked them, and when I'd written other stories and had published two and been selected for an anthology of young writers, one of those anthologies whose table of contents one rereads ten years after its publication and feels fear and sadness, I found myself once more with the living Argentine writer, and I worked up the courage to interrupt a conversation about the woman who hadn't come to clean the stairs for two weeks, and I told him that I listened to him every night. I don't remember how I said it exactly, but I remember the words 'nights' and 'apartment' and 'write' and 'I know' and 'writer', and I remember his bewildered, worried face, and now I actually do remember that he answered his son had a fever, and he'd spent his nights dozing on the couch and getting up a few times a night to take the boy's temperature or simply curl up at his side and think that everything would pass quickly. He also told me that during those days he hadn't been able to write anything, and for the first time in his life, this hadn't mattered to him at all. I lowered my head and asked him how the boy was now, and he said fine and showed me a truck he'd just bought him. The truck was red and had a hose, and it came with a few firefighters who seemed ready to cross the flames of hell to save a boy from sickness and death. I stood there, not knowing what to say, and the living Argentine writer even had to give me a light push so that I'd leave the elevator for my apartment. A few weeks later, I left the country, and a little while later the living Argentine writer did, too. He kept writing, and so did I; and at the source of all of that was an involuntary education and a mystery and a commandment that I'd learned from him without his knowledge and that I'd never tell him, no matter how many times I ran into him again. Once, though, I asked him if he'd had a secret teacher, too, someone to imitate at least through a total surrender to literature and its contradictory demands, and the living Argentine writer handed me a copy of a book by a dead Argentine writer and smiled and I, at least this once, I thought things always happened this way, that the writers we love often serve us through their comfort and example without their ever knowing it, and in this sense, they're as imaginary as the characters or lands they imagine and people. ■

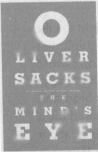

The Mind's Eye *Oliver Sacks*

The best-selling author of *The Man Who Mistook His Wife for a Hat* examines our experience of the visual world. One day in 2005, Oliver Sacks became aware of a dazzling light in his visual field; just two days later a malignant tumour in one eye was diagnosed. Alongside his subsequent journal entries of living with cancer, Oliver Sacks writes about people who have lost visual abilities, such as how we recognize individual faces or see in three dimensions.

Picador | HB

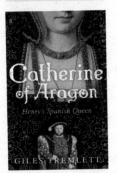

Catherine of Aragon *Giles Tremlett*

From the author of *Ghosts of Spain*, the *Guardian*'s Madrid correspondent, comes a glorious account of the life of the Spanish infanta who became Queen of England and changed the course of history.

Faber & Faber £20 | HB

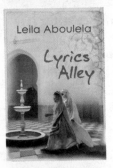

Lyrics Alley *Leila Aboulela*

A lyrical and deeply moving novel by a twice Orange Prize-longlisted rising star, set in pre-Independence Sudan, Egypt and post-war Britain. A sweeping tale that dramatizes the conflicts between modernity and tradition that are being fought within Islam today. Leila Aboulela won the Caine Prize for African Writing in 2000. Her short fiction was recently featured in *Granta* magazine.

Weidenfeld & Nicolson £12.99 | PB

The Mexican Suitcase *Photographers: Robert Capa, Gerda Taro and David Seymour*

In December 2007 three tattered cardboard boxes arrived at the International Center of Photography in New York. Contained in this 'Mexican Suitcase' were the legendary Spanish Civil War negatives of Capa, Taro and Seymour that had disappeared from Capa's studio at the beginning of WWII. These rolls of film constitute an inestimable record of photographic innovation and war photography.

Steidl ICP £70 | HB

The Sixty-Five Years of Washington

Juan José Saer Translated from the Spanish by Steve Dolph

It's October 1960 in a seaside Argentinian city, and 'the Mathematician' is just back from Europe. He runs into Ángel Leto, a relative newcomer to Santa Fe, and they settle into a long conversation about Washington Noriega's sixty-fifth birthday party – a party neither of them attended. *The Sixty-Five Years of Washington* is a brilliant comedy and a moving narrative about the lost generations of Argentina.

Open Letter Books $14.95 | PB

A Novel Bookstore *Laurence Cossé*

Ivan and Francesca dream of opening a bookstore that shuns the latest best-sellers and sells nothing but good novels. Their dreams come true, but the consequences may be deadly.

The *San Francisco Chronicle* calls Cossé's tribute to reading and bookselling 'marvelous and stimulating'. 'Eminently readable, *A Novel Bookstore* is a love letter to the novel and a profound exploration of human nature.' – *Library Journal*

Europa Editions $16.00 | PB

The Rest is Jungle and Other Stories

Mario Benedetti Translated from the Spanish by Harry Morales

In this exquisite new short-story collection, celebrated Uruguayan writer Mario Benedetti affords us a beguiling glimpse of a world in flux. Addressing subjects ranging from love and middle-class frustration in the city to the pain of exile, the stories in *The Rest is Jungle* transport the reader from the cafes of Montevideo to the fault lines that divide nations and people.

Host Publications $15.00 | PB

While the Women Are Sleeping

Javier Marías Translated from the Spanish by Margaret Jull Costa

A dozen unforgettable stories, haunted by slippery figures in anomalous situations – ghosts, spies, bodyguards, criminals – by 'one of the most original writers at work today' (Wyatt Mason, *New York Times Book Review*). 'Sexy, contemplative, elusive and addictive' – *San Francisco Bay Guardian*. 'In the space of ten or twenty pages, Marías contrives to write a novel.' – *Nouvel Observateur*

New Directions $ 21.95 | HB

The Society of Authors Grants

The Society is offering grants to published authors who need funding to assist in the writing of their next book. Writers of fiction, non-fiction and poetry may apply. The grants are provided by the Authors' Foundation and the K. Blundell Trust.

Closing date: 30 April 2011

Full details from:
website: www.societyofauthors.org
email: info@societyofauthors.org

or send an SAE to:
Paula Johnson, The Society of Authors
84 Drayton Gardens
London SW10 9SB

FINANCIAL ASSISTANCE FOR WRITERS

The Royal Literary Fund

Grants and Pensions are available to published authors of several works who are in financial difficulties due to personal or professional setbacks.

Applications are considered in confidence by the General Committee every month.

For further details please contact:
Eileen Gunn, General Secretary
The Royal Literary Fund
3 Johnson's Court
London EC4A 3EA
Tel 020 7353 7159
email: egunnrlf@globalnet.co.uk
website: www.rlf.org.uk
Registered Charity No. 219952

Shadow Catchers: Camera-less Photography

V&A, London
13 October 2010 – 20 February 2011
www.vam.ac.uk/shadowcatchers

This exhibition shows the work of five contemporary artists – Floris Neusüss, Pierre Cordier, Susan Derges, Garry Fabian Miller and Adam Fuss – who work without a camera to create images on photographic paper by casting shadows, manipulating light or chemically treating the surface of the paper.

Sponsored by
♥ BARCLAYS
WEALTH

Norman Rockwell's America

Dulwich Picture Gallery, London
15 December 2010 – 27 March 2011
www.dulwichpicturegallery.org.uk

The first Norman Rockwell exhibition in Britain. Norman Rockwell was the best-known illustrator of the 20th century. He lived and worked through one of the most eventful periods in the nation's history and his paintings vividly chronicle those times.

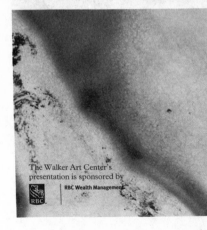

Yves Klein: With the Void, Full Powers

Walker Art Center, Minneapolis
23 October 2010 – 13 February 2011
www.walkerart.org

A visionary and a provocateur, Yves Klein took the European art scene by storm, radically defying common notions of art with bold attempts to paint with fire and monochrome experiments in International Klein Blue. This acclaimed retrospective presents more than two hundred paintings, sculptures, drawings, photographs and films – a revolutionary body of work on view in the US for the first time in nearly thirty years.

The Walker Art Center's presentation is sponsored by
RBC. RBC Wealth Management

NOTES ON TRANSLATORS

Daniel Alarcón, author of two story collections, won the 2009 International Literature Prize for his novel *Lost City Radio* (Harper). He has translated works by Mario Bellatin and Santiago Roncagliolo. He was selected as one of *Granta*'s Best of Young American Novelists in 2007. He lives in Oakland, California.

Peter Bush's most recent translations include Leonardo Padura's *Havana Fever* (Bitter Lemon) and Najat El Hachmi's *The Last Patriarch* (Serpent's Tail). His work has appeared in *The New York Review of Books*. Forthcoming translations include Juan Goytisolo's *Níjar Country* (Lumen Books), *Exiled from Almost Everywhere* (Dalkey Archive Press) and Teresa Solana's *A Shortcut to Paradise* (Bitter Lemon).

Nick Caistor was awarded the Valle-Inclán Prize for translation from Spanish in 2006 and 2008. He is currently translating an Argentinian thriller for MacLehose Press, a Spanish revisiting of Joyce's *Ulysses* for Dalkey Archive Press, Felix Palma's *The Map of Time* for

HarperCollins and Idelfonso Falcones's *The Hand of Fatima* for Transworld.

Margaret Jull Costa has translated the works of José Saramago and is the regular translator of Javier Marías. Her most recent translations are Marías's *Your Face Tomorrow* (Vintage/New Directions), Saramago's *The Elephant's Journey* (Harvill Secker/Harcourt Brace) and Bernardo Atxaga's *Seven Houses in France* (forthcoming from Harvill Secker/Graywolf Press).

Carolina De Robertis is the author of *The Invisible Mountain* (HarperCollins/ Knopf), which won the 2010 Rhegium Julii Debut Prize and has been translated into twelve languages. Her translation of Alejandro Zambra's *Bonsai* (Melville House) was named one of the Ten Best Translated Books of 2008 by the website *Three Percent*.

Lisa Dillman translates from Spanish and Catalan and teaches at Emory University, Atlanta. She has translated works by Andreu Carranza, José Somoza, Gioconda Belli and Eugenio Cambaceres and co-edited

Spain: A Traveler's Literary Companion (Whereabouts Press). Her most recent translations include Juan Filloy's *Op Oloop* (Dalkey Archive Press), nominated for Open Letter's Best Translated Fiction of 2010, and Juan Eslava Galán's *The Mule* (Bantam). She is also currently working on Christopher Domínguez Michael's *Personal Dictionary of Mexican Literature, 1955-2005.*

Edith Grossman has been the recipient of numerous awards and honours for her work. She recently completed a translation of Luis de Góngora's *Solitudes*, to be published by Penguin in 2011, and is currently working on Antonio Muñoz Molina's most recent novel, tentatively titled *The Depths of Time*, for Houghton Mifflin Harcourt. She lives in Manhattan and has two sons, both of whom are musicians.

Richard Gwyn translates from Spanish and Catalan and is the author of six books of poetry and two novels: *The Colour of a Dog Running Away* (Parthian/ Anchor) and *Deep Hanging Out*

(Snowbooks). His work has appeared in more than ten languages. A memoir, *The Vagabond's Breakfast*, will be published in May 2011 (Alcemi).

Janet Hendrickson teaches Spanish at the University of Iowa. Her translation of *The Future is Not Ours*, an anthology of twenty young Latin American fiction writers, will be published in 2012 (Open Letter Books). Her translations have appeared in *Zoetrope: All-Story, n+1* and *Words Without Borders*, among others.

Tanya Huntington Hyde is a painter, writer and translator based in Mexico City. Her work has been published in *Comment is Free, Letras Libres, Metropolitan* and *Literal: Latin American Voices*, where she is managing editor. Her book *Return/El regreso* (Literal) was published in 2009 and her translations of stories by Sergio Pitol, José Emilio Pacheco and Efrén Hernández have been included in the anthology *Sun, Stone, and Shadows* (Fondo de Cultura Económica).

Anna Kushner translates from Spanish, French and Portuguese.

She is the translator of the novels *The Halfway House* by Guillermo Rosales (New Directions), *Jerusalem* by Gonçalo Tavares (Dalkey Archive Press/W.W. Norton) and *The Autobiography of Fidel Castro* by Norberto Fuentes (Dalkey Archive/W.W. Norton).

Mara Faye Lethem has recently translated *Learning to Lose* by David Trueba (Portobello/Other Press), *Cold Skin* by Albert Sánchez Piñol (Canongate) and works by Juan Marsé, Javier Calvo and Pablo De Santis. Her translation of Patricio Pron's *Ideas*, which originally appeared in *The Paris Review*, has been chosen for *The Best American Non-Required Reading 2010*.

Alfred Mac Adam is a professor of Latin American literature at Barnard College, Columbia University. He has translated works by Alejo Carpentier, Julio Cortázar, José Donoso, Carlos Fuentes, Juan Carlos Onetti, Fernando Pessoa, Osvaldo Soriano and Mario Vargas Llosa, and most recently *Season of Ash* by Jorge Volpi (Open Letter).

Megan McDowell is the translator of *The Private Lives of Trees* by Alejandro Zambra (Open Letter Press). She has also translated works by Chilean authors Juan Emar and Álvaro Bisama. Her work can be found in *Words Without Borders*, *Translation Review*, *St Petersburg Review* and *Vice* magazine. She lives in Durham, North Carolina.

Anne McLean translates Spanish and Latin American novels, short stories and memoirs by authors including Julio Cortázar, Javier Cercas, Evelio Rosero and Tomás Eloy Martínez. Recent translations include *The Secret History of Costaguana* by Juan Gabriel Vásquez (Bloomsbury/Riverhead) and *Oblivion: A Memoir* by Héctor Abad (Old Street).

Valerie Miles is the publishing director of Duomo Ediciones and, together with Aurelio Major, one of the founding co-editors of *Granta en español*. She has written for *La Vanguardia*, *The Paris Review* and *ABCD* and is a professor on the postgraduate programme for literary translation at the Pompeu i Fabra University, Barcelona.

Samantha Schnee is the founding editor of the website *Words Without Borders*, which translates, publishes and promotes international literature. Most recently she has translated works by Carmen Boullosa, including the essay 'Writing in Spanish in New York' for the New York Historical Society, and the screenplay *Las Paredes Hablan*, directed by Antonio Zavala. Her translations from the Spanish have appeared in the *New York Times Magazine, Bomb* and *The Nation*.

Katherine Silver is an award-winning translator of Spanish and Latin American literature and the co-director of the Banff International Literary Translation Centre in Canada. She has translated works by Horacio Castellanos Moya and César Aira for New Directions, and Daniel Sada for Graywolf Press.

Natasha Wimmer has translated Roberto Bolaño's *2666* (Picador/ FSG) and *Antwerp* (Picador/New Directions). Her translation of Bolaño's essay collection *Between Parentheses* will be published in 2011 (Picador/New Directions).

Frank Wynne, who translates from both French and Spanish, has translated authors including Michel Houellebecq, Yasmina Khadra, Ahmadou Kourouma, Marcelo Figueras and Almudena Grandes. He was awarded the IMPAC Prize (2002), the Independent Foreign Fiction Prize (2005) and the Scott Moncrieff Prize (2008). Forthcoming works include the memoirs of Claude Lanzmann and a lost masterpiece by Andrés Caicedo.

Contributing Editors
Diana Athill, Peter Carey, Sophie Harrison, Isabel Hilton, Blake Morrison, John Ryle, Lucretia Stewart, Edmund White